MW01106125

Corporate Governance as a Limited Legal Concept

European Company Law Series

VOLUME 4

The CECL-book series on European company law is closely linked to the bimonthly journal *European Company Law* ('ECL'), also published by Kluwer Law International. The persons comprising the ECL's editorial board and the editors of the CECL-book series are one and the same. The aims and objectives of CECL can be found at <www.cecl.nl>. The series covers subjects of company law in a broad sense, including insolvency, co-determination and securities law. The editorial board ensures that all parts of this series are well written, of sufficient scientific depth and, at the same time, useful for legal practitioners and academics alike. The board's credo is that international and comparative law should never degenerate into a theoretical *l'art pour l'art*-exercise, but must always be subservient to the requirement of practical applicability and a further development of the law.

KLUWER LAW INTERNATIONAL

Corporate Governance as a Limited Legal Concept

Cornelis de Groot

Leiden University, The Netherlands

Wolters Kluwer
Law & Business

AUSTIN   BOSTON   CHICAGO   NEW YORK   THE NETHERLANDS

Published by:
Kluwer Law International
PO Box 316
2400 AH Alphen aan den Rijn
The Netherlands
Website: www.kluwerlaw.com

Sold and distributed in North, Central and South America by:
Aspen Publishers, Inc.
7201 McKinney Circle
Frederick, MD 21704
United States of America
Email: customer.care@aspenpubl.com

Sold and distributed in all other countries by:
Turpin Distribution Services Ltd.
Stratton Business Park
Pegasus Drive, Biggleswade
Bedfordshire SG18 8TQ
United Kingdom
Email: kluwerlaw@turpin-distribution.com

Printed on acid-free paper.

ISBN 978-90-411-2873-7

Printed in Great Britain.

Table of Contents

Introduction

[1] Corporate governance is about the regulation of the corporate form. Corporate governance requires a rethinking of the roles of the board and management of (especially listed) corporations and of the role of the shareholders of these corporations. This rethinking of the regulation of the corporate form seeks to guarantee that corporations best serve the purpose of enhancing shareholder value in the long term. What corporate governance entails, or to put it in other words what 'good' corporate governance is, may be derived from an abundance of sources. These include statutory regulation, listing rules, and corporate governance codes and guidelines. Two corporate governance codes are at the centre of much of the discussion in this book. These are The Dutch Corporate Governance Code adopted in the Netherlands and The Combined Code on Corporate Governance adopted in the United Kingdom. However, corporate governance should not be studied from such 'static' sources as codes and guidelines, statutory regulation and listing rules alone. The 'dynamics' of corporate governance come to life when other sources are also taken into account. Among these are reports and judgments that deal with specific instances where investigators or courts were asked to analyze corporate governance issues in concrete cases. This accounts for the build-up of this book. Chapters are divided in two parts (A and B): the first part gives a general overview of the subject discussed in the chapter, the second part illustrates and supplements the general overview with other sources of corporate governance.[1]

Underlying this book are two assumptions. The first is that the concept of 'good' corporate governance is not a concept that is dramatically different from one jurisdiction to another but represents an international phenomenon that has to a reasonable extent the same characteristics everywhere. Therefore, although the law in the Netherlands plays a paramount role in this book, it is supplemented by

---

1. In the case of chapters 4 and 5: three.

corporate governance sources from other jurisdictions (e.g. The Combined Code on Corporate Governance) that are treated on a par. The second is that there are a number of issues that make up the brunt of corporate governance. To extent that a listed corporation follows the corporate governance rules required from those subjects it may be said to be in line with 'good' corporate governance. Collectively, these corporate governance rules form the characteristics of 'good' corporate governance.

This book identifies a number of rules that together constitute 'good' corporate governance and raises the question whether – and if so, to what extent – these rules of 'good' corporate governance are capable of being legally enforced. If they are not, (rules of) 'good' corporate governance would have but limited relevance as a legal concept and would represent foremost a set of expectations on how corporations should be organized ideally. If they are, however, (rules of) 'good' corporate governance would not just be a concept that is embedded in organizational theory, but a full-fledged legal concept. The reports and judgments on corporate governance issues discussed in this book are intended to help answer that question. Also, in the fall of 2008 signs of a crisis in the financial sector became manifest.[2] The ensuing financial crisis has turned into an economic crisis as well. The investigation conducted in this book could also shed light on the question whether one can rely on rules of 'good' corporate governance as a tool to counter such crises.

Chapter 1 of this book does not discuss a core subject of corporate governance as such, but some general issues concerning corporate governance in an attempt to formulate a working definition of corporate governance. Other chapters do go into a number of core subjects of corporate governance.[3] Chapter 3 deals with the 'centralized administration' of a corporation, i.e. its board and management. Chapter 4 is concerned with the composition and functioning of corporate boards; this chapter also contains (model) Corporate Governance Guidelines of the board of directors of the imaginary ABC Corporation that are derived from a number of corporate governance guidelines adopted by the boards of directors of US listed corporations. Chapter 6 is concerned with risks. Chapter 7 is about executive directors' remuneration, and chapter 8 is concerned with personal ethics. The subject discussed in chapter 9 are public takeover bids. Chapter 10 discusses investor relations. Chapters 2 and 5 deal with two specific features of statutory corporate law in the Netherlands that have relevance for corporate governance: the so-called 'right of inquiry' and the so-called 'mandatory organizational arrangement' respectively. The 'right of inquiry' is a legal procedure that gives (among others) shareholders the opportunity to challenge inter alia a corporation's corporate governance framework in a court. The 'mandatory organizational arrangement' is an arrangement that regulates the functioning of corporate boards of some corporations in a specific way.

---

2. W. Vermeend, De kredietcrisis (Amsterdam: Lebowski, 2008), at 7.
3. An issue not dealt with in this book – as it requires specific attention – is the connection between corporate governance and group law: cf. on that matter S.M. Bartman, *Voorbij NV en BV* (Deventer: Kluwer, 2004).

The sources of corporate governance discussed in this book are from a number of jurisdictions, first and most important the Netherlands, and second inter alia the United Kingdom and the United Stated. This distinction coincides with the fact that corporate law in the Netherlands is sometimes described as reflecting a 'Rhineland' stakeholder-oriented model of law whereas corporate law in the United Kingdom and in the United States is sometimes described as reflecting an 'Anglo-American' shareholder-oriented model of law. At the same time, both the Netherland and the United States are host to courts that are versed in interpreting corporate law: the Chamber of Business Affairs in the Netherlands and the Court of Chancery and the Supreme Court of the State of Delaware.[4]

---

4. In this book full and abbreviated references in footnotes are renewed each chapter.

Chapter 1

Corporate Governance

I.   CHARACTERIZATION AND DEFINITION

[2] The phrase corporate governance emerged probably somewhere after 1975 in corporate law.[5] Today, corporate governance is no longer a mere phrase but has developed into a concept that is part of corporate law. This is reflected in the titles of articles, books, corporate governance codes and guidelines, reports and all sorts of other documents. This chapter tries to find a working definition of the concept. Part A of this chapter consists of the following paragraphs: *corporate governance and corporate law, the corporate form, corporate governance and the European Union, corporate governance codes and guidelines,* and *rethinking corporate governance.*

A.   CORPORATE GOVERNANCE AND CORPORATE LAW

[3] As a concept, corporate governance is largely part of that branch of the law that can be called company law. Company law is part of a much larger realm of the law that can be called economic law. The purpose of economic law is the regulation of economic activities. Economic law encompasses subjects like antitrust law, financial law, intellectual property law, labor law, the law of the European Community

---

5. B. Garratt, *Thin on Top: Why Corporate Governance Matters and How to Measure and Improve Board Performance* (London: Nicholas Brealey Publishing, 2003); A.F.M. Dorresteijn & C. de Groot, 'Corporate Governance Codes: Origins and Perspectives', in *European Company Law in Accelerated Progress*, ed. S.M. Bartman (Alphen aan den Rijn: Kluwer Law International, 2006), 31-57 (also published in *European Company Law* (2004), 43-56).

and of the World Trade Organization, and company law. Economic activities may
be undertaken by all sorts of legal entities, ranging from the simple sole proprietorship to the listed corporation. The purpose of company law is to regulate these
legal entities. The connection between the economy and company law was already
recognized in a report on corporate governance published in the United Kingdom
in 1992, the Cadbury Report, that states that '[a] country's economy depends on the
drive and efficiency of its companies'.[6] Because company law is concerned with
the regulation of legal entities, it is to a large extent more of a procedural and
organizational nature than containing rules of substance. As concerns the phrase
company law, it should be noted that the scope of company law is wider than just
companies. Some of the legal forms addressed by company law are (1) the sole
proprietorship, (2) partnerships,[7] and (3) the 'company' or 'corporation'.[8] As
concerns the third category, two types can be distinguished. The first type is
mostly used to organize small or medium-sized businesses. It is known as the
private limited company, or – in the Netherlands – the *besloten vennootschap*
('BV'). The second type, that is mostly used to organize large-scale businesses, is
known as the public limited company ('Plc'), or – in the Netherlands – the
naamloze vennootschap ('NV'). This second type is the so-called corporate
form that may be compared to the US corporation ('Corp.' or 'Inc.'). Whereas
the term company makes it less clear what is meant as this phrase denotes two
types of legal structures, the term corporation is more exact as it refers to one
specific type only. This is important because corporate governance has as its
prime object corporations, to be more exact listed corporations. Where corporations are concerned, company law is replaced by the narrower field of corporate
law. And corporate law is the place where corporate governance is most abun-
dantly present.

Corporate law, itself part of company law, may be as difficult to master as any
part of economic law. There are several reasons for this:

– Corporate law makes use of abstract concepts (e.g. well-founded reasons to
  doubt good policy and mismanagement) and abstract rules (e.g. the business
  judgment standard and the anti-frustration and breakthrough rules), whose
  meaning cannot be derived simply from common parlance.

---

6. 'The Financial Aspects of Corporate Governance', drawn up by the Committee on the Financial
   Aspects of Corporate Governance (December 1992, by the name of the committee's chairperson
   this report is also called the Cadbury report), 1.1, <www.ecgi.org> codes & principles → index
   of all codes; cf. the (Dutch) Corporate Governance Code Monitoring Committee, 'Report on
   Compliance with The Dutch Corporate Governance Code' (over 2004), at 4:
       'Well-managed companies are of crucial importance to the health and competitiveness of
   the economy. The income and well-being of millions of people and the value of their pensions
   and investments depend directly on the performance of companies and their governance'
   (<www.commissiecorporategovernance.nl> information in English).
7. Partnerships may include general partnerships and limited partnerships.
8. Between the partnership and the company or corporation may be legal forms like the limited
   liability partnership ('LLP') and the limited liability company ('LLC').

- Corporate law is not just law but has a policy component too, especially where competences lie with (quasi-)governmental bodies like specialized courts and takeovers panels.[9]
- Corporate law lacks a central paradigm, because its purpose is to regulate legal entities against the background of ever-changing economic circumstances.[10]
- Corporate law is concerned with corporations that are often engaged in cross-border economic activities and therefore cannot be studied from sources derived from one national jurisdiction solely.[11]

One way to understand corporate law is to study it not from individual concepts or rules, and not just from the case law of specialized courts and takeover panels, but from a specifically chosen angle. Such an angle should link up with corporate law as a means to regulate the way in which legal entities engage in economic activities. One such angle could be to study not legal forms as such, but concentrate on any number of legal entities combined into a group relationship. This angle studies the concept of the group.[12] Another angle could be to study the corporate form against the background of the demands on its functioning as the entity that is most apt to engage in today's international economic activities. Meeting these demands reveals a large number of characteristics of a well-functioning corporation. These characteristics, when combined, amount to corporate governance.

B.   THE CORPORATE FORM

[4] Going as it were upward from the simple sole proprietorship, through partnerships, up to private limited companies and corporations, three developments occur.[13] *On a legal level*, somewhere along the ladder legal entities start having legal personality. Legal personality gives an entity a legal status separate from

---

9. P. van Schilfgaarde, 'De Hoge Raad, ABN AMRO en LaSalle', *Nederlands Juristenblad* (2007), 1950-1956.
10. L. Timmerman, 'Kroniek van het vennootschapsrecht', *Nederlands Juristenblad* (2004), 1629-1636.
11. J.W. Cioffi & S.S. Cohen, 'The State, Law and Corporate Governance: The Advantage of Forwardness', in *Corporate Governance and Globalization: Long Range Planning Issues*, eds S.S. Cohen & G. Boyd (Cheltenham: Edward Elgar Publishing Limited, 2000), 307-349; M.L. Kroeze, 'Kroniek van het vennootschapsrecht', *Nederlands Juristenblad* (2007), 2219-2232.
12. This angle is e.g. pursued by S.M. Bartman & A.F.M. Dorresteijn, *Van het concern*, (Deventer: Kluwer, 2006).
13. R. Kraakman, 'The Durability of the Corporate Form', in *The Twenty-First-Century Firm: Changing Economic Organization in International Perspective*, ed. P. DiMaggio (Princeton: Princeton University Press, 2001), 147-160; P.L. Davies, *Introduction to Company Law* (Oxford: Oxford University Press, 2002); C. de Groot, 'Can Corporate Governance Contribute to Sustainable Development', in *Neo-liberal Globalism and Social Sustainable Globalisation*, ed. E.C. Nieuwenhuys (Leiden: Brill Academic Publishers, 2006), 195-214; C. de Groot, 'The Function of Corporate Boards: Toward a New State of Affairs?', *European Company Law* (2007), 4-9.

those who participate in it. This allows the entity to take on obligations and incur liabilities in its own name. Added to that, legal personality allows limited liability, which means that the obligations and liabilities of the entity in principle cannot be enforced against its participants. *Also on a legal level*, at some point legal entities start having an issued share capital that is divided into transferable shares. The fact that an entity has a share capital gives investors of capital an easily available opportunity to invest directly in the entity by buying shares, without having to enter into elaborate contractual relationships. Furthermore, the transferability of the shares gives investors the possibility to enter and leave the entity, while the activities of the entity continue uninterruptedly. These two developments that occur on a legal level are likely to be introduced in combination when the stage of the company form has been reached. At this level, the investors of capital have become shareholders. *On a sociological level*, rather than on a legal level, a third development takes places. Somewhere along the ladder a separation occurs between the investors of capital on the one hand and the administration of the entity on the other hand. This separation amounts to a division of labor whereby investing opportunities become distinct from the entity's administration. This division of labor makes it possible that several groups of participants are involved in the entity in their own right. The investors of capital entrust the administration of the entity to specialized decision makers. This administration consists of the entity's directors and managers. This third development is likely to have been completed when the stage of the corporate form has been reached. The investors of capital have the value of their investment as their prime interest. This is why they have entitlements to the corporation's profits in the form of payment of dividends while it exists as well as to the residual assets should it be liquidated. The investors of capital invest in the corporation but retain some rights to exert influence over corporate affairs, although limited to major issues. The latter is understandable because greater involvement of the investors of capital would undermine the very benefits of specialized decision making. The prime interest of the directors and managers lies in the remuneration they are awarded for their efforts and in having a secure and stable working environment. The directors form one or two corporate boards, where the 'ultimate management authority' of the entity is vested.[14] In a corporation that is organized along the lines of a unitary board structure there is one 'unitary' board (the board of directors – the 'board' – that consists of executive directors and non-executive directors), whereas in a corporation that is organized along the lines of a dual board structure there is a 'dual' board that falls into two boards (the 'management board' that consists of executive directors, and the 'supervisory board' that consists of non-executive directors).[15] The managers are an array of high level personnel who are engaged in decision making on behalf of the entity, but are not board members. Together, the directors and managers of the corporation

---

14. R. Kraakman (2001), 147-160 (at 150).
15. Also: one-tier board structure or one-tier board system, and two-tier board structure or two-tier board system; in a dual board structure the non-executive directors may also be referred to as supervisory directors.

constitute – what may be called – the corporation's 'centralized or specialized management'.[16] As an alternative, the term 'centralized administration' could be used.[17] This latter phrase avoids the use of the term management, as that term is also used to denote the corporation's executive directors and managers collectively, making management in this sense a part of the centralized administration.

C.   CORPORATE GOVERNANCE AND THE EUROPEAN UNION

[5] Corporate governance issues have not gone unnoticed at the level of the European Union. In September 2001 the European Commission set up the High Level Group of Company Law Experts. This Group issued two reports. The first was the Report of the High Level Group of Company Law Experts on Issues Relating to Takeover Bids (January 2002), and the second and final was the Report of the High Level Group of Company Law Experts on A Modern Regulatory Framework for Company Law in Europe (November 2002). The first report played a role in the adoption by the European Parliament and the Council of the European Union of directive 2004/25/EC on takeover bids.[18] The second report prompted the Commission in 2003 to publish an Action Plan on company law and corporate governance.[19] This Action Plan formulated two Community policy objectives and identified a number of areas where initiatives could be undertaken. The policy objectives are strengthening shareholders' rights and protection of third parties, and fostering efficiency and competition of business. The areas where initiatives could be undertaken go beyond corporate governance issues. They include capital maintenance and alteration, corporate groups and pyramids, corporate restructuring and mobility, and the introduction of a European Private Company. In the field of corporate governance related issues they include modernizing the board of directors, strengthening shareholders' rights, enhancing corporate governance disclosure, and coordinating corporate governance efforts of the Member States. The Action Plan has resulted in several legal instruments on corporate governance issues, notably a recommendation on the remuneration of directors, a recommendation on the role of non-executive directors and of board committees, and a directive on shareholders' rights.[20] Furthermore, the European Commission has set up two new advisory bodies to assist the Commission in its work. These are the

---

16. P.L. Davies (2002), at 13, capitalization deleted.
17. C. de Groot (2007), 4-9 (at 5).
18. 'Directive 2004/25/EC of the European Parliament and of the Council of 21 April 2004 on Takeover Bids', OJEU 2004 L 142/12-23 (text with EEA relevance); C. de Groot, *Bescherming en breakthrough bij overname* (Amsterdam: Rozenberg Publishers, 2004), at 53.
19. 'Communication from the Commission to the Council and the European Parliament of 21 May 2003: Modernising Company Law and Enhancing Corporate Governance in the European Union: A Plan to Move Forward' (Com (2003) 284 final).
20. 'Commission Recommendation of 14 December 2004 Fostering an Appropriate Regime for the Remuneration of Directors of Listed Companies (2004/913/EC)', OJEU 2004 L 385/55-59 (text with EEA relevance); 'Commission Recommendation of 15 February 2005 on the Role of

European Corporate Governance Forum and the Group of Non-Governmental Experts on Corporate Governance and Company Law.[21] The remit of the Forum is 'to examine best practices in Member States with a view to enhancing the convergence of national corporate governance codes and providing advice to the Commission'. The role of the Group is 'to provide technical advice to the Commission on the Commission's initiatives in the field of corporate governance and company law'. Other legal instruments that contain corporate governance related issues are a directive on statutory audits of annual accounts and consolidated accounts, and a directive on annual accounts and consolidated accounts.[22] The directive on statutory audits of annual accounts and consolidated accounts establishes rules concerning the statutory audit of annual and consolidated accounts by statutory auditors and audit firms. The directive deals with issues like approval, continuing education and mutual recognition, registration, professional ethics, independence, objectivity, confidentiality and professional secrecy, quality assurance, public oversight, and the appointment and dismissal of statutory auditors and audit firms. The directive on annual accounts and consolidated accounts relates to 'the duty to ensure that the financial information included in a company's annual accounts and annual reports gives a true and fair view'. As far as the broad issue of corporate groups and pyramids is concerned, the Commission staff working document on the proportionality between capital and control in listed companies of 12 December 2007 went into so-called 'Control-Enhancing-Mechanisms (CEMs)' that are 'institutional arrangements (e.g. taken by the listed company itself) creating a discrepancy in the relation between financial ownership and voting power with the result that a shareholder can increase his control without holding a proportional stake of equity'.[23] Such CEMs are comparable to pyramid structures and shareholder agreements that serve 'to reinforce controlling shareholders' power'. On the basis of this staff working document, the Commission decided not to take action on this issue. On the whole, apart from directive 2004/25/EC

Non-Executive or Supervisory Directors of Listed Companies and on the Committees of the (Supervisory) Board (2005/162/EC)', OJEU 2005 L 52/51-63 (text with EEA relevance); 'Directive 2007/36/EC of the European Parliament and of the Council of 11 July 2007 on the Exercise of Certain Rights of Shareholders in Listed Companies', OJEU 2007 L 184/17-24.

21. Press release of 18 October 2004, IP/04/1241: 'Corporate Governance: Commission Creates European Forum to Promote Convergence in Europe'; 'Commission decision of 28 April 2005 Establishing a Group of Non-Governmental Experts on Corporate Governance and Company Law', OJEU 2005 L 126/40-42.

22. 'Directive 2006/43/EC of the European Parliament and of the Council of 17 May 2006 on Statutory Audits of Annual Accounts and Consolidated Accounts, Amending Council Directives 78/660/EEC and 83/349/EEC and Repealing Council Directive 84/253/EEC', OJEU 2006 L 157/87-107 (text with EEA relevance); 'Directive 2006/46/EC of the European Parliament and of the Council of 14 June 2006 Amending Council Directives 78/660/EEC on the Annual Accounts of Certain Types of Companies, 83/349/EEC on Consolidated Accounts, 86/635/EEC on the Annual Accounts and Consolidated Accounts of Banks and Other Financial Institutions and 91/674/EEC on the Annual Accounts and Consolidated Cccounts of Insurance Undertakings', OJEU 2006 L 224/1-7 (text with EEA relevance).

23. Commission Staff Working Document of 12 December 2007: 'Impact Assessment on the Proportionality between Capital and Control in Listed Companies' (SEC(2007) 1705).

on takeover bids, the Community efforts in the field of corporate governance do not contain standards that had not already developed as standards of 'good' corporate governance anyhow.

D.   Corporate Governance Codes and Guidelines

[6] Regulation in the field of corporate governance can be found in a number of sources.[24] Among these are statutory regulation, listing rules, court judgments and all kinds of reports on corporate governance. Another important source are documents in the form of corporate governance codes and guidelines.[25] These come in two varieties. The first are nationwide documents that regulate the corporate governance framework of all listed corporations in a given jurisdiction. They can – conveniently – be called corporate governance *codes*. The second are documents adopted by the unitary or dual board of a corporation that regulate the corporate governance framework of a specific corporation. They can – conveniently – be called corporate governance *guidelines*.

1.   Corporate Governance Codes

[7] Examples of corporate governance codes are in the United Kingdom The Combined Code on Corporate Governance, drawn up by the Financial Reporting Council (version of June 2008, originally July 2003), and in the Netherlands The Dutch Corporate Governance Code, drawn up by the Corporate Governance Committee (December 2003, by the name of the committee's chairperson this committee is also called the Tabaksblat Committee).[26] Both codes specifically address listed corporations.[27] The Combined Code on Corporate Governance is the successor to three reports: The Financial Aspects of Corporate Governance, drawn up by the Committee on the Financial Aspects of Corporate Governance (December 1992, by the name of the committee's chairperson this report is also called the Cadbury Report), Directors' Remuneration, drawn up by the Study Group on Directors' Remuneration (July 1995, by the name of the study group's chairperson this rapport is also called the Greenbury Report), and the Final Report, drawn up by the Committee on Corporate Governance (January 1998, by the name of the committee's chairperson this report is also called the Hampel Report).[28] The Dutch Corporate Governance Code is the successor to the Recommendations on Corporate

---

24. A.F.M. Dorresteijn & C. de Groot (2006), 31-57; C. de Groot (2006), 195-214.
25. H.H. Voogsgeerd, *Corporate governance codes: markt- of rechtsarrangement?* (Deventer: Kluwer, 2006).
26. 'The Combined Code on Corporate Governance', <www.frc.org.uk> corporate governance; 'The Dutch Corporate Governance Code: Principles of Good Corporate Governance and Best Practice Provisions', <www.commissiecorporategovernance.nl> corporate governance code.
27. 'The Combined Code on Corporate Governance', Preamble, 3; 'The Dutch Corporate Governance Code', Preamble, 1.
28. <www.ecgi.org> codes & principles → index of all codes.

Governance in the Netherlands, Recommendations for Sound Management, Effective Supervision and Accountability, drawn up by the Committee on Corporate Governance (June 1997, by the name of the committee's chairperson this committee is also called the Peters Committee).[29] The build-up of The Combined Code on Corporate Governance and The Dutch Corporate Governance Code is very similar. The Combined Code consists of main principles, supporting principles and (concrete) code provisions. The Dutch Corporate Governance Code distinguishes between principles and (concrete) best practice provisions. The latter code states that '[t]he principles may be regarded as reflecting the latest general views on good corporate governance, which now enjoy wide support', whereas the best practice provisions 'reflect the national and international "best practices" and may be regarded as an elaboration of the general principles of good corporate governance'.[30] Both codes give listed corporations some measure of discretion in the application of the concrete corporate governance provisions by allowing corporations to depart from them. As The Combined Code on Corporate Governance puts it: 'While it is expected that companies will comply wholly or substantially with [all of the Code's] provisions, it is recognised that non-compliance may be justified in particular circumstances'.[31] And as The Dutch Corporate Governance Code states: 'Listed companies may depart from the best practice provisions. [Departure] is not in itself objectionable and indeed may even be justified in certain circumstances'.[32] The possibility of departure from the concrete corporate governance provisions is known as the 'comply or explain' approach.[33] In accordance with this formulation, departure must be explained.[34]

The 'comply or explain' approach is also recognized at the level of the European Union:[35]

> 1. A company whose securities are admitted to trading on a regulated market [. . .] shall include a corporate governance statement in its annual report. That

---

29. <www.commissiecorporategovernance.nl> archief → commissie peters.
30. 'The Dutch Corporate Governance Code', Preamble, 4 and 5.
31. 'The Combined Code on Corporate Governance', Preamble, 2; cf. Preamble, 3:
    'The Listing Rules require UK companies listed on the Main Market of the London Stock Exchange to describe in the annual report and accounts their corporate governance from two points of view, the first dealing generally with their adherence to the Code's main principles, and the second dealing specifically with non-compliance with any of the Code's provisions'.
32. 'The Dutch Corporate Governance Code', Preamble, 5.
33. 'The Combined Code on Corporate Governance', Preamble, 2; 'The Dutch Corporate Governance Code', Preamble, 6.
34. 'The Combined Code on Corporate Governance', Preamble, 2 and 5; 'The Dutch Corporate Governance Code', Preamble, 7.
35. 'Directive 2006/46/EC of the European Parliament and of the Council of 14 June 2006 Amending Council Directives 78/660/EEC on the Annual Accounts of Certain Types of Companies, 83/349/EEC on Consolidated Accounts, 86/635/EEC on the Annual Accounts and Consolidated Accounts of Banks and Other Financial Institutions and 91/674/EEC on the Annual Accounts and Consolidated Accounts of Insurance Undertakings', OJEU 2006 L 224/1-7 (text with EEA relevance): Article 1 ('Amendments to Directive 78/660/EEC'): Directive 78/660/EEC is hereby amended as follows: 7. the following Article shall be inserted: Article 46a.

statement shall be included as a specific section of the annual report and shall contain at least the following information:

(a) a reference to:
    (i) the corporate governance code to which the company is subject, and/or
    (ii) the corporate governance code which the company may have voluntarily decided to apply, and/or
    (iii) all relevant information about the corporate governance practices applied beyond the requirements under national law.
    Where points (i) and (ii) apply, the company shall also indicate where the relevant texts are publicly available; where point (iii) applies, the company shall make its corporate governance practices publicly available;

(b) to the extent to which a company, in accordance with national law, departs from a corporate governance code referred to under points (a)(i) or (ii), an explanation by the company as to which parts of the corporate governance code it departs from and the reasons for doing so. Where the company has decided not to apply any provisions of a corporate governance code referred to under points (a)(i) or (ii), it shall explain its reasons for doing so.

Other corporate governance codes have a similar build-up, although sometimes with deviations. In Australia, the ASX Corporate Governance Principles and Recommendations consist of principles, recommendations, and commentary and guidance.[36] The recommendations are governed by the comply or explain approach (called the 'if not, why not?' approach in the code), the commentary and guidance offers background, highlights certain aspects and provides suggestions.[37] The code mentions size as a specific circumstance that may lead a corporation to depart from corporate governance provisions: 'The ASX Corporate Governance Council recognises that the range in size and diversity of companies is significant and that smaller companies from the outset may face particular issues in following all Recommendations'.[38] The Belgian Code on Corporate Governance consists likewise of principles, provisions to which the comply or explain approach

---

36. 'Corporate Governance Principles and Recommendations', adopted by the ASX Corporate Governance Council, convened by the Australian Securities Exchange (August 2007, the successor to the 'Principles of Good Corporate Governance and Best Practice Recommendations' (March 2003)), <www.asx.com.au> listed companies → corporate governance.
37. 'ASX Corporate Governance Principles and Recommendations', Disclosure of corporate governance practices (following the 'if not, why not?' approach).
38. 'ASX Corporate Governance Principles and Recommendations', Disclosure of corporate governance practices (following the 'if not, why not?' approach).

applies, and guidelines, to which the comply or explain approach does not apply.[39]
The German Corporate Governance Code contains three kinds of provisions. These
are provisions of general purport, provisions in the form of recommendations, and
provisions in the form of suggestions.[40] As concerns the stipulations of general
purport the code states that these are 'provisions that enterprises are compelled to
observe under applicable law' anyhow. The code allows corporations to depart
from the recommendations, but corporations 'are then obliged to disclose this'. The
suggestions 'can be departed from without disclosure'. The New Zealand corporate
governance code, Corporate Governance in New Zealand, is built up of principles
and guidelines; added to that are key findings from consultation as well as the
opinion of the Securities Commission of New Zealand.[41]

In the Action Plan on company law and corporate governance published by the
European Commission in 2003 the Commission stated that '[t]here is little indi-
cation that the development of a European corporate governance code as an additional layer between principles developed at the international level and codes
adopted at national level would offer significant added value'. In this respect
the Commission referred to the OECD Principles of Corporate Governance.[42]

---

39. 'The Belgian Code on Corporate Governance', drawn up by the Corporate Governance Com-
    mittee (December 2004), <www.corporategovernancecommittee.be> English → code; 'The
    Belgian Code on Corporate Governance', Preamble, 4:
       'Smaller listed companies, in particular those new to listing, as well as young growth
    companies, may judge that some provisions are disproportionate or less relevant in their case.
    Also, holding companies and investment companies may need a different board structure, which
    may affect the relevance of some provisions'.
40. 'German Corporate Governance Code', drawn up by the Regierungskommission Deutscher
    Corporate Governance Kodex (February 2002 (subsequently amended), by the name of the
    chairperson of the Regierungskommission the code is also called the Cromme Code),
    <www.corporate-governance-code.de> English; 'German Corporate Governance Code', Fore-
    word: the recommendations are marked by the word 'shall', the suggestions are marked words
    such as 'should' or 'can'.
41. 'Corporate Governance in New Zealand: Principles and Guidelines' (February 2004, drawn up
    by the Securities Commission of New Zealand, <www.sec-com.govt.nz> publications → other
    publications; 'Corporate Governance in New Zealand', Foreword:

    'this document is in nine sections, each with four parts.

    1. The Principle – the high level objective which all entities should aim to achieve in
        each area of corporate governance. Entities should report on how they have
        achieved each of the Principles.
    2. Guidelines – structures or processes intended to help entities achieve each Principle.
        Some guidelines are more suited to certain types of entity, some to all entities. They
        are suggested ways of achieving the Principles. However, entities need not report
        against each guideline, including if the relevant Principle is achieved in another way.
    3. Key findings from consultation – the main points expressed by respondents to the
        consultation.
    4. Securities Commission View – the Commission's view on the issue, and the ratio-
        nale behind the Principle and guidelines'.

42. Now the 'OECD Principles of Corporate Governance' (2004): <www.oecd.org> browse (by
    topic) → corporate governance.

Nationwide corporate governance codes may have a considerable length. The Combined Code on Corporate Governance consists of 17 main principles, 26 supporting principles and 48 code provisions, and The Dutch Corporate Governance Code consists of 21 principles and 113 best practice provisions. The Cadbury Report contained a Code of Best Practice that consisted of 19 provisions; the Greenbury Report also contained a Code of Best Practice (the 'Greenbury Recommendations') that consisted of 39 provisions. The Hampel Report supported the results of its predecessors for the most part.[43] Therefore, it drafted only a small number of corporate governance principles.[44] The number of principles totaled 17. The Committee on Corporate Governance (that drew up the Hampel Report) furthermore announced its intention to bring together the existing and its own conclusions on good corporate governance into a combined 'set of principles and code'.[45] It did so in May 2000, by issuing The Combined Code, Principles of Good Governance and Code of Best Practice.[46] This code consisted of 17 principles and 48 code provisions. Finally, the report of the Peters Committee contained an appendix that consisted of 40 recommendations.

In the Netherlands, the government has set up the Monitoring Committee Corporate Governance Code.[47] The Monitoring Committee's remit is to advance the topicality and workability of The Dutch Corporate Governance Code.[48] The Committee shall at least once every year issue a report on the application of the code and on the adequacy of the code in the light of (international) corporate governance standards and practices.[49] The Committee can give its views on the way the code is being applied,[50] but does not have the power to amend the code.[51] In December 2005 the Committee issued a Report on Compliance with The Dutch Corporate Governance Code (this report dealt with compliance in 2004), in December 2006 the Committee issued its Second Report on Compliance with the Dutch Corporate Governance Code (this report dealt with compliance in 2005), and in December 2007 the Committee issued its Third Report on Compliance with the Dutch Corporate Governance Code (this report dealt with compliance in 2006).[52] Also, in May 2007 the Committee issued an Advisory Report on the Company-Shareholder Relationship and on the Scope of the Code, and in June 2008 the Committee issued a Report on the Evaluation and Updating of the Dutch

---

43. Hampel Report, 1.7.
44. Hampel Report, 1.20 and 2.1.
45. Hampel Report, 1.22-1.24.
46. '[D]erived by the Committee on Corporate Governance from the Committee's Final Report and from the Cadbury and Greenbury Reports', <www.ecgi.org> codes & principles → index of all codes.
47. Decree of 6 December 2004 (Establishing the Monitoring Committee Corporate Governance Code), Staatscourant 14 December 2004, nr. 241 page 11; C. de Groot, 'De opvattingen van de Monitoring Commissie Corporate Governance Code', *Onderneming en Financiering* (2007) issue 76, 42-50.
48. Article 2 of the decree.
49. Article 5 of the decree.
50. Article 5 of the decree.
51. Explanatory remarks to Article 5 of the decree.
52. <www.commissiecorporategovernance.nl> information in English.

Corporate Governance Code.[53] Finally, in December 2008 the Monitoring Committee presented an amended version of the Dutch Corporate Governance Code to the Dutch government for its consideration.[54]

2.   Corporate Governance Guidelines

[8] In the USA the New York Stock Exchange Listed Company Manual applies to corporations that are listed on the New York Stock Exchange.[55] In this Manual section 3 deals with 'Corporate responsibility'. This section itself consists of a number of Sections, some of which are subdivided into subsections. In Section 301 the manual states that 'every listed company is expected to follow certain practices aimed at maintaining appropriate standards of corporate responsibility, integrity and accountability to shareholders', and that section 3 as a whole 'describes the Exchange's policies and requirements with respect to independent directors, shareholders' voting rights, and other matters affecting corporate governance'. From these phrases it would seem to follow that the Manual understands corporate responsibility and corporate governance to be closely related. Section 303A deals with 'Corporate governance standards'. Among these are subsections 303A.01 ('Independent Directors'): 'Listed companies must have a majority of independent directors', 303A.03 ('Executive Sessions'): 'To empower non-management directors to serve as a more effective check on management, the non-management directors of each listed company must meet at regularly scheduled executive sessions without management', 303A.04 ('Nominating/Corporate Governance Committee'): 'Listed companies must have a nominating/corporate governance committee composed entirely of independent directors', 303A.05 ('Compensation Committee'): 'Listed companies must have a compensation committee composed entirely of independent directors', 303A.06 ('Audit Committee'): 'Listed companies must have an audit committee that satisfies the requirements of Rule 10A-3 under the Exchange Act', and 303A.14 ('Website Requirement'): 'Listed companies must have and maintain a publicly accessible website'. Thus, the Manual itself formulates a number of corporate governance standards, but in subsection 303A.09 ('Corporate Governance Guidelines') also requires that '[l]isted companies must adopt and disclose corporate governance guidelines'. These corporate governance guidelines must address at least the following issues: 'Director qualification standards', 'Director responsibilities', 'Director access to management and, as necessary and appropriate, independent advisors', 'Director compensation', 'Director orientation and continuing education', 'Management succession', and 'Annual performance evaluation of the board'. Understandably, corporate governance guidelines adopted by (the board of) a corporation do not

---

53. <www.commissiecorporategovernance.nl> information in English; The Dutch government is preparing a bill in reaction to the reports of the Monitoring Committee Corporate Governance Code.
54. <www.commissiecorporategovernance.nl>.
55. <www.nyse.com> nyse regulation → listed companies.

distinguish between principles and concrete provisions of corporate governance and do not make use of the comply or explain approach. These guidelines directly reflect the opinion of the corporation that adopted them.[56]

E.   RETHINKING CORPORATE GOVERNANCE

[9] The purpose of corporate law is to regulate the corporate form. Regulation in the field of corporate governance is an important aspect of corporate law. This would suggest that corporate governance too simply has the regulation of the corporate form as its purpose. However, such a characterization of corporate governance would reduce corporate governance to just being part of corporate law and would disregard any distinguishing features that corporate governance might have. Also, it would not explain why the concept of corporate governance has come to the fore with so much force. The predecessors to The Combined Code on Corporate Governance as well as The Dutch Corporate Governance Code highlight some features of corporate governance. According to the Hampel Report '[t]he single overriding objective shared by all listed companies, whatever their size or type of business, is the preservation and the greatest practicable enhancement over time of their shareholders' investment'.[57] The same thought is reflected in The Dutch Corporate Governance Code that states that 'the company endeavors to create long-term shareholder value'.[58] Corporate Governance tries to further this by addressing specific aspects of the regulation of the corporate form in a very specific way. The aspects addressed by corporate governance are outlined in the Cadbury and Hampel reports. The Cadbury Report defines corporate governance as 'the system by which companies are directed and controlled',[59] to which the Hampel Report adds that '[this definition] puts the directors of a company at the centre of any discussion on corporate governance, linked to the role of the shareholders, since they appoint the directors'.[60] And as for the specific way in which these issues are addressed by corporate governance, The Dutch Corporate Governance Code refers to 'the two pillars on which good corporate governance rests'.[61] These are 'integrity and transparency of decision-making by the management board', and 'proper supervision thereof, including accountability for such supervision'. The elements integrity, transparency, proper supervision and accountability may be thought of to imply a renewed evaluation of the roles of the unitary or dual board and of the shareholders. These four elements could then be considered as

---

56. An important US document are the 'Principles of Corporate Governance 2005', drawn up by the Business Roundtable (November 2005), 'an association of chief executive officers of leading US companies with $4.5 trillion in annual revenues and more than 10 million employees', <www.businessroundtable.org> task forces and issues → corporate governance.
57. Hampel Report, 1.16.
58. 'The Dutch Corporate Governance Code', Preamble, 3.
59. Cadbury Report, 2.5.
60. Hampel Report, 1.15.
61. 'The Dutch Corporate Governance Code', Preamble, 3.

the modern means to enhance shareholder value in the long term. Thus, corporate governance is about rethinking the corporate form and its regulation. From these sources, the following working definition of corporate governance can be derived: corporate governance is the regulation of the corporate form that – by rethinking corporate law with the purpose of guaranteeing the enhancement of shareholder value in the long term – addresses the roles of the corporation's centralized administration (the unitary or dual board and the managers) and of the corporation's shareholders, by specifically taking into account elements like integrity, transparency, proper supervision and accountability.

There are many definitions of corporate governance, so this is neither the only nor the definitive one.[62] Although this definition is rather narrow, it reaffirms the link between corporate governance and corporate law and at the same time allows the concept of corporate governance to embrace aspects as important as integrity, transparency, proper supervision and accountability. However, in order to bring this definition to life, it is necessary to realize that corporate governance is not just a legal term but is also embedded in organizational theory.

1.   Corporate Governance as a Legal Concept

[10] Corporate governance is – apart from being embedded in organizational theory (see below) – a legal concept. This may simply be derived from the fact that listed corporations may be obliged under law to apply the rules contained in a corporate governance code. Thus, Article 2:391 section 5 of the Dutch Civil Code empowers the government to enact that listed corporation shall apply The Dutch Corporate Governance Code. On the basis of this statutory provision the government issued a decree that obliges listed corporations to go into 'the application of the principles and best practice provisions [of The Dutch Corporate Governance Code] that are directed at the management board or the supervisory board' in the annual report, and to give an explanation when they did not apply one of these principles or best practice provisions and/or do not intend to do so.[63] Here the 'comply or explain' approach has been given a legal basis.[64] It follows from the foregoing that *application* of the relevant provisions in The Dutch Corporate Governance Code is not confined to the situation where a listed corporation decides on *full compliance* with those provisions but also includes the situation where a listed corporation decides on *departure* from those provisions by either *not observing* those provisions or *otherwise observing* those provisions. Full compliance and departure (non-observation and observation otherwise) are the allowed

---

62. A.F.M. Dorresteijn & C. de Groot (2006), 31-57.
63. Decree of 23 December 2004 to set further provisions on the contents of the annual accounts, Staatsblad 2004, 747; Article 3 of the decree.
64. S.M. Bartman, 'De code-Tabaksblat: een juridisch lichtgewicht', *Ondernemingsrecht* (2004), 123-126; M. Das, 'Geldt de Code?', *Ondernemingsrecht* (2004), 126-129; J.B. Huizink, A.J.M. Klein Wassink & S.E. Zijlstra, 'De Nederlandse Corporate Governance Code in de wet: statisch, dynamisch of problematisch', *Nederlands Juristenblad* (2004), 425-430; R. Abma, 'De commissie-Tabaksblat en haar code', *Tijdschrift voor Ondernemingsbestuur* (2005), 7-10.

ways of application of The Dutch Corporate Governance Code. Departure, however, must be explained. The (Dutch) Monitoring Committee Corporate Governance Code argued in its Second Report on Compliance with the Dutch Corporate Governance Code (over 2005) that explanation by a corporation of departure from provisions in The Dutch Corporate Governance shall meet criteria of intelligibility, verifiability, legitimacy and plausibility.[65]

Under The Dutch Corporate Governance Code responsibility 'for the corporate governance structure of the company and compliance with this code' falls to the management board and the supervisory board of the corporation together (Principle I). This cannot come as a surprise, because '[g]ood entrepreneurship, including integrity and transparency of decision-making by the management board, and proper supervision thereof, including accountability for such supervision' form the basis of corporate governance.[66] In order to be able to understand what good entrepreneurship within the meaning of the code is, it is necessary to consider how the code answers one important question: in whose interest should a corporation operate?[67] There are several views on this issue.[68] According to the shareholder-oriented model of corporate law the corporation is run in the interest of the shareholders primarily. This view is based on the idea that the interest of the shareholders should come first because they have invested in the corporation. In the stakeholder-oriented model of corporate law the corporation is run in the interests of both the shareholders and other stakeholders. These other stakeholders may include the corporation's employees, its creditors, its suppliers, customers and clients; beside that, the stakeholder-oriented model may place emphasis on a corporation's responsibilities toward government agencies, special interest groups, the environment and the wider community the corporation is part of. This view is based on the idea that a corporation is not just a vehicle for creating shareholder value but should be aware of its broader responsibilities and must contribute to sustainable development because it is part of society. On the surface of things, it would seem that The Dutch Corporate Governance Code adheres to the stakeholder-oriented model of corporate law. The code thinks of a corporation as 'a long-term form of collaboration between the various parties involved'.[69] In the opinion of the code, '[t]he stakeholders are the groups and individuals who directly or indirectly influence (or are influenced by) the achievement of the aims of the company. In other words employees, shareholders and other providers of capital,

---

65. Corporate Governance Code Monitoring Committee, 'Second Report on Compliance with the Dutch Corporate Governance Code' (over 2005), at 27-29.
66. 'The Dutch Corporate Governance Code', Preamble, 3.
67. A.F.M. Dorresteijn & C. de Groot (2006), 31-57.
68. A.W.A. Boot & R. Soeting, 'De onderneming in een spagaat', *Maandblad voor Accountancy en Bedrijfseconomie* (2004), 178-184; J.M. Dine, 'Executive Pay and Corporate Governance in the UK: Slimming the Fat Cats?', *European Company Law* (2006), 75-85; A.F.M. Dorresteijn & C. de Groot (2006), 31-57.
69. 'The Dutch Corporate Governance Code', Preamble, 3.

suppliers and customers, but also government and civil society'.[70] However, in the end the code does not adhere to the stakeholder-oriented model to the full. The code states: 'the company *endeavours* to create long-term shareholder value'.[71] As far as the other stakeholders are concerned, '[t]he management board and supervisory board should *take account of* the interests of the different stakeholders'.[72] This middle way between the shareholder-oriented and the stakeholder-oriented models is also known as the enlightened shareholder view.[73]

2.   Corporate Governance and Organizational Theory

[11] Corporate governance is – apart from being a legal concept (see above) – embedded in organizational theory. This is already clear from an expression as 'the corporate governance framework' of a corporation. Roberts describes the organization of corporations by using the phrase PARC.[74] PARC stands for the words *people, architecture, routines* and *culture*. These words may be used to consider corporate governance from the angle of organizational theory. Corporate governance would then imply that the executive directors and the non-executive directors must be equal to their duties and fit the criteria that are laid down in a profile (*people*). This also comes to the fore in The Dutch Corporate Governance Code that requires that the supervisory board 'shall prepare a profile of its size and composition, taking account of the nature of the business, its activities and the desired expertise and background of the supervisory board members'.[75] Also the design of the board, or both the management board and the supervisory board, must meet certain demands (*architecture*). According to The Dutch Corporate Governance Code the supervisory board (if it consists of more than four members) shall set up from among its members three key committees: an audit committee, a remuneration committee and a selection and appointment committee.[76] Furthermore, the executive directors and the non-executive directors must adhere to certain procedures (*routines*). The Dutch Corporate Governance Code outlines e.g. what to do in the event of an (apparent) complex of interests or a conflict

---

70. 'The Dutch Corporate Governance Code', Preamble, 3.
71. 'The Dutch Corporate Governance Code', Preamble, 3, emphasis added.
72. 'The Dutch Corporate Governance Code', Preamble, 3, emphasis added.
73. J. Rickford, 'Forthcoming Change in Corporate Law in the UK: The British Company Law Review and beyond (Part 1)', *Ondernemingsrecht* (2002), 325-332; cf. E. Berglöf & E.-L. von Thadden, 'The Changing Corporate Governance Paradigm: Implications for Developing and Transition Economies', in *Corporate Governance and Globalization: Long Range Planning Issues*, eds S.S. Cohen & G. Boyd (Cheltenham: Edward Elgar Publishing Limited, 2000), 275-306.
74. J. Roberts, *The Modern Firm: Organizational Design for Performance and Growth* (Oxford, Oxford University Press, 2004).
75. 'The Dutch Corporate Governance Code', best practice provision III.3.1.
76. 'The Dutch Corporate Governance Code', principle III.5 and best practice provisions III.5.1-III.5.13.

of interests involving an executive director or a non-executive director.[77] Finally, the board, or the management and supervisory boards, must exude high-standard norms and values (*culture*): in any organization the tone at the top is essential and should e.g. reflect the importance of integrity. On this thought, The Dutch Corporate Governance Code refers to the corporation having 'a code of conduct which should, in any event, be published on the company's website' and to employees having 'the possibility of reporting alleged irregularities of a general, operational and financial nature in the company to the chairman of the management board or to an official designated by him, without jeopardising their legal position'.[78] Among these four elements of corporate governance derived from organizational theory *people* and *architecture* on the one hand, and *routines* and *culture* on the other hand are closely connected. The purpose of the first pair (*people* and *architecture*) is that the unitary or dual board can exercise its *functions* effectively. The purpose of the second pair (*routines* and *culture*) is to guarantee that the unitary or dual board adheres to correct *processes*. The first pair forms – as a matter of speech – the passive part of corporate governance, because it emphasizes the persons who make up and the design of the board as such. The second pair forms – as a matter of speech – the active part of corporate governance, because it demands that the board takes an active stand. Passive corporate governance is concerned with e.g. the functions of the corporation's centralized administration and the composition and functioning of corporate boards. Active corporate governance requires the board of a corporation to do things. Examples of this are that a corporation shall take care about risk management,[79] develop a policy on executive remuneration,[80] make sure that the executive directors, non-executive directors, managers and employees may refer to a code of conduct,[81] can handle public takeover bids, and be concerned about investor relations. The fact that corporate governance is also embedded in organizational theory underlines the 'dynamics' of corporate governance as these dynamics may well result from the fact that corporate governance is not just a legal concept. These dynamics of corporate governance can best be derived from studying, next corporate governance codes, statutory regulation and listing rules, sources of corporate governance that reveal these dynamics. These sources are most importantly reports and judgments that deal with instances where investigators or courts were asked to analyze corporate governance issues in specific cases. They reveal how corporate governance comes to life in practice. Thus, both this and each of the chapters that follow are built up of two parts: part A gives a general overview of the subject discussed and part B

---

77. 'The Dutch Corporate Governance Code', principle II.3 and best practice provisions II.3.2-II.3.4, and principle III.6 and best practice provisions III.6.1-III.6.3 and III.6.5.
78. 'The Dutch Corporate Governance Code', best practice provision II.1.3 and best practice provision II.1.6 (II.1.7 in the amended version of The Dutch Corporate Governance Code).
79. 'The Dutch Corporate Governance Code', principle II.1 and best practice provisions II.1.3-II.1.5 and III.1.6.
80. Article 2:135 section 1 of the Dutch Civil Code; 'The Dutch Corporate Governance Code', principle II.2-2.
81. 'The Dutch Corporate Governance Code', best practice provision II.1.3.

illustrates and supplements that discussion by investigating the dynamics of corporate governance.[82]

These are some of the issues addressed by corporate governance: the corporation's centralized administration (discussed in chapter 3), the composition and functioning of corporate boards (discussed in chapter 4), risks (discussed in chapter 6), executive directors' remuneration (discussed in chapter 7), personal ethics (discussed in chapter 8), public takeover bids (discussed in chapter 9), and investor relations[83] (discussed in chapter 10). Chapters 2 and 5 deal with specific elements of corporate law in the Netherlands: the so-called 'right of inquiry' and the so-called 'mandatory organizational arrangement'.

II.   CASE STUDIES

A.   AN INTRODUCTION TO RESTORING TRUST

[12] The report *Restoring Trust* may serve as a first example of a document that deals with a number of issues that make up corporate governance. It deals with the events surrounding the US corporation WorldCom, Inc.

[13] The US corporation WorldCom, Inc. ('WorldCom') operated one of the world's largest communications networks. In 2002 it appeared that WorldCom had overstated earnings by more than USD 3,8 billion. Thereafter, the US Securities and Exchange Commission ('SEC') filed suit against WorldCom. WorldCom and the SEC entered into a settlement whereby the court would issue an injunction. Under the terms of the injunction WorldCom and its successor MCI, Inc. ('MCI') were required to implement all recommendations that were contained in a report on the governance of WorldCom. The investigation that resulted in this report was undertaken by R.C. Breeden. The report is *Restoring Trust*. *Restoring Trust* 'seeks to identify the weaknesses in the Company's internal governance practices that made it vulnerable to the abuses that took place, or allowed them to continue undetected and unchecked for a considerable time'.[84] Further, *Restoring Trust* contains a large number of recommendations. Although directed at WorldCom and MCI, the report states that the issues that it addresses are of interest to all publicly held corporations.[85]

---

82. In the case of chapters 4 and 5: three.
83. Also: shareholder relations.
84. 'Restoring Trust: Report to the Hon. Jed S. Rakoff, the United States District Court for the Southern District of New York on Corporate Governance for the Future of MCI, Inc.', prepared by Richard C. Breeden, Corporate Monitor ('Restoring Trust', August 2003), <www.ecgi.org> codes & principles → index of all codes.
85. The events surrounding WorldCom are also discussed in S. Hamilton & A. Micklethwait, *Greed and Corporate Failure: The Lessons from Recent Disasters* (Houndmills: Palgrave Macmillan, 2006), 59-80.

B.   Results of the Review in Restoring Trust

[14] The review of the governance of WorldCom showed that although WorldCom had grown rapidly through acquisitions, it had done little to integrate the companies it had acquired. Like other corporations that operated communications networks, WorldCom's revenues had declined because fixed line services were being substituted by wireless services. Yet, WorldCom had overstated its profits, something that investors were unaware of. *Restoring Trust* speaks of 'capitalization of "line costs", misuse of reserves and other accounting tricks'. Also, WorldCom had overstated its net worth as shown on the balance sheet. In the words of the report, 'more than 75% of the assets reported on the Company's balance sheet turned out to be accounting helium rather than tangible sources of net worth'. Some of this could be accredited to the fact that controls for the preparation and publication of financial results were not functioning or did not even exist. First, WorldCom's internal accounting and finance department had its functions dispersed over many locations, and – absent systems to prevent or expose alterations that were made – at the corporation's headquarters financial figures could be adjusted manually. Second, WorldCom's internal audit department was too small, and its personnel lacked training and experience.

All of this took place against the background of a failing corporate governance framework. WorldCom's CEO 'was allowed nearly imperial reign over the affairs of the Company, without the board of directors exercising any apparent restraint on his actions, even though he did not appear to possess the experience or training to be remotely qualified for his position'. According to *Restoring Trust*, the CEO pursued wealth, and handed out stock options and retention grants to senior managers who were loyal to him. The CEO was personally involved in a number of business activities that required bank loans that he collateralized by WorldCom stock he held. When in the late 1990's stock value of telecom corporations began to fall, this posed great difficulties for him. To counter these problems, the CEO arranged for WorldCom to give him personal loans and guarantees. When the board finally fired the CEO, it granted him elaborate severance arrangements consisting of a severance award 'along with other perks such as use of corporate planes and offices and insurance benefits'. Notably, on the surface of things WorldCom's corporate governance framework made an excellent impression. A majority of the members of the board of WorldCom were independent non-executive directors, the board had established board committees, and WorldCom had separated the positions of CEO and chairperson of the board. But the board met only quarterly in brief sessions. This allowed little more than the mere ratification of proposals. Likewise, the board's audit committee spent no more than three to six hours per year in fulfilling its main responsibilities. The board 'did not act like it was in control of the Company's overall direction'. For example, WorldCom grew rapidly through acquisitions that it acquired at high prices. It had to make enough money to pay back its debts, but the board paid little attention to managing WorldCom's liquidity risks. And as result of WorldCom's growth, '[c]ontrol risks also grew exponentially as new companies were acquired and management failed to integrate systems, networks, commission plans or other areas of operations'.

C.   RECOMMENDATIONS IN RESTORING TRUST

[15] The recommendations contained in *Restoring Trust* are divided over ten parts in the report. Part I focuses on the board of directors, part II on board leadership and the chairman of the board, and parts III and IV on board compensation and executive compensation respectively.[86]

1.   The Board of Directors

[16] As concerns the board of directors, the report recommends that the number of directors of MCI should range between eight and twelve, and that all members of the board except the CEO should be independent directors. The board should meet at least eight but rather ten times per year, and two or three meetings should be held at corporate locations other than the corporation's headquarters. At each board meeting, the independent directors should meet in a separate session for some time to discuss among themselves corporate affairs without the CEO being present. Once every year, the CEO should present before the board a '"State of the Company" presentation'. With the exception of the CEO, directors should not serve for more than ten years or past the age of 75. Qualification standards for independent directors should:

   (i) require a preponderance of members to have minimum experience serving on boards of publicly held business entities,
   (ii) require absence of conflicts of interest,
   (iii) set a maximum limit on the number of public company boards on which the director sits, and
   (iv) establish other qualifications deemed appropriate by the board.

2.   Board Leadership and the Chairman of the Board

[17] On the matter of board leadership, the report discusses the 'Chairman and CEO' structure that is traditionally followed by most US listed corporations. In this structure, the positions of CEO and chairperson of the board are held by one person. Two drawbacks this structure may have are the concentration of power in the hands of one individual and the work overload that she may have to cope with. In the opinion of the report, for the structure to work it needs the creation of the position

---

86. Part V deals with the audit committee, part VI with the governance committee, part VII with the compensation committee, part VIII with the risk management committee, part IX with general corporate issues, and part X with legal and ethics programs.

of 'lead director' to guarantee independent board leadership. However, this has a drawback too, as it makes one independent non-executive director (who is designated lead director) more important than the others. The report contrasts the 'Chairman and CEO' structure with the structure that is commonly followed in Europe and in particular in the United Kingdom whereby the positions of CEO and chairperson of the board are separated. WorldCom operated along those lines, but its chairperson did not have real powers. This structure has potential drawbacks because it will not work when the chairperson is disengaged, and will not work either when the chairperson becomes too engaged because she may then be regarded as a rival of the CEO. However, the structure's main advantage lays in better checks and balances that it offers. Therefore, 'the separation of the role of board leadership from management leadership seems desirable for MCI', but the powers, duties and responsibilities of the independent chairperson should be clearly defined. The chairperson should also be assisted by a small separate staff. The report recommends that a non-executive chairperson of the board should hold this position for not more than six years.

3. Board Compensation and Executive Compensation

[18] In the opinion of the report, executive directors' compensation should be paid in cash for at least 50%, and preferably 60 to 75%. Given the fact that compensation in the form of stock options may generate windfall benefits or may induce directors 'to hype the stock', the report favors equity compensation in the form of stock grants over stock options. The construction of awards in the form of stock grants could have the form of a certain pre-set amount of money that is being paid in shares rather than the form of a certain pre-set number of shares that are being given. Further, such stock grants should be linked to performance criteria.[87] The report further recommended that non-executive directors should be required to invest at least 25% of their compensation in shares of the corporation to be held for at least six months after leaving the corporation, and that executive directors (and senior managers) should be required to hold on to at least 75% of the compensation that was awarded to them in the form of shares in the corporation for at least six months after leaving the corporation.

In the opinion of the report, non-executive directors should receive only cash compensation and should not be granted stock options or equity grants. Although stock options and equity grants are thought to align the interests of directors with those of shareholders, this 'is more illusory than real' because the real benefit that shareholders enjoy is mostly the long term growth of the value of their investment whereas recipients of stock options especially benefit mostly from short term share price fluctuations. Non-executive directors' compensation should reflect both time

---

87. '[S]uch as (i) profitability, (ii) tangible net worth, (iii) strength of balance sheet ratios, (iv) return on assets or equity, (v) growth in net income or EBITDA, (vi) cost reductions, (vii) growth in market share or other hurdles that reflect the creation of real economic value'.

commitment and the fact that non-executive directors may serve on a limited number of board only. At the same time, setting the level of non-executive directors' compensation too high might reduce their willingness to confront the executive directors or to resign. For MCI, non-executive directors' compensation could have 'a recommended level of not less than $150,000 per year'.

D.   Introduction to the North American Catholic v.
                      Gheewalla Case

[19] The judgment of the Supreme Court of the State of Delaware in the *North American Catholic v. Gheewalla* case shows that debates on abstract concepts like the shareholder-oriented model of corporate law versus the stakeholder-oriented model of corporate law may have consequences for the application of corporate law (even if those concepts are not referred to expressly).

[20] North American Catholic Educational Programming Foundation, Inc. ('NACEPF'), Hispanic Information and Telecommunications Network, Inc., Instructional Telecommunications Foundation, Inc. ('ITF') and a number of affiliates of ITF held licenses issued by the Federal Communications Commission to use certain radio waves in the spectrum of 'Instruction Television Fixed Service'. In 2000 these lessees formed the ITFS Spectrum Development Alliance, Inc. (the 'Alliance') and in 2001 entered into an agreement with Clearwire Holdings, Inc. ('Clearwire'). Under the agreement the Alliance members would allow Clearwire to acquire those licenses as the Alliance members would not exercise their rights of first refusal when the terms of the licenses expired, and Clearwire would pay the Alliance members the sum of over USD 24,3 million. However, in 2002, following the events surrounding WorldCom, Inc. ('WorldCom') – also licensed to use certain radio waves – it appeared that the market for radio waves would collapse as a result of a surplus of radio waves that would become available from World-Com. Clearwire then entered into negotiations with the Alliance members to dissolve its obligations. These negotiations ended in Clearwire settling with the Alliance members but not with NACEPF.

E.   The Decision of the Delaware Supreme Court

[21] NACEPF filed actions against three directors of Clearwire, Rob Gheewalla, Gerry Cardinale, and Jack Daly. NACEPF argued that these directors had been able to control Clearwire because – although they constituted only a minority on Clearwire's board – they were also 'employed by [Goldman Sachs & Co. ('Goldman Sachs')] and served on the Clearwire Board of Directors at the behest of Goldman Sachs' that funded Clearwire.[88] In the opinion of Clearwire these directors, who

---

88. Formulation by the Delaware Supreme Court.

controlled Clearwire, had inter alia breached their *fiduciary duties* to NACEPF because the fact that 'Clearwire was either insolvent or in the "zone of insolvency,"' had as a consequence that they owed such duties to NACEPF who, although not a shareholder of Clearwire, was a substantial creditor of Clearwire.[89] These actions were dismissed by the Court of Chancery of the State of Delaware. The plaintiff appealed, but in its judgment of 18 May 2007 the Supreme Court of the State of Delaware affirmed the judgment of the Court of Chancery.[90] As to the question when a corporation is either insolvent or in the zone of insolvency, the Supreme Court referred to the considerations of the Court of Chancery:[91]

> that insolvency may be demonstrated by either showing (1) 'a deficiency of assets below liabilities with no reasonable prospect that the business can be successfully continued in the face thereof,' or (2) 'an inability to meet maturing obligations as they fall due in the ordinary course of business.' (footnotes deleted),

also referring to the fact that the Court of Chancery had 'concluded that NACEPF had satisfactorily alleged facts which permitted a reasonable inference that Clearwire operated in the zone of insolvency during at least a substantial portion of the relevant periods'.[92] In general terms the Supreme Court considered that 'Delaware corporate law provides for a separation of control and ownership. The directors of Delaware corporations have "the legal responsibility to manage the business of a corporation for the benefit of its shareholders owners." Accordingly, fiduciary duties are imposed upon the directors to regulate their conduct when they perform *that* function',[93] and therefore '[i]t is well established that the directors owe their fiduciary obligations to the corporation and its shareholders'.[94] However, the Supreme Court added:

> When a corporation is *solvent*, those [fiduciary] duties may be enforced by its shareholders, who have standing to bring *derivative* actions on behalf of the corporation because they are the ultimate beneficiaries of the corporation's growth and increased value. When a corporation is *insolvent*, however, its creditors take the place of the shareholders as the residual beneficiaries of any increase in value. Consequently, the creditors of an *insolvent* corporation have standing to maintain derivative claims against directors on behalf of the corporation for breaches of fiduciary duties. The corporation's insolvency 'makes the creditors the principal constituency injured by any fiduciary breaches that diminish the firm's value.' Therefore, equitable considerations give creditors

89. Formulation by the Delaware Supreme Court.
90. Supreme Court of the State of Delaware 18 May 2007 (North American Catholic v. Gheewalla); <www.courts.delaware.gov> opinions → 2007, 5/18/07 North American Catholic v. Gheewalla 521, 2006.
91. Formulation by the Delaware Supreme Court.
92. Footnote deleted.
93. Footnotes deleted.
94. Footnote deleted.

standing to pursue derivative claims against the directors of an insolvent corporation. Individual creditors of an insolvent corporation have the same incentive to pursue valid derivative claims on its behalf that shareholders have when the corporation is solvent (footnotes deleted).

This case, however, did not involve a derivative claim, but NACEPF 'asserted a *direct* claim against the director Defendants for alleged breaches of fiduciary duty when Clearwire was insolvent'. The Supreme Court did not accept that such a direct claim exists:

> Recognizing that directors of an insolvent corporation owe direct fiduciary duties to creditors, would create uncertainty for directors who have a fiduciary duty to exercise their business judgment in the best interest of the insolvent corporation. To recognize a new right for creditors to bring direct fiduciary claims against those directors would create a conflict between those directors' duty to maximize the value of the insolvent corporation for the benefit of all those having an interest in it, and the newly recognized direct fiduciary duty to individual creditors. Directors of insolvent corporations must retain the freedom to engage in vigorous, good faith negotiations with individual creditors for the benefit of the corporation. Accordingly, we hold that individual *creditors* of an *insolvent* corporation have *no right to assert direct* claims for breach of fiduciary duty against corporate directors. Creditors may nonetheless protect their interest by bringing derivative claims on behalf of the insolvent corporation or any *other* direct nonfiduciary claim [...] that may be available for individual creditors (footnote deleted).[95]

The Supreme Court repeatedly formulated that the basis of such nonfiduciary claims of creditors could be 'a direct claim arising out of contract or tort', more specifically 'protection through contractual agreements, fraud and fraudulent conveyance law, implied covenants of good faith and fair dealing, bankruptcy law, general commercial law and other sources of creditor rights',[96] and 'the protections afforded by their negotiated agreements, their security instruments, the implied covenant of good faith and fair dealing, fraudulent conveyance law, and bankruptcy law'.

F.   EVALUATION

[22] *Restoring Trust* offers a neat illustration of a number of (corporate governance) issues that may cause problems for corporations or even their downfall. These issues include problems relating to integration after making acquisitions, declining revenues following technological developments, but also overstating net

---

95. Therefore, '[t]he creditors of a Delaware corporation that is either insolvent or in the zone of insolvency have no right, as a matter of law, to assert direct claims for breach of fiduciary duty against its directors'.
96. Footnote deleted.

worth and profits, non-existence or non-functioning of risk management and control systems, board performance, the role of board committees and of the CEO, director independence and (executive) director compensation. If anything, *Restoring Trust* underlines the importance of 'good' corporate governance as a means to enhance shareholder value in the long term and preserve the well-being of the corporation for all stakeholders. In relation to the shareholder- versus stakeholder-oriented models of corporate law are concerned, the Supreme Court of the State of Delaware stated in *North American Catholic v. Gheewalla* that the prime duty of directors is 'the legal responsibility to manage the business of a corporation for the benefit of its shareholders owners'. Only in specific circumstances the interests of other stakeholders may take precedence, in particular the interests of the creditors of a corporation that is insolvent or in the zone of insolvency.

Chapter 2
Legal Remedies

I. THE 'RIGHT OF INQUIRY' IN THE NETHERLANDS
    AS AN EXAMPLE

[23] The corporate form, or corporation, has several characteristics. In legal terms, corporations are characterized by having legal personality and an issued share capital that is divided into transferable shares. These features, however, cannot serve to distinguish corporations definitively from other legal entities as they are also found in the legal form that is mostly used in small or medium-sized businesses, the private limited company. In sociological terms however, corporations have a characteristic that distinguishes them from private limited companies. This feature is the separation of investing opportunities in the corporation for investors of capital from the administration of the corporation that is undertaken by its directors and managers (collectively called the corporation's centralized administration). This characteristic makes it possible that several groups of participants are involved in the corporation in their own right and with their own interests. The investors of capital are given investing opportunities without the need to be concerned about the administration of the corporation themselves, and the directors and managers of the corporation are specialized decision makers who in return for their work receive remuneration. Although especially this last sociological feature may have contributed to the fact that the corporation is the dominant legal form for organizing large-scale businesses world-wide,[97] it also brings with it some drawbacks of the corporate form.[98]

---

97. R. Kraakman, 'The Durability of the Corporate Form', in *The Twenty-First-Century Firm: Changing Economic Organization in International Perspective*, ed. P. DiMaggio (Princeton: Princeton University Press, 2001), 147-160.
98. C. de Groot, 'Can Corporate Governance Contribute to Sustainable Development', in *Neoliberal Globalism and Social Sustainable Globalisation*, ed. E.C. Nieuwenhuys (Leiden: Brill Academic Publishers, 2006), 195-214.

One of these is the so-called 'agency problem'. The agency problem may well be the cause of much corporate litigation, especially shareholder litigation. Corporate and shareholder litigation may be used to attempt to enforce rules of 'good' corporate governance. Corporate and shareholder litigation may involve proceedings where (former) directors are held liable for conduct that is at variance with 'good' corporate governance. Such actions may be instigated by the corporation or in some jurisdictions by shareholders on behalf of the corporation. The latter are so-called derivative actions. Derivative action have led to much case law of e.g. the Court of Chancery of the State of Delaware and – on appeal – of the Supreme Court of the State of Delaware.[99] Corporate and shareholder litigation may also involve proceedings before specialized authorities such as takeover panels. Examples of takeover panels are the Panel on Takeovers and Mergers in the United Kingdom,[100] the Takeovers Panel in Australia,[101] the Takeovers Panel in New Zealand,[102] the Übernahmekommission in Austria,[103] and the Übernahmekommission in Switserland.[104] Part A of this chapter consists of the following paragraphs: *the agency problem* and *the 'right of inquiry'*. The 'right of inquiry' is a judicial process in the Netherlands before a specialized court that to a large extent facilitates corporate and shareholder litigation.[105]

A.   THE AGENCY PROBLEM

[24] The agency problem goes back to the separation of investing opportunities in the corporation from the administration of the corporation.[106] This separation implies that the investors of capital entrust the running of the corporation to the directors and managers but cannot be sure that these directors and managers will always act in the investors' best interests.[107] The agency problem translates this into a more fundamental issue that is characteristic of the corporate form.

---

99. B.F. Assink, *Rechterlijke toetsing van bestuurlijk gedrag* (Deventer: Kluwer, 2007).
100. <www.thetakeoverpanel.org.uk>.
101. <www.takeovers.gov.au>.
102. <www.takeovers.govt.nz>.
103. <www.takeover.at>.
104. <www.takeover.ch>.
105. On the 'right of inquiry': P.G.F.A. Geerts, *Enkele formele aspecten van het enquêterecht* (Deventer: Kluwer, 2004); G.J.H. van der Sangen, 'Het enquêterecht als bron van nieuw ondernemingsrecht?', *Tijdschrift voor Ondernemingsbestuur* (2004), 33-45 and 82-93; M.M. Tuijtel, 'The Dutch Inquiry Proceedings: A Unique Instrument for Minority Protection from a Comparative Law Perspective', *European Company Law* (2005), 90-99.
106. H. Hansmann & R. Kraakman, 'Agency Problems and Legal Strategies', in R. Kraakman et al., *The Anatomy of Corporate Law: A Comparative and Functional Approach* (Oxford: Oxford University Press, 2004), 21-31.
107. R. Kraakman (2001), 147-160; J.G.C.M. Galle, 'Toezicht op de naleving van corporategovernance-regelgeving', *Tijdschrift voor Ondernemingsbestuur* (2006), 219-227; C. de Groot (2006), 195-214; B.T.M. Steins Bisschop, 'Beloningssystemen: de ongerechtvaardigde hypothese van parallelle belangen tussen aandeelhouders en bestuurders', *Tijdschrift voor*

This is the issue of the separation of ownership and control. This is to be understood basically as the situation where the *ownership* by the shareholders of the shares they hold *in* the corporation does not imply *control* by the shareholders *over* the corporation, as real control is not in the hands of the corporation's shareholders but in the hands of the corporation's directors and managers.[108] At the outset, the agency problem is especially acute in listed corporations where it results from the fact that the corporation's shares are traded on one or several regulated markets.[109] At the same time, the focus on listed corporations has the effect that the agency problem may present itself in three ways.[110] *First*, a listed corporation may have numerous and dispersed shareholders. In that case, individual shareholders on their own are unable to exert influence over the way the directors and managers of the corporation handle the affairs of the corporation, and come across practical difficulties when they want to exert such influence together with fellow shareholders. This case (it could be referred to as the 'polypsonic' case) is the basic example of the agency problem as there is a confrontation of the shareholders and the directors and managers. A solution could be to think out mechanisms that serve to align the interests of the directors and managers of the corporation with the interests of the shareholders. But it is not the only case. *Second*, a listed corporation may have large block holding shareholders. In that case, the directors and managers of the corporation and these block holding shareholders may be tempted to run the affairs of the corporation in close co-operation, to the detriment of minority shareholders. In this case (it could be called the 'oligopsonic' case), a remedy could be found in the protection of minority shareholders. *Third*, a listed corporation may be confronted by a public takeover bid by one shareholder or several shareholders acting in concert. In that case, the directors and managers of the corporation may want to entrench themselves in an attempt to counter the public takeover bid by making use of defensive measures and relying on defensive constructions. In this case (the 'monopsonic' case) an anti-frustration rule might come to the aid of a prospective bidder to counter these defensive measures and a breakthrough rule might come to the aid of a successful bidder to counter these defensive constructions.

Central to all these cases is that the general meeting of shareholders does not function properly as a controlling and decision-making mechanism. Under these

Ondernemingsbestuur (2006), 50-59; C. Knoops, 'Transparantie in de beloningen van topbestuurders', *Maandblad voor Accountancy en Bedrijfseconomie* (2008), 314-316.

108. A.F.M. Dorresteijn & C. de Groot, 'Corporate Governance Codes: Origins and Perspectives', in *European Company Law in Accelerated Progress*, ed. S.M. Bartman (Alphen aan den Rijn: Kluwer Law International, 2006), 31-57 (also published in *European Company Law* 2004, 43-56); C. de Groot, 'The Level and Composition of Executive Remuneration: A View from the Netherlands', *European Company Law* (2006), 11-17.
109. C. de Groot (2006), 11-17.
110. E. Berglöf & E.-L. von Thadden, 'The Changing Corporate Governance Paradigm: Implications for Developing and Transition Economies', in *Corporate Governance and Globalization: Long Range Planning Issues*, eds S.S. Cohen & G. Boyd (Cheltenham: Edward Elgar Publishing Limited, 2000), 275-306; C. de Groot (2006), 11-17.

circumstances, it is no surprise that shareholders may be tempted to institute legal proceedings. Corporate litigation, especially shareholder litigation, is an important element of corporate law. In the Netherlands, there exists a remarkable judicial process that highly facilitates corporate litigation. This judicial process is the so-called 'right of inquiry'. The provisions on the right of inquiry are laid down in Book 2 of the Dutch Civil Code. Book 2 of the Dutch Civil Code deals with 'Legal persons'. It consist of nine Titles (some of which are divided into sections): Title 1: General provisions, Title 2: Associations, Title 3: Cooperative societies and mutual insurance societies, Title 4: Corporations, Title 5: Private limited companies, Title 6: Foundations, Title 7: Merger and division, Title 8: Dispute resolution by compulsory transfer of shares or compulsory acquisition of shares, and the right of inquiry, Title 9: The annual accounts and the annual report. The provisions on the 'right of inquiry' are laid down in Articles 2:344 through 2:359 of the Dutch Civil Code. Legal proceedings under the 'right of inquiry' take place before the *ondernemingskamer*. The Dutch term *ondernemingskamer* may be translated as Chamber of Business Affairs, Companies and Business Chamber, Companies and Business Court or Enterprise Court.[111] Technically, the Chamber of Business Affairs is a division of the Court of Appeals at Amsterdam (one of the five Courts of Appeals in the Netherlands). Although part of the Court of Appeals at Amsterdam, the Chamber of Business Affairs acts as the court of first instance under the provisions on the 'right of inquiry' in Book 2 of the Dutch Civil Code.

B.   THE 'RIGHT OF INQUIRY'

[25] The provisions on the 'right of inquiry' give shareholders (and holders of depository receipts) two successive rights in respect of a corporation (and also of a private limited company). First, shareholders are entitled to ask the Chamber of Business Affairs to find well-founded reasons to doubt good policy on the part of the corporation, and – if the court so finds – appoint one of several persons to investigate the policy and the course of affairs of the corporation. Second, shareholders are entitled to ask the Chamber of Business Affairs to conclude that the report drawn up by the investigator(s) shows that there has been mismanagement on the part of the corporation, and – if the court so concludes – order measures in respect of the corporation.

Under Articles 2:344 through 2:346 of the Dutch Civil Code one or several shareholders (or holders of depository receipts) who alone or together represent at

---

111.   On the Chamber of Business Affairs: M. Josephus Jitta et al., *The Companies and Business Court from a Comparative Law Perspective* (Deventer: Kluwer, 2004); J.B. Jacobs, 'The Role of Specialized Courts in Resolving Corporate Governance Disputes in the United States and in the EU: An American Judge's Perspective', *Ondernemingsrecht* (2007), 80-85; M.J. Kroeze, 'The Companies and Business Court as a Specialized Court', *Ondernemingsrecht* (2007), 86-91; L. Timmerman, 'Company Law and the Dutch Supreme Court', *Ondernemingsrecht* (2007), 91-95.

least one tenth of the issued share capital, or – in the alternative – who alone or together hold shares (or depository receipts) that have a nominal value of at least EUR 225,000 are entitled to ask the Chamber of Business Affairs to appoint one of several persons to investigate the policy and the course of affairs of the corporation (or private limited company). Before bringing the matter to the Chamber of Business Affairs, the applicants must – in accordance with Article 2:349 section 1 – bring their concerns about the policy or the course of affairs of the corporation to the attention of the management board and the supervisory board, and allow these boards a reasonable amount of time to investigate these concerns and take measures in response. When the applicants fail to do so, the Chamber of Business Affairs will declare the application inadmissible. In accordance with Article 2:350 section 1 the Chamber of Business Affairs finds for the applicants if it finds well-founded reasons to doubt good policy on the part of the corporation (and dismisses the application if it does not find well-founded reasons to doubt good policy). When the Chamber of Business Affairs finds for the applicants it may appoint one or several persons to investigate the policy and the course of affairs of the corporation, either in its entirety, or with regard to specific parts or a specific period. The Chamber of Business Affairs sets the amount of money that the investigation may cost at the most; the corporation must pay the costs of the investigation (Article 2:350 section 3). The investigators may examine all documentation of the corporation and have access to all property of the corporation; the executive directors and the non-executive directors of the corporation, and all persons who are employed by the corporation, must answer questions asked by the investigators (Article 3:351 section 1). The investigators must deposit the report of the investigation at the registry of the Chamber of Business Affairs (Article 3:353 section 1). The report is open for inspection by the corporation, the applicants, and – if the court so decides – other persons (Article 3:353 section 2). The original applicants (and in case the report was open for inspection to them other shareholders (or holders of depository receipts) who meet the requirements of Articles 2:344 through 2:346) are entitled to ask the Chamber of Business Affairs to order measures in respect of the corporation (Article 3:355 section 1). In accordance with Article 2:355 section 1 the Chamber of Business Affairs finds for the applicants if it concludes that the report drawn up by the investigator(s) shows that there has been mismanagement on the part of the corporation (and dismisses the application if it does not conclude mismanagement). When the Chamber of Business Affairs finds for the applicants it may order one or more of the following measures: (a) suspension or annulment of decisions of the members of the management board or the supervisory board, of the general meeting of shareholders or of any other organ of the corporation, (b) suspension or dismissal of one or more executive directors or non-executive directors, (c) temporary appointment of one or more executive directors or non-executive directors, (d) temporary departure from provisions in the articles of association as specified by the court, (e) temporary transfer of shares to a trustee, and even (f) dissolution of the corporation (Article 3:356). Decisions of the Chamber of Business Affairs are subject to appeal lodged with the High Court (Article 2:359).

In its judgment of 10 January 1990, on appeal from a decision of the Chamber of Business Affairs, the High Court gave some important clarifications of the provisions on 'the right of inquiry'.[112] Referring to the legislative history the High Court considered that the purposes of the 'right of inquiry':

> are not just the restructuring and restoration of sounds relations by means of measures that serve to reorganize the enterprise of the legal person concerned, but also bringing matters into the open and establishing responsibility for mismanagement that may exist, while the possibility of prevention [...] cannot be ruled out either.

The High Court also considered that mismanagement on the part of organs of the corporation or on the part of members of those organs is a contributing factor to the conclusion that there is mismanagement on the part of the corporation, and that the question whether there is mismanagement on the part of the management board (or the executive directors) or the supervisory board (or the non-executive directors) must be answered by taking into account the circumstances under which decisions had to be made at the time. Although, in the opinion of the High Court, a random mistake will not be considered mismanagement normally, the term mismanagement must not be construed to include structural behavior only. Therefore, even one specific act can constitute mismanagement, in particular when that act has had severe consequences. Also, mismanagement is an objective term: when mismanagement on the part of the corporation is derived from mismanagement on the part of the management board (or the executive directors) or the supervisory board (or the non-executive directors), it is not dependent on personal culpability on the part of the executive directors or non-executive directors. Likewise, the conclusion that there is mismanagement on the part of the corporation is not dependent on the existence of damage. Further, the High Court supported the Chambers of Business Affairs in its reasoning that the phrase mismanagement may be paraphrased conveniently as behavior that is in violation of 'elementary principles of responsible entrepreneurship'.

One provision concerning the 'right of inquiry' deserves special attention. This is Article 2:349a section 2 of the Dutch Civil Code. Under this provision, the applicants who have asked the Chamber of Business Affairs to appoint one of several persons to investigate the policy and the course of affairs of the corporation may also ask the court to order interim measures in respect of the corporation from the moment they filed their application. The Chamber of Business Affairs may order any measure that is warranted by 'the state of affairs of the corporation or the interest of the inquiry'. This wording gives the Chamber of Business Affairs broad latitude to intervene in the policy or the course of affairs of a corporation from an early stage on. The interim measures the Chamber of Business Affairs may order are not confined to range that the definitive measures of Article 2:356 may order. Normally, the duration of interim measures runs parallel to the duration of the

---

112. High Court 10 January 1990, NJ 1990, 466 (*Ogem*), translation of considerations of the court by the author.

proceedings before the Chambers of Business Affairs, after which they may be replaced by the measures ordered under Article 2:355 section 1 in case the court concludes that there has been mismanagement on the part of the corporation.

II.   CASE STUDIES

A.   Introduction to the Getronics Case

[26] The legal proceedings concerning Getronics NV are an example of the use of the 'right of inquiry' as a means of shareholder litigation.

[27] Getronics NV ('Getronics') was a listed corporation established in the Netherlands. Getronics provided services in the field of information and communication technology. In 1999 Getronics took over Wang Laboratories Inc. In order to finance this takeover Getronics issues two series of convertible bonds and negotiated a line of credit with a banking consortium. The first series of convertible bonds had a value of EUR 350 million and was to be paid back or converted in 2004; the second series had a value of EUR 500 million and was to be paid back or converted in 2005. The line of credit had a value of EUR 500 million and expired in 2004. Part of the credit agreement was the formulation of financial ratios that Getronics had to meet each year by 30 June and 31 December. Failure to meet these ratios would constitute an 'event of default' that would make the credit fall due immediately, which would in turn constitute an 'event of default' that would make the two series of bonds fall due immediately.

In 2001 market conditions deteriorated. This had negative consequences on the financial results of Getronics, forcing Getronics to start looking – to no effect – for a strategic partner. Because Getronics expected that bondholders would prefer repayment on their bonds over converting their bonds into shares in 2004 and 2005 at the set price, it lowered the conversion prices in 2001 and began re-buying bonds in 2002. Also, Getronics sold a US subsidiary company in 2002. In August 2002 the share price of Getronics fell sharply. Thereafter the management board of Getronics decided to restructure the debt position of Getronics. There were a number of alternatives to do so, among which was selling Getronics Human Resource Solutions BV, another subsidiary company. The management board was not in favor of this solution, as this subsidiary was profitable and generated a stable cash flow. Therefore, the management board decided that the restructuring was to be effected by issuing new shares, by an offer to existing bondholders to sell their bonds in return for money, shares or new bonds, and by a replacing the line of credit. This decision was approved by the supervisory board, in spite of its anxiety for the dilution of shares it would cause. The offer to the existing bondholders (the 'Invitation to Tender', 'ITT') was dependent on the condition that at least 57,5% of the bondholders would accept the offer. However, this condition was not met. The management board and the supervisory board of Getronics took different views on the next steps to be taken. The management board preferred adjusting the ITT, but

the supervisory board preferred disinvesting or finding a bidder that was prepared
to make a takeover bid on Getronics – again because of the anxiety for the dilution
of shares that adjusting the ITT would cause. However, in February 2003 the
supervisory board went along with the management board and approved the
'Revised Invitation to Tender' ('RITT') drawn up by the management board.
But also that month, the members of the management board resigned following
a decision, as was stated in a press release, 'taken by the Supervisory Board after
consultation with the Board of Management and [...] based on a difference of
opinion on how to manage the Company'. The new management board that was
appointed was not a strong supporter of the RITT. Eventually, at the end of March
2003, the new management board and the supervisory board terminated the RITT
because they would not be able to get the approval of the general meeting of
shareholders for amending the articles of association as would be necessary to
implement the RITT.

B.   THE DECISION OF THE CHAMBER OF BUSINESS AFFAIRS
                      TO DISMISS THE APPLICATION

[28] On 14 November 2003 Vereniging van Effectenbezitters ('DIA') together
with 225 shareholders filed an application with the Chamber of Business Affairs
under the provisions on the 'right of inquiry' in the Book 2 of the Dutch Civil
Code.[113] They asked the Chamber of Business Affairs to find well-founded reasons
to doubt good policy on the part of Getronics and appoint persons to investigate the
policy and the course of affairs of Getronics from 1 July 2000 through 1 July 2003.
DIA et al. basically argued that Getronics had neglected the interests of its shareholders for the interests of its bondholders and the interests of the banking consortium. In its judgment of 2 September 2004 the Chamber of Business Affairs
dismissed the application.[114] In general terms the court considered:

> that in matters as brought to the fore by DIA et al. (like the intended restruc-
> turing of the financial position of a corporation, the moment on which external
> advisors need to be consulted and the level of influence that the views and
> advice of these advisors can or must have) the management of a corporation
> has a wide margin of discretion. For these are issues that are open to debate,
> also among prudent executive officers. This implies that these issues will not
> easily give rise to (suspicion of) the conclusion that there are well-founded
> reasons to doubt good policy.

DIA et al. had based their application on a number of concerns. One of these
concerns was that Getronics, before embarking on the ITT, had not considered
alternatives like disinvesting, and that after the failure of the ITT Getronics had

---

113. 'Dutch Investors' Association', abbreviated in Dutch 'VEB', <www.veb.net>.
114. Chamber of Business Affairs 2 September 2004, JOR 2004, 271 (*Getronics*), translation of
     considerations of the court by the author.

embarked on the RITT rather that considering such alternatives. The Chamber of Business Affairs considered that before opting for the ITT the management board and the supervisory board had in fact considered alternatives. Also, choosing for the ITT could not be held against them: 'Choices like these involve weighing advantages and disadvantages. Weighing the ramifications of these advantages and disadvantages is always open to debate'. Furthermore, before opting for the RITT the management board and the supervisory board had also considered alternatives. Added to that, they had to decide within a short period of time and the management board clearly favored the RITT: 'for a supervisory board it is difficult to rebut as incorrect the perception of management that considers this the way to go forward [. . .]; besides, there are no indications that facts were presented by the management board to the supervisory board either incorrectly or incompletely'. Another concern was that Getronics in the course of restructuring its debt position had replaced its line of credit on unfavorable terms. On this matter the court considered that:

> Getronics has [. . .] given a plausible explanation that the New Credit it had [. . .] negotiated fitted the intended restructuring of its debt position, as advocated by its management board at the time. The fact that the new credit facility might have been less favorable on a number of points than the existing one does not imply [. . .] that replacing it constitutes well-founded reasons to doubt good policy. Getronics had established certain priorities and was entitled to do so. That (re)negotiations with banks do not yield advantages only, certainly not in the situation in which Getronics found itself at the time, is a reality that cannot be ignored.

C.   INTRODUCTION TO THE VERSATEL CASE

[29] The legal proceedings concerning Versatel Telecom International NV are an example of the use of Article 2:349a section 2 of the Dutch Civil Code that allows the Chamber of Business Affairs to order interim measures in respect of a corporation.

D.   THE JUDGMENT OF THE CHAMBER OF BUSINESS AFFAIRS
          OF 27 SEPTEMBER 2005

[30] Versatel Telecom International NV ('Versatel') was established in 1995 in the Netherlands as a provider of broadband media services, mainly in the fields of internet and television. It was a listed company that operated through several subsidiary companies. Tele2 AB was a corporation established in Sweden that was also engaged in the field of telecommunication services. It too was a listed company that operated through several subsidiary companies. One of these was Tele2 Finance BV ('Tele2 Finance'). On 14 September 2005 Tele2 Finance made a

public takeover bid for the shares and convertible bonds of Versatel for EUR 1,3 billion. The success of this bid would result in Versatel becoming a subsidiary company of Tele2 Finance. According to the offer document the Tele2 group intended to de-list Versatel in case the bid was successful and convert Versatel into a private limited company. In this respect, the Tele2 group had developed several scenarios, as explained in the offer document:

- If Tele2 Finance were to acquire at least 95% of the capital of Versatel, it would initiate proceedings under Article 2:92a of the Dutch Civil Code against the remaining shareholders and squeeze out this remaining minority;
- If Tele2 Finance were to acquire less than 95% of the capital of Versatel, it would enter into a complete merger with Versatel, with Tele2 Finance as the transferee company and Versatel as the transferor company that would cease to exist. On the part of Versatel, the decision to merge with Tele2 Finance could be made by a resolution of the general meeting of shareholders by a simple majority vote. Following the takeover, Tele2 Finance – although in this scenario not having 95% of the capital of Versatel – would be able to cast so many votes in the general meeting of shareholders of Versatel that the required majority could be easily reached.

The management board and the supervisory board of Versatel basically recommended the bid by calling it 'reasonable and fair'. The bid was also backed by the largest shareholder of Versatel, Talpa Capital BV, established in the Netherlands, that held 41,65% of the capital of Versatel to the effect that Talpa had entered into an 'Irrevocable Undertaking' to tender all shares it held. On 29 September 2005 an extraordinary general meeting of shareholders was scheduled to discuss the bid and take decisions in anticipation of the bid being declared unconditional.

In a standard complete merger, the shareholders of the company that ceases to exits (in this case Versatel) become as a result of the merger shareholders of the transferee company (in this case Tele2 Finance). But when a so-called 'triangular merger' takes place, the shareholders of the company that ceases to exits become as a result of the merger shareholders of another company that is part of the group of the transferee company. The offer document referred specifically to this type of merger, indicating that the shareholders of Versatel would not become shareholders of Tele2 Finance but of Tele2 Netherlands Holding BV ('Tele2 Netherlands Holding'). In the case of a standard complete merger, where the remaining minority of the shareholders of Versatel would become shareholders of Tele2 Finance, their total participation in Tele2 Finance could well be more than 5% of the capital of Tele2 Finance. But in the case of a triangular merger, where the remaining minority of the shareholders of Versatel would become shareholders of Tele2 Netherlands Holding instead, their total participation in Tele2 Netherlands Holding could well be less than 5% of the capital of Tele2 Netherlands Holding. As a result of this, a triangular merger would for the Tele2 group have the advantage that in the aftermath of the public takeover bid, the group could still squeeze out the remaining minority.

E.   THE DECISION OF THE CHAMBER OF BUSINESS AFFAIRS
                                TO DISMISS THE APPLICATION FOR INTERIM MEASURES

[31] On 20 September 2005 five shareholders of Versatel ('Centaurus et al.') filed an
application with the Chamber of Business Affairs under the provisions on the 'right
of inquiry' in the Book 2 of the Dutch Civil Code.[115] They asked the Chamber of
Business Affairs to find well-founded reasons to doubt good policy on the part of
Versatel as concerns the public takeover bid by Tele2 Finance and appoint persons to
investigate the policy and the course of affairs of Versatel, and to order interim
measures. In its judgment of 27 September 2005 the Chamber of Business Affairs
dismissed the application for interim measures.[116] According to their own statement,
Centaurus et al. held approximately 13,6% of the capital of Versatel and belonged to
the (minority of) shareholders that might not want to accept the public takeover bid.
Centaurus et al. argued inter alia that because Tele2 Finance would most likely not be
able to make use of Article 2:92a of the Dutch Civil Code following the takeover, the
scenario whereby Tele2 Finance and Versatel would enter into a triangular merger
that also involved Tele2 Netherlands Holding was an unacceptable means to circum-
vent the normal scope of Article 2:92a of the Dutch Civil Code. And, as they argued,
the mere announcement of this scenario was intended to force them into accepting the
public takeover bid. The Chamber of Business Affairs considered however, that
the arguments advanced by Centaurus et al. failed to appreciate the purpose of the
squeeze out provision of Article 2:92a of the Dutch Civil Code that could hardly
be circumvented as this provision serves the interests of a majority shareholder in the
first place. In the opinion of the court, by their arguments Centaurus et al.:

> fail to recognize the purpose of the squeeze out provision [. . .] which is to
> offer a way out for the majority shareholder when she unwantedly finds herself
> in a situation where a small minority of shareholders gives her trouble, e.g. in
> the sense that annual general meetings of shareholders must be convened and
> the formalities that are necessary to call an annual general meeting of share-
> holders must be observed to the full, in the sense that the exemption to draw up
> the annual accounts does not apply, and in the sense that she must take into
> account the interests of the minority shareholder(s) in establishing a policy on
> paying dividend and in entering into contracts with a not wholly owned
> subsidiary company.

To this the Chamber of Business Affairs added that Centaurus et al. had failed to
refute that the Tele2 group had a legitimate interest that following the inclusion of
Versatel into the Tele2 group it did not wish to be confronted with minority

---

115. Centaurus Capital Limited (established in the United Kingdom), SG Amber Fund (established
in the United Kingdom), Arnhold & S. Bleichroeder Advisers LLC (established in the United
States), Mellon HBV Alternative Strategies Limited (established in the United Kingdom), and
Barclays Capital Securities Limited (established in the United Kingdom).
116. Chamber of Business Affairs 27 September 2005, JOR 2005, 272 (*Versatel*), translation of
considerations of the court by the author; affirmed by the High Court in its judgment of 14
September 2007, JOR 2007, 237 (*Versatel I*).

shareholders any longer. This implied in the circumstances of the case that the intended triangular merger could not be considered to be at odds with the purpose of the merger provisions.

F.   THE JUDGMENT OF THE CHAMBER OF BUSINESS
                       AFFAIRS OF 14 DECEMBER 2005

[32] On 29 September 2005 the extraordinary general meeting of shareholders of Versatel took several decisions in anticipation of the bid being declared unconditional. These decisions were supported by Talpa, but rejected by most of the other shareholders that attended the meeting, including Centaurus et al. The extraordinary general meeting of shareholders dismissed the serving members of the board of supervisors of Versatel and appointed four new non-executive directors. All persons appointed were employed as executive officers elsewhere in the Tele2 group. The extraordinary general meeting of shareholders also conditionally appointed an executive director. This appointment was conditional upon the resignation of the current executive director becoming effective and Tele2 Finance declaring the bid unconditional. The new executive director was also employed as an executive officer elsewhere in the Tele2 group. On 14 October 2005 Tele2 Finance and Versatel disclosed the results of the bid: approximately 74% of the shares had been tendered and as a result Tele2 Finance would declare the bid unconditional; on 1 November 2005 Tele2 Finance announced that also after the acceptance closing date of the bid shares had been tendered as a result of which Tele2 Finance held 82,39% of the shares of Versatel. On 15 December 2005 another extraordinary general meeting of shareholders of Versatel was scheduled to take the decision to appoint one extra non-executive director from outside the Tele2 group as a means of going part of the way to meet the interests of the minority shareholders, but also to take the decision to allow the supervisory board of Versatel to deviate from best practice provision III.6.2 of The Dutch Corporate Governance Code. Under this provision '[a] supervisory board member shall not take part in a discussion and/or decision-making on a subject or transaction in relation to which he has a conflict of interest with the company'.

G.   THE DECISION OF THE CHAMBER OF BUSINESS
                       AFFAIRS TO ORDER INTERIM MEASURES

[33] On 2 December 2005 Centaurus et al. filed a second application with the Chamber of Business Affairs in which they asked the court to order interim measures. This time, the Chamber of Business Affairs did order interim measures.[117]

---

117. Chamber of Business Affairs 14 December 2005, JOR 2006, 7 (*Versatel*), translation of considerations of the court by the author.

In respect of the decisions taken by the first extraordinary general meeting of shareholders held on 29 September 2005 the court considered that:

> well-founded reasons to doubt good policy on the part of a company, i.c. Versatel, may exist when, by a complex of interests of some of those who are part of the organs of the company, there is a danger that the interest of all who are involved in the company are not being weighed correctly, among whom in this case are to be reckoned the minority shareholders of Versatel (or some of them) in particular.

In the opinion of the Chamber of Business Affairs, this danger had become 'manifest' because the appointment of the new members of the supervisory board of Versatel, all from within the Tele2 group, and the appointment of the new executive director of Versatel, also from within the Tele2 group (in the words of the Chamber of Business Affairs a 'de facto executive co-director'), had created a situation in which the interests of the minority shareholders could not be protected adequately. In respect of the decisions to be taken by the extraordinary general meeting of shareholders to be held on 15 December 2005 the Chamber of Business Affairs considered that, although Versatel following the bid being declared unconditional had become a group company within the Tele2 group, Versatel was still in a transitional period characterized by opposite interests of minority of shareholders and the group. In the opinion of the court:

> In such a situation the starting point must be found in principle III.6 of The Dutch Corporate Governance Code and the accompanying best practice provisions, that lay down that any complex of interests or apparent complex of interests between the company and members of the supervisory board shall be avoided, and that a member of the supervisory board shall not take part in a discussion and/or decision-making on a subject or transaction in relation to which she has a conflict of interest with the company. This occurs in any event in case the decision making relates to transactions with a company where the non-executive director is employed as an executive director or is a non-executive director.

Not only did the Chamber of Business Affairs prohibit Versatel's general meeting of shareholders from voting on or deciding on any departure from The Dutch Corporate Governance Code, it also appointed three extra non-executive directors to exercise – to the exclusion of the other non-executive directors – the authority of the supervisory board in respect of transactions with companies of the Tele2 group. The Chamber of Business Affairs amplified this as implying that these three non-executive directors would also have the exclusive power to represent Versatel in all transactions with companies belonging to the Tele2 group, including representing Versatel in transactions concerning the proposed triangular merger.

These judgments were followed by judgments of 24 March 2006 (in which the Chamber of Business Affairs once more ordered interim measures),[118] 8 December 2006 (in which the Chamber of Business Affairs dismissed the application to find

---

118. Chamber of Business Affairs 24 March 2006, JOR 2006, 98 (*Versatel*).

well-founded reasons to doubt good policy and appoint persons to investigate the policy and the course of affairs of Versatel),[119] and 12 February 2007 (in a renewed application to find well-found reasons to doubt good policy and appoint persons to investigate the policy and the course of affairs of Versatel the Chamber of Business Affairs dismissed an application for interim measures).[120]

H.   THE DECISION OF THE HIGH COURT TO AFFIRM THE JUDGMENT
                    OF THE CHAMBER OF BUSINESS AFFAIRS OF 14 DECEMBER 2005
                    ON THE ISSUE OF DEPARTURE FROM THE DUTCH
                    CORPORATE GOVERNANCE CODE

[34] Tele2 Finance lodged an appeal with the High Court against the judgment of the Chamber of Business Affairs of 14 December 2005. Tele2 Finance argued that the Chamber of Business Affairs had – now that Versatel had become a group company within the Tele2 group – incorrectly prohibited Versatel's general meeting of shareholders from voting or deciding on any departure from The Dutch Corporate Governance Code, in particular principle III.6 and the accompanying best practice provisions. In the opinion of Tele2 Finance the fact that Versatel had become a group company could be a reason to substantiate departure from those provisions. The High Court, however, dismissed the appeal by Versatel.[121] The High Court took as a starting point that in the circumstances of the case 'the interest that the Tele2 group wants to take effect within Versatel and the interest of the minority shareholders do not coincide just like that, and that it is obvious that there is fear that the latter interest will not be fully taken into account when the composition of the supervisory board is such that Tele2 AB primarily has its own representatives on that board'. The High Court further considered:

> It appears that the Chamber of Business Affairs had in mind Article 2:8 of the Dutch Civil Code [a legal person and those who are involved in its organization shall exercise due care in relation to each other's interests] and the rule following from that provision that the corporation must exercise due care in relation to the interests of all its shareholders and must prevent that an unacceptable complex of interests arises [...]. [...] in order to be able to assume the existence of conflicts of interests in a case as the one under discussion it suffices that the non-executive directors concerned are so much involved in irreconcilable interests that there may be reasonable doubt whether they will be guided in their doings solely by the interest of the corporation and its affiliated enterprise [...]. [...] The decision [of the Chamber of Business Affairs] is to be understood that it does not follow from [...] the code that the demands formulated in III.6 of the code never apply to a group

---

119. Chamber of Business Affairs 8 December 2006, JOR 2007, 41 (*Versatel*).
120. Chamber of Business Affairs 12 February 2007, JOR 2007, 69 (*Versatel*).
121. High Court 14 September 2007, JOR 2007, 239 (*Versatel III*), translation of considerations of the court by the author.

company, but that this depends on the circumstances of the case. In the opinion of the Chamber of Business Affairs the circumstances are such that – in the light of the fact that there are minority shareholders who have little influence over the policy of the corporation – the demands that must be met by the supervisory organ of a corporation in general keep applying even now Versatel has become a group company. This judgment [. . .] is neither incomprehensible nor incorrectly motivated.

I.   The Decision of the High Court to Affirm the Judgment
           of the Chamber of Business Affairs of 14 December 2005
           on the Issue of the Power to Represent Versatel

[35] Versatel also lodged an appeal with the High Court against the judgment of the Chamber of Business Affairs of 14 December 2005. The grounds for the appeal by Versatel were two-pronged. First, Versatel interpreted the amplification by the Chamber of Business Affairs of its judgment as a reference to Article 2:146 of the Dutch Civil Code. Under this provision, whenever any executive director of a corporation has a conflict of interests with the corporation, the power to represent the corporation in matters concerning that conflict of interests shall fall to the non-executive directors. In the opinion of Versatel, the Chamber of Business Affairs would have had this provision in mind because the newly appointed executive director of Versatel was an executive officer elsewhere in the Tele2 group and therefore had a conflict of interests with Versatel concerning transactions in relation to the proposed triangular merger. Second, Versatel referred to Article 2:356 of the Dutch Civil Code that outlines the measures the Chamber of Business Affairs may order in respect of a corporation if it concludes that there has been mismanagement on the part of the corporation. Under Article 2:356 subsection c the Chamber may temporarily appoint one of more executive or non-executive directors. Under Article 2:356 subsection d the Chamber may order temporary departure from provisions in the articles of association as specified by the court. Article 2:356 subsection d does not give the Chamber the possibility to order departure from statutory law. From the combination of these provisions, Versatel derived that the Chamber of Business Affairs could appoint three non-executive directors as an interim measure (cf. Article 2:356 subsection c), but could not give the power to represent Versatel in all transactions with companies belonging to the Tele2 group to these three non-executive directors exclusively: such a power would under statutory law be a power of the supervisory board as a whole and therefore the Chamber of Business Affairs could not allocate such a power to the three non-executive directors it had appointed to the exclusion of the supervisory board as such (cf. Article 2:146 and the effect of Article 2:356 subsection d). The High Court, however, dismissed the appeal by Versatel.[122] In its reasoning, the High

---

122.   High Court 14 September 2007, JOR 2007, 238 (*Versatel II*), translation of considerations of
       the court by the author.

Court stressed the special character of interim measures ordered by the Chamber of Business Affairs on the basis of Article 2:349a section 2 of the Dutch Civil Code as opposed to measures ordered on the basis of Article 2:355:

> It follows from the legislative history [. . .] that Article 2:349a of the Dutch Civil Code was intended to allow the Chamber of Business Affairs a separate possibility to order interim measures for the duration of the legal proceedings connected to the circumstances in which the corporation finds itself, or in the interest of the investigation into the policy and the course of affairs of a corporation as referred to in Article 2:345 of the Dutch Civil Code, that is not restricted to, and is separate from, the measures referred to in Article 2:356 of the Dutch Civil Code. These measures, as opposed to the exhaustive list of measures stated in Article 2:356, have a temporary character. They may imply [. . .] that the power to take decisions on certain subjects or to represent the corporation in matters concerning these subjects falls exclusively to non-executive directors appointed by the Chamber of Business Affairs [. . .].

Chapter 3

The Corporation's Centralized Administration

I.

THE EVOLVING ROLES OF THE BOARD AND
MANAGEMENT

[36] A characteristic of the corporate form is that the investors of capital are no longer involved in the administration of the corporation. The responsibility for the administration lies with the unitary or dual board and with the managers that together form the corporation's centralized administration. In a unitary board structure there is one board of directors that consists of executive and non-executive directors. In a dual board structure there are two boards: the management board consisting of executive directors and the supervisory board consisting of non-executive directors. The managers are high level personnel who are not board members. Management consists of the executive directors and the managers collectively. Together, the unitary or dual board and the managers – as the corporation's centralized administration – perform a number of functions. Traditionally, these are the functions of strategy setting, policy implementation, and supervision.[123] This chapter considers the way in which the roles of the unitary or dual board and the managers have evolved with respect to performing these functions. The result of this evolution has been that a new function has arisen: the function of monitoring management.[124] Part A of this chapter consists of the following paragraphs: *the traditional functions of the centralized administration* and *toward monitoring management*.

---

123. C. de Groot, 'The Function of Corporate Boards: Toward a New State of Affairs?', *European Company Law* (2007), 4-9.
124. C. de Groot (2007), 4-9.

A.   THE TRADITIONAL FUNCTIONS OF THE CENTRALIZED
                ADMINISTRATION

1.   In a Unitary Board Structure

[37] The most general function of a corporation's centralized administration is that
of *setting the corporation's strategy*. In a unitary board structure, this function is
performed by the board. Main principle A.1 of The Combined Code on Corporate
Governance states that '[e]very company should be headed by an effective board,
which is collectively responsible for the success of the company'.[125] Supporting
principle A.1 adds to this that '[t]he board should set the company's strategic aims'.
The fact that strategy setting is the collective responsibility of the board implies
that not only the executive directors are involved in this, but the non-executive
directors as well. Or, in the formulation of supporting principle A.1 of The Combined Code, '[a]s part of their role as members of a unitary board, non-executive
directors should constructively challenge and help develop proposals on strategy'.[126]
Policy implementation is the executive function. Understandably, in a unitary
board structure this function is performed by the executive directors. But because
there are only a limited number of executive directors, they are assisted by the
managers in performing this function. This means that the function of policy
implementation is performed by management. This is reflected in supporting
principle A.1 of The Combined Code under which '[t]he board should [. . .] ensure
that the necessary financial and human resources are in place for the company to
meet its objectives'. *The supervisory function* is performed by the non-executive
directors. Their supervision is directed at the executive directors. Although The
Combined Code does not refer specifically to the non-executive directors supervising the executive directors, it does refer in supporting principle A.1 to the fact
that the non-executive directors 'have a prime role in appointing, and where
necessary removing, executive directors, and in succession planning'. The way
in which the three basic functions of strategy setting, policy implementation and
supervision are divided over the unitary board and the managers in a unitary board
structure may pose a dilemma for the non-executive directors. They are at the same
time involved in setting the corporation's strategy with the executive directors as
well as in supervising those same executive directors.[127]

---

125.   'The Combined Code on Corporate Governance', drawn up by the Financial Reporting Coun-
       cil (version of June 2008, originally July 2003), <www.frc.org.uk> corporate governance.
126.   The origin of non-executive directors is that of 'part-time directors', who 'can bring a breadth
       of experience and knowledge of commerce, industry or finance generally to discussions
       of major matters of policy at board meetings. Also their connections with other companies
       or sources of finance are useful when the company is expanding into new ventures':
       R.R. Pennington, 'Management Structures and Functions in English Law', in *Quo Vadis,
       Ius Societatum?*, ed. P. Zonderland (Deventer: Kluwer, 1972), 151-164 (at 153).
127.   S. Dumoulin, 'De positie van niet-uitvoerend bestuurders in het monistisch bestuursmodel',
       Ondernemingsrecht (2005), 266-272.

2. In a Dual Board Structure

[38] In a dual board structure, the general function of *setting the corporation's strategy* is performed by the management board that consists of the executive directors. Thus, in accordance with principle II.1 of The Dutch Corporate Governance Code, '[t]he role of the management board is to manage the company'.[128] Understandably, the executive directors are also responsible for *policy implementation*. The same principle explains that managing the corporation 'means, among other things, that [the management board] is responsible for achieving the company's aims, strategy and policy, and results', or – in the words of the amended version of the Dutch Corporate Governance Code – 'that it is responsible for achieving the company's aims, the strategy and associated risk profile, the development of results and corporate social responsibility issues that are relevant to the enterprise'. Again, because there are only a limited number of executive directors, they are assisted by the managers in performing this function, meaning again that the function of policy implementation is performed by management. The code, however, does not mention the role of the managers in policy implementation specifically. *The supervisory function* is performed by the non-executive directors who form the supervisory board. They direct their supervision at the executive directors. The supervisory function of the non-executive directors and the direction of supervision at the executive directors are reflected in a number of provisions in The Dutch Corporate Governance Code. Under principle II.1, '[t]he management board is accountable [...] to the supervisory board [and] shall provide the supervisory board in good time with all information necessary for the exercise of the duties of the supervisory board'. And principle III.1 states that '[t]he role of the supervisory board is to supervise the policies of the management board and the general affairs of the company and its affiliated enterprise, as well as to assist the management board by providing advice'.[129] The way in which the three basic functions of strategy setting, policy implementation and supervision are divided over the dual board and the managers in a dual board structure protects the non-executive directors from the dilemma posed to the non-executive directors in a

---

128. 'The Dutch Corporate Governance Code: Principles of Good Corporate Governance and Best Practice Provisions', drawn up by the Corporate Governance Committee (December 2003, by the name of the committee's chairperson this committee is also called the Tabaksblat Committee), <www.commissiecorporategovernance.nl> corporate governance code.
129. The Dutch Corporate Governance Code, best practice provision III.1.6 reads:
    'The supervision of the management board by the supervisory board shall include:
    (i) achievement of the company's objectives;
    (ii) corporate strategy and the risks inherent in the business activities;
    (iii) the structure and operation of the internal risk management and control systems;
    (iv) the financial reporting process;
    (v) compliance with the legislation and regulations'.

    M.W. den Boogert, 'De raad van commissarissen onder de nieuwe corporate governance code,' *Ondernemingsrecht* (2004), 113-116.

unitary board structure. In a dual board structure, the non-executive directors are only involved in supervising the executive directors.

However, the difference between the functioning of the centralized administration in a dual board structure and in a unitary board structure should not be exaggerated. Dual boards have come to function like unitary board because in dual board corporations there is a tendency for supervisory boards to become involved in strategy setting.[130] This implies that the role of the non-executive directors in a dual board structure more and more resembles the role of the non-executive directors in a unitary board structure. The Dutch Corporate Governance Code recognizes this development explicitly. In accordance with best practice provision II.1.2 '[t]he management board shall submit to the supervisory board for *approval*: a) the operational and financial objectives of the company; b) the strategy designed to achieve the objectives; c) the parameters to be applied in relation to the strategy, for example in respect of the financial ratios',[131] to which the amended version of the Dutch Corporate Governance Code adds: 'd) corporate social responsibility issues that are relevant to the enterprise'. This provision implies that the management board can no longer set the strategy of the corporation itself, but must do so together with the supervisory board.

B.   TOWARD MONITORING MANAGEMENT

[39] Traditionally, the centralized administration of a corporation performed three functions. In a unitary board structure the unitary board was responsible for setting the corporation's strategy. The executive function of policy implementation was performed by the executive directors and the managers. The non-executive directors were responsible for supervising the executive directors. In a dual board structure the management board was responsible for strategy setting. Policy implementation was performed by the executive directors and the managers. The role of the non-executive directors was to supervise the executive directors. However, this picture has changed. It was already noted that dual boards have come to resemble unitary boards. But there is another development that is even more profound. This development occurs in both unitary and dual board corporations. It amounts to a

---

130.   H. Beckman, 'Enkele losse gedachten bij en over commissaris, toezicht en controle', *Onder-nemingsrecht* (2005), 251-252; M.W. den Boogert, 'De vergeten band tussen raad van commissarissen en algemene vergadering: de Januskop van de commissaris', *Ondernemingsrecht* (2005), 252-257; A.F.M. Dorresteijn & C. de Groot, 'Corporate Governance Codes: Origins and Perspectives', *European Company Law in Accelerated Progress*, ed. S.M. Bartman (Alphen aan den Rijn: Kluwer Law International, 2006), 31-57 (also published in *European Company Law* (2004), 43-56); C. de Groot, 'Can Corporate Governance Contribute to Sustainable Development', in *Neo-liberal Globalism and Social Sustainable Globalisation*, ed. E.C. Nieuwenhuys (Leiden: Brill Academic Publishers, 2006), 195-214; Ch.E. Honée, 'Bestuursvorm (one-tier of two-tier) en verantwoording', in *Verantwoording aan Hans Beckman*, eds M.J. Kroeze et al. (Deventer: Kluwer, 2006), 215-224; C. de Groot (2007), 4-9.
131.   Emphasis added.

fading away of the distinction between policy implementation and strategy setting. In both unitary and dual board corporations there is a tendency for the executive directors and the managers to expand the role they have in policy implementation into a role of strategy setting as well. The consequence of this is that not only the function of policy implementation but also the function of strategy setting are likely to be performed to a large degree by the executive directors and the managers collectively, that is by management. This is primarily a consequence of size, especially in a large corporation that is organized in a multidivisional form,[132] or is the holding company of a corporate group that has subsidiaries worldwide.[133] As Davies puts it: 'In large global businesses [...] the board can manage the company only in the rather broad sense of setting overall corporate strategy and monitoring the effectiveness of its execution by non-board management',[134] which is in conformity with 'the modern view from the business school that the role of the boards of large companies is to set and monitor the execution of the company's business strategy, not to take every business decision needed to implement that strategy'.[135] The overall result of this development is that there seems to exist a division between the unitary or dual board on the one hand and management on the other hand. The executive directors are in the middle of this, torn between being board members and part of management at the same time. For the unitary or dual board this leads to the emergence of a new function. This new function is that of monitoring management.[136] By assuming this function, boards protect their position as the corporation's main organ as opposed to management. The tendency of the functioning of corporate boards toward assuming as their prime role the monitoring of management can be found both in predecessors to The Combined Code on Corporate Governance and in several corporate governance codes. Code provision 1.1 of the Code of Best Practice in the Cadbury Report stated that '[t]he board should [...] monitor the executive management'.[137] And the Hampel Report argued that '[t]he prime responsibility of the board of directors is to determine the broad strategy of the company and to ensure its implementation'.[138] The Combined Code, having stated in supporting principle A.1 that '[t]he board's role

---

132. J. Roberts, *The Modern Firm: Organizational Design for Performance and Growth* (Oxford: Oxford University Press), 2004, at 1.

133. S. Dumoulin, 'De positie van niet-uitvoerend bestuurders in het monistisch bestuursmodel', *Ondernemingsrecht* (2005), 266-272.

134. P.L. Davies, *Introduction to Company Law* (Oxford: Oxford University Press, 2002), at 14.

135. P.L. Davies (2002), at 157.

136. P.J.N. Halpern, 'Systemic Perspectives on Corporate Governance Systems', in *Corporate Governance and Globalization, Long Range Planning Issues*, eds S.S. Cohen & G. Boyd (Cheltenham: Edward Elgar Publishing Limited, 2000), 1-58; C. de Groot (2007), 4-9.

137. 'The Financial Aspects of Corporate Governance', drawn up by the Committee on the Financial Aspects of Corporate Governance (December 1992, by the name of the committee's chairperson this report is also called the Cadbury Report), <www.ecgi.org> codes & principles → index of all codes.

138. 'Final Report', drawn up by the Committee on Corporate Governance (January 1998, by the name of the committee's chairperson this report is also called the Hampel Report), 3.11, <www.ecgi.org> codes & principles → index of all codes.

is to provide entrepreneurial leadership of the company', elaborates this by adding that '[t]he board should [. . .] review management performance'. The code repeats this in respect of the non-executive directors: 'Non-executive directors should scrutinise the performance of management in meeting agreed goals and objectives and monitor the reporting of performance'. According to the ASX Corporate Governance Principles and Recommendations,[139] establishing the roles of the board and senior executives is '[f]undamental to any corporate governance structure'.[140] Principle 1 elaborates this by stating that good corporate governance requires to '[l]ay solid foundations for management and oversight', and to 'establish and disclose the respective roles and responsibilities of board and management'. The code suggests that corporate boards 'adopt a formal statement of matters reserved to them or a formal board charter that details their functions and responsibilities', which also means that '[t]here should be a formal statement of the areas of authority delegated to senior executives'.[141] In a comparable way, code provision A.1.1. of The Combined Code on Corporate Governance requires that '[t]here should be a formal schedule of matters specifically reserved for [the board's] decision'. To a large extent, the function of monitoring management can be understood as a combination of the traditional functions of strategy setting and supervision. This new function is performed by the executive directors and the non-executive directors together. Its supervisory part is directed at management. This poses a dilemma for the executive directors especially. They are at the same time involved in policy implementation with the managers as well as in monitoring those same managers.

II.   CASE STUDY

A.   Introduction to the Laurus Case

[40] The *Laurus* case gives an example of a corporation with a dual board structure where the functioning of both the management board and the supervisory board was criticized by the Chamber of Business Affairs.

[41] Laurus NV ('Laurus') was a listed corporation established in the Netherlands. It was the result of a merger in 1998 of De Boer Unigro NV and Vendex Food Groep BV. Laurus operated a large number of superstores in the Netherlands, Belgium and Spain that sold foodstuffs. It employed approximately 40.000

---

139. 'Corporate Governance Principles and Recommendations', adopted by the ASX Corporate Governance Council, convened by the Australian Securities Exchange (August 2007, the successor to the 'Principles of Good Corporate Governance and Best Practice Recommendations' (March 2003)), <www.asx.com.au> listed companies → corporate governance.
140. 'ASX Corporate Governance Principles and Recommendations', Corporate Governance in Australia.
141. 'ASX Corporate Governance Principles and Recommendations', Recommendation 1.1, Commentary and guidance.

employees. Around 30.000 employees worked in the Netherlands, and around 10.000 employees worked in Belgium and Spain. The management board of Laurus originally consisted of the CEO and the CFO. This board directed the group management team. The supervisory board of Laurus originally consisted of eight members. The superstores managed by Laurus in the Netherlands were highly diversified. Laurus ran up-market stores with brand names Super de Boer and Konmar, middle-market stores with the brand name Edah and low-market stores with the brand name Basismarkt. Furthermore, Laurus ran a number of local grocery stores with the brand name Spar. In 2000, Laurus acquired additional superstores with brand names Groenwoudt, Nieuwe Weme and Lekker&Laag. Laurus's diversified range of up-market, middle market and low-market super-stores made up its 'three formula' strategy. Following the retirement of the CEO in 2000, a successor was appointed, the CFO was replaced and a third member of the management board was appointed. The management board of Laurus, with the approval of the supervisory board, embarked on a course to recast the 'three formula' strategy into a 'one formula' strategy. This operation was called the 'Businessplan Groenland'. It consisted of reconstructing the Super de Boer, Konmar, Edah, Groenwoudt, Nieuwe Weme and Lekker&Laag stores into new style Konmar stores between 2001 and 2003. Critical in this plan was the 'go no-go' decision that was to be made following the restyling of the first stores between May and September 2001. Laurus expected the financial resources that it needed for the operation to come from inter alia selling its Basismarkt and Spar chains, from lower operating costs by integrating logistics, distribution and IT systems, and from the increased turnover in its new style integrated stores. At the end of 2000 and the beginning of 2001 there were first signs that the business plan was not succeeding as expected. Laurus's group controller felt that he could not take responsibility for the business plan any more and terminated his contract, and the CFO was replaced once more (to be replaced again after four months). Selling the Basismarkt stores proved difficult and did not generate enough money. Also, when Laurus announced it would relocate its headquarters, a large group of employees left the corporation. In January 2001 the supervisory board of Laurus established an audit committee. This committee concluded that Laurus's manage-ment information systems and internal risk management and control systems were not working properly. Also, Laurus had to start renegotiating its line of credit extended by a banking consortium. The first new style Konmar superstores that were opened in May 2001 experienced supply and IT difficulties. Finally, during the first and second quarters of 2001 the operating results of Laurus in the Neth-erlands as well as in Belgium and Spain declined. As a result of all of these events the management board ended the 'Businessplan Groenland'. In August 2001 the supervisory board appointed one of its members as delegated supervisory board member to be in close contact with the management board, suspended the CEO and appointed a new CEO. In October 2001 the banking consortium demanded that Laurus should seek either a strategic partner or find a bidder that was prepared to make a takeover bid. Following negotiations between Laurus and the French cor-poration Casino Guichard Perrachon SA ('Casino'), that also sold foodstuffs,

Laurus and Casino agreed that Laurus would issue a large number of shares to Casino and become a subsidiary company of Casino. This intention was made public in a press release on 22 May 2002, and the takeover was accepted by a large majority of the shareholders of Laurus on 28 June 2002.

B.   THE DECISION OF THE CHAMBER OF BUSINESS
          AFFAIRS TO CONCLUDE MISMANAGEMENT

[42] In May 2002 several shareholders of Laurus filed an application with the Chamber of Business Affairs under the provisions on the 'right of inquiry' in the Book 2 of the Dutch Civil Code. These shareholders asked the Chamber of Business Affairs to find well-founded reasons to doubt good policy on the part of Laurus and to appoint persons to investigate the policy and the course of affairs of Laurus. In its judgment of 22 May 2002 the Chamber of Business Affairs ordered an investigation into the policy and the course of affairs of Laurus from 1 January 2000 onward.[142] The report of the investigation distinguished between phases I and II of the course of affairs of Laurus. Phase I was the period from 1 January 2000 through August 2001, phase II was the period from August 2001 through June 2002. Following this investigation in February 2003 two shareholders of Laurus filed application with the Chamber of Business Affairs in which they asked the court to find mismanagement on the part of Laurus on the basis of the report of the investigation as concerns phase I (and order measures), and to order an additional investigation as concerns phase II. In its judgment of 16 October 2003 the Chamber of Business Affairs found mismanagement as concerns phase I and ordered an additional investigation as concerns phase II.[143] Here, the decision as concerns phase I is of interest. The Chamber of Business Affairs considered that the decision of Laurus to recast its 'three formula' strategy into a 'one formula' strategy was in itself solid and feasible. It was, however, both in terms of operations and finance highly ambitious, and its success depended on a number of parameters as outlined in the business plan. At the same time, crucial conditions in the fields of financing, accounting information systems and logistics had never been met to a sufficient degree. Further, the appeal that the new style integrated stores would have on customers had not been tested seriously. The Chamber of Business Affairs found mismanagement on the part of Laurus and in reaching this conclusion took into account the roles of both the management board and the supervisory board. In respect of the management board the court considered:

> By continuing to carry the business plan into effect beyond a point of no acceptable return in spite of all negative signs, the management board has taken irresponsible risks that ultimately endangered the continued existence of

---

142. Chamber of Business Affairs 22 May 2002, JOR 2002, 116 (*Laurus*).
143. Chamber of Business Affairs 16 October 2003, JOR 2003, 260 (*Laurus*), translation of considerations of the court by the author.

Laurus [...]. [...] The only conclusion that can be drawn from this is that the policy of the management board of Laurus with respect to the Businessplan Groenland constitutes mismanagement.

In respect of the supervisory board the Chamber of Business Affairs considered that in a corporation that is organized along the lines of a dual board structure, the prevailing opinion on good corporate governance in the Netherlands is that a supervisory board may in principle rely of information provided by the management board on request or unsolicited. The Chamber of Business Affairs noted that the management board of Laurus had expressed an optimistic view of the Businessplan Groenland constantly and against its better judgment, and that the supervisory board had intervened with force in July-August 2001. Against this background, the Chamber of Business Affairs considered the question whether the supervisory board should have intervened at an earlier stage in response to signs that it should have picked up. In this respect the court considered that:

> As the supervisory board must have been aware of too, the choice for the business plan was very ambitious and its execution depended on holding a steady course. It was well known that finances depended on speedy disinvestment of non core activities and on growth of profits from the recasting of the business itself. Furthermore, [...] the continued execution of the business plan was not made dependent on examination that could have resulted in adjusting this execution or bringing it to a halt.

In the opinion of the Chamber of Business Affairs, 'it could have been expected from the supervisory board [...] that it would be more actively engaged in its supervisory role than under normal conditions of continuity'. The Chamber of Business Affairs noted that the supervisory board had failed to formulate conditions that would have allowed for emergency measures, that as early as the beginning of 2001 the results and financing of the business plan were at variance with the original forecast, and that the publication of the annual report on the year 2000 in March 2001 was the moment that should have made clear that a worst case scenario was developing. The Chamber of Business Affairs also noted that the board of supervisors should have given more weight to the fact that the new CEO had no experience with retail and that there had been three CFOs within a short period of time. The Chamber of Business Affairs concluded from these elements that the board of supervisors should have tightened up its supervisory role at the end of March 2001 at the latest, 'and that the board of supervisors, by failing to do so, is to that extent responsible too for the mismanagement found'.

Chapter 4

The Composition and Functioning of Corporate Boards

I. HOW CORPORATE BOARDS FUNCTION

[43] Corporate governance codes, including The Combined Code on Corporate Governance and The Dutch Corporate Governance Code, hold various provisions on the composition and functioning of corporate boards.[144] Part A of this chapter deals with the following subjects that corporate governance codes may deal with: *board composition and board functioning* in general as well as more concrete issues like *reinforcing monitoring: director independence* and *reshaping supervision: board committees*.

A. BOARD COMPOSITION AND BOARD FUNCTIONING

1. Directors, (Senior) Management, Executives and Officers

[44] The centralized administration of a corporation consists of the corporation's unitary or dual board and the managers. In a unitary board structure there is one board of directors. This unitary board consists of both executive directors and non-executive directors. In a dual board structure there are two boards. This dual board

---

144. 'The Combined Code on Corporate Governance', drawn up by the Financial Reporting Council (version of June 2008, originally July 2003), <www.frc.org.uk> corporate governance; 'The Dutch Corporate Governance Code: Principles of Good Corporate Governance and Best Practice Provisions', drawn up by the Corporate Governance Committee (December 2003, by the name of the committee's chairperson this committee is also called the Tabaksblat Committee), <www.commissiecorporategovernance.nl> corporate governance code.

falls into the management board consisting of executive directors and the supervisory board consisting of non-executive directors. *Management* consists of the corporation's executive directors and its managers (the managers are high level personnel who are not board members). Both the executive directors and the managers may be referred to as 'executives'. Some executives are board members and thereby executive directors, other executives are not board members but managers. The executive directors and the highest level ('senior') managers may collectively be referred to as *senior management*. The term 'officer' would seem to refer to the directors (both the executive directors and the non-executive directors) together with the highest level managers. Therefore the executive officers would be the executive directors and the highest level managers. Thus, senior management consists of the executive officers.

There is an abundance of names that the members of senior management (the executive officers) may have. Any of these may or may not be board members. These names include the chief accounting officer, chief administrative officer, chief client executive officer, chief compliance officer, chief credit officer, chief financial officer (CFO), chief human resources officer, chief information officer, chief innovation officer, chief legal officer, chief marketing officer, chief operating officer (COO), chief organization officer, chief restructuring officer, chief risk officer, chief sales officer, chief security officer, chief strategic officer, chief strategy officer, chief tax officer, chief technical officer, and chief technology officer. Other executives may have names like the comptroller, general auditor, general counsel, secretary, and treasurer.

A corporation may award a member of senior management (the executive officers) the title president, as in 'President and CEO' or 'President and COO'. Below the president, there may be one of more members of senior management with the title vice president, or also with the titles senior (executive) vice president and executive vice president.

2.   The CEO and the Chairperson

[45] Among the executives the chief executive officer ('CEO') has a special place.[145] The CEO is the executive director who shall give leadership to management. Next the CEO other executives may serve on the board, but many executives will not be board members.[146] Among the directors the chairperson has a special place. The chairperson shall ensure the proper functioning of the board if she is chairperson of a unitary board and shall ensure the proper functioning of the supervisory board if she is chairperson of a supervisory board. In a unitary board structure the question arises whether the CEO of a corporation may serve as chairperson of the board of the corporation at the same time. In accordance with

---

145.   In English usage: 'managing director': P.L. Davies, *Introduction to Company Law* (Oxford: Oxford University Press, 2002), at 111.
146.   P.L. Davies 2002, at 111; L. Bebchuk & J. Fried, *Pay without Performance: The Unfulfilled Promise of Executive Compensation* (Cambridge: Harvard University Press, 2004), at 64.

main principle A.2 of The Combined Code on Corporate Governance '[t]here should be a clear division of responsibilities at the head of the company between the running of the board and the executive responsibility for the running of the company's business. No one individual should have unfettered powers of decision'. The code clearly favors that the positions of CEO and chairperson of the board should not be held by the same person: 'The roles of chairman and chief executive should not be exercised by the same individual. The division of responsibilities between the chairman and chief executive should be clearly established, set out in writing and agreed by the board' (code provision A.2.1). Also, '[a] chief executive should not go on to be chairman of the same company. If exceptionally a board decides that a chief executive should become chairman, the board should consult major shareholders in advance and should set out its reasons to shareholders at the time of the appointment and in the next annual report' (code provision A.2.2). Comparably, in accordance with best practice provision III.4.2 of The Dutch Corporate Governance Code '[t]he chairman of the supervisory board shall not be a former member of the management board of the company'.

In accordance with principle III.4 and best practice provision III.4.1 of The Dutch Corporate Governance Code the chairperson of the supervisory board 'monitors the proper functioning of the supervisory board and its committees' (and shall make sure that 'the supervisory board elects a vice-chairman' and that 'the committees of the supervisory board function properly'),[147] 'arranges for the induction and training programme for the members' of the supervisory board (making sure that 'the supervisory board members follow their induction and education or training programme'),[148] 'determines the agenda', 'chairs the supervisory board meetings', 'arranges for the adequate provision of information to the members' of the supervisory board (making sure that 'the supervisory board members receive in good time all information which is necessary for the proper performance of their duties'),[149] 'ensures that there is sufficient time for making decisions' (so that 'there is sufficient time for consultation and decision-making by the supervisory board'), 'initiates the evaluation of the functioning of the

---

147. Under The Combined Code on Corporate Governance, supporting principle A.2 '[t]he chairman is responsible for leadership of the board, ensuring its effectiveness on all aspects of its role and setting its agenda. The chairman is also responsible for ensuring that the directors receive accurate, timely and clear information. The chairman should ensure effective communication with shareholders. The chairman should also facilitate the effective contribution of non-executive directors in particular and ensure constructive relations between executive and non-executive directors'.

148. Under The Combined Code on Corporate Governance, supporting principle A.5 '[t]he chairman should ensure that the directors continually update their skills and the knowledge and familiarity with the company required to fulfil their role', and under code provision A.5.1 '[t]he chairman should ensure that new directors receive a full, formal and tailored induction on joining the board. As part of this, the company should offer to major shareholders the opportunity to meet a new non-executive director'.

149. Under The Combined Code on Corporate Governance, supporting principle A.5 '[t]he chairman is responsible for ensuring that the directors receive accurate, timely and clear information'.

supervisory board and the management board' (making sure that 'the performance of the management board members and supervisory board members is assessed at least once a year'), 'acts on behalf of the supervisory board as the main contact for the management board' (making sure that 'the supervisory board has proper contact with the management board'),[150] and 'ensures the orderly and efficient conduct of the general meeting of shareholders'. In the performance of all these duties the chairperson shall be assisted by company secretary who shall also assist the (supervisory) board as a whole (best practice provision III.4.3):[151] 'The company secretary should be responsible for advising the board through the chairman on all governance matters' (supporting principle A.5), and '[a]ll directors should have access to the advice and services of the company secretary, who is responsible to the board for ensuring that board procedures are complied with' (code provision A.5.3).

3. Appointments and Incompatibilities

[46] In accordance with main provision A.4 of The Combined Code on Corporate Governance '[t]here should be a formal, rigorous and transparent procedure for the appointment of new directors to the board'. This implies that '[a]ppointments to the board should be made on merit and against objective criteria. Care should be taken to ensure that appointees have enough time available to devote to the job', and '[t]he board should satisfy itself that plans are in place for orderly succession for appointments to the board and to senior management, so as to maintain an appropriate balance of skills and experience within the company and on the board' (supporting principle A.4). Under main provision A.7 '[a]ll directors should be submitted for re-election at regular intervals, subject to continued satisfactory performance. The board should ensure planned and progressive refreshing of the board', meaning that '[a]ll directors should be subject to election by shareholders at the first annual general meeting after their appointment, and to re-election thereafter at intervals of no more than three years' (code provision A.7.1). Although '[n]on-executive directors may serve longer than nine years (e.g. three three-year terms), subject to annual re-election', '[a]ny term beyond six years (e.g. two three-year terms) for a non-executive director should be subject to particularly rigorous review, and should take into account the need for progressive refreshing of the board' (code provision A.7.2). In accordance with best practice provision II.1.1 of The Dutch Corporate Governance Code the maximum duration of the term of office of an executive director on appointment is four years and on reappointment the maximum duration of her term of office shall likewise

---

150. '[A]nd the works council (or central works council)'.
151. And: 'The company secretary shall, either on the recommendation of the supervisory board or otherwise, be appointed and dismissed by the management board, after the approval of the supervisory board has been obtained'; cf. 'The Combined Code on Corporate Governance', code provision A.5.3: 'Both the appointment and removal of the company secretary should be a matter for the board as a whole'.

not exceed four years at a time. Best practice provision III.3.5 states that '[a] person may be appointed to the supervisory board for a maximum of three 4-year terms'. Under code provision A.4.5 '[t]he board should not agree to a full time executive director taking on more than one non-executive directorship in a FTSE 100 company nor the chairmanship of such a company'. Under best practice provision II.1.7 an executive director shall need the approval of the supervisory board for her appointment as a non-executive director of another listed corporation and may serve as a non-executive director with no more than two listed corporations.[152] She may not serve as chairperson of the supervisory board of a listed corporation. Under best practice provision III.3.4 '[t]he number of supervisory boards of Dutch listed companies of which an individual may be a member shall be limited to such an extent that the proper performance of his duties is assured', meaning that 'the maximum number is five, for which purpose the chairmanship of a supervisory board counts double'.

4. Various Provisions on Board Composition and Board Functioning

[47] In accordance with supporting principle A.3 of The Combined Code on Corporate Governance '[t]he board should not be so large as to be unwieldy. The board should be of sufficient size that the balance of skills and experience is appropriate for the requirements of the business and that changes to the board's composition can be managed without undue disruption'. In accordance with principle III.3 of The Dutch Corporate Governance Code '[e]ach supervisory board member shall be capable of assessing the broad outline of the overall policy' and 'shall have the specific expertise required for the fulfilment of the duties assigned to the role designated to him'; also, '[t]he composition of the supervisory board shall be such that it is able to carry out its duties properly'.[153] To these ends, the supervisory board shall under best practice provision III.3.1 'prepare a profile of its size and composition, taking account of the nature of the business, its activities and the desired expertise and background of the supervisory board members'. The foregoing implies that '[a]t least one member of the supervisory board shall be a financial expert, in the sense that he has relevant knowledge and experience of financial administration and accounting for listed companies or other large legal entities' (best practice provision III.3.2). 'The supervisory board shall draw up a retirement schedule in order to avoid, as far as possible, a situation in which many supervisory board members retire at the same time' (best practice provision III.3.6).

---

152. Best practice provision II.1.8 in the amended version of The Dutch Corporate Governance Code.
153. The amended version of The Dutch Corporate Governance Code adds to this:

    'The supervisory board shall aim for a diverse composition in terms of such factors as gender and age'.

In accordance with main principle A.5 of The Combined Code on Corporate Governance '[a]ll directors should receive induction on joining the board and should regularly update and refresh their skills and knowledge'. In accordance with principle III.1 of The Dutch Corporate Governance Code the supervisory board shall be 'responsible for the quality of its own performance'. Following appointment, each non-executive director shall follow an 'induction programme, which, in any event, covers general financial and legal affairs, financial reporting by the company, any specific aspects that are unique to the company and its business activities, and the responsibilities of a supervisory board member', as well as 'further training or education during [her] period of appointment' where necessary (best practice provision III.3.3). Under code provision A.1.1 '[t]he board should meet sufficiently regularly to discharge its duties effectively'. A non-executive director 'who [is] frequently absent shall be called to account for this' (best practice provision III.1.5). Also, '[t]he supervisory board and its individual members each have their own responsibility for obtaining all information from the management board and the external auditor that the supervisory board needs', '[t]he supervisory board may require that certain officers and external advisers attend its meetings', and '[i]f the supervisory board considers it necessary, it may obtain information from officers and external advisers of the company' (best practice provision III.1.9). Likewise, '[t]he board should be supplied in a timely manner with information in a form and of a quality appropriate to enable it to discharge its duties' (main principle A.5), and '[m]anagement has an obligation to provide [accurate, timely and clear] information but directors should seek clarification or amplification where necessary' (supporting principle A.5). 'The board should ensure that directors, especially non-executive directors, have access to independent professional advice at the company's expense where they judge it necessary to discharge their responsibilities as directors' (code provision A.5.2). At least once a year the supervisory board shall discuss without executive directors being present both 'its own functioning and that of its individual members, and the conclusions that must be drawn on the basis thereof' and 'the functioning of the management board as an organ of the company and the performance of its individual members, and the conclusions that must be drawn on the basis thereof' (best practice III.1.7). Likewise, '[t]he board should undertake a formal and rigorous annual evaluation of its own performance and that of its committees and individual directors' (main principle A.6); '[i]ndividual evaluation should aim to show whether each director continues to contribute effectively and to demonstrate commitment to the role' (supporting principle A.6). The supervisory board shall under best practice provision III.1.1 draw up a set of regulations on '[t]he division of duties within the supervisory board and the procedure of the supervisory board' (this set of regulations shall in any event consider relations with the management board and the general meeting of shareholders),[154] and shall under best practice provision III.1.2 draw up and insert into the annual report of the corporation

---

154. '[A]nd the works council, where relevant'.

'a report of the supervisory board' describing its activities in the financial year. Under code provision A.1.1 '[t]he annual report should include a statement of how the board operates'. 'Where directors have concerns which cannot be resolved about the running of the company or a proposed action, they should ensure that their concerns are recorded in the board minutes. On resignation, a non-executive director should provide a written statement to the chairman, for circulation to the board, if they have any such concerns' (code provision A.1.4). A non-executive director 'shall retire early in the event of inadequate performance, structural incompatibility of interests, and in other instances in which this is deemed necessary by the supervisory board' (best practice provision III.1.4).[155] In accordance with code provision A.1.5 '[t]he company should arrange appropriate insurance cover in respect of legal action against its directors'.

When the board, or the management or supervisory board, formally convenes, it meets 'in executive session'.

5. The Senior Independent Director[156]

[48] In accordance with code provision A.1.2 of The Combined Code on Corporate Governance '[t]he annual report should identify' not only the chairperson, but also 'the deputy chairman (where there is one) [and] the senior independent director'. Under code provision A.3.3. '[t]he board should appoint one of the independent non-executive directors to be the senior independent director'. 'Led by the senior independent director, the non-executive directors should meet without the chairman present at least annually to appraise the chairman's performance [. . .] and on such other occasions as are deemed appropriate' (code provision A.1.3),[157] and '[t]he senior independent director should be available to shareholders if they have concerns which contact through the normal channels of chairman, chief executive or finance director has failed to resolve or for which such contact is inappropriate' (code provision A.3.3).

B. Reinforcing Monitoring: Director Independence

[49] Traditionally, the three functions of the unitary or dual board of a corporation were strategy setting (in a unitary board traditionally performed by the executive directors and the non-executive directors together and in a dual board since more recently also performed by the executive directors and the non-executive directors

---

155. And in accordance with The Dutch Corporate Governance Code, best practice provision III.6.7 '[a] supervisory board member who temporarily takes on the management of the company, where the management board members are absent or unable to fulfil their duties, shall resign from the supervisory board'.
156. In US usage: lead director, lead independent director or presiding director.
157. Under The Combined Code on Corporate Governance, code provision A.6.1 '[t]he non-executive directors, led by the senior independent director, should be responsible for performance evaluation of the chairman, taking into account the views of executive directors'.

together), policy implementation (performed by the executive directors assisted by the managers) and supervision (performed by the non-executive directors). However, the main function of the unitary or dual board of a corporation has developed into monitoring management. This function can to a large extent be understood as a combination of the traditional functions of strategy setting and supervision. The function of monitoring management is performed by the executive directors and the non-executive directors together. For the unitary or dual board of a corporation to be able to perform the functions of monitoring management properly, it needs to be composed of members who 'are able to act critically and independently of one another [...] and any particular interests',[158] and are 'independent in character and judgement', devoid of 'relationships or circumstances which are likely to affect, or could appear to affect, the director's judgement'.[159] This notion has also led to the concept of director independence that must make sure that directors 'take decisions objectively in the interests of the company',[160] 'guided by the interests of the company and its affiliated enterprise'.[161] Performing the function of monitoring management independently implies especially that directors do not have a too close relationship with the managers of the corporation and do not favor the interests of certain shareholders of the corporation they may have ties with. Under the concept of director independence a sufficient number of directors shall be independent directors as opposed to non-independent directors. Because the executive directors are part of management the concept of director independence cannot apply to them. The concept therefore means that a sufficient number of non-executive directors shall be independent non-executive directors as opposed to non-independent non-executive directors.[162]

Director independence may be regulated in three ways.[163] The *first* is a principle-based approach where a non-executive director is considered independent if the board (or the supervisory board), taking into account all circumstances, determines that she has no material relationship with the corporation and is therefore independent. This approach is followed in The Combined Code on Corporate Governance. The code contains a number of more or less well-defined criteria on

---

158. 'The Dutch Corporate Governance Code', principle III.2.
159. 'The Combined Code on Corporate Governance', code provision A.3.1.
160. 'The Combined Code on Corporate Governance', supporting principle A.1.
161. 'The Dutch Corporate Governance Code', principle III.1.
162. Cf. also the 'Commission Recommendation of 15 February 2005 on the Role of Non-Executive or Supervisory Directors of Listed Companies and on the Committees of the (Supervisory) Board (2005/162/EC)', OJEU 2005 L 52/51-63 (text with EEA relevance). M.J. Kroeze, 'Onafhankelijkheid van commissarissen', *Ondernemingsrecht* 2005: 272-278, H. Koster, 'Independent Non-executive Directors: The Way forward', *Ondernemingsrecht* (2006), 414-419.
163. A.F.M. Dorresteijn & C. de Groot, 'Corporate Governance Codes: Origins and Perspectives', in *European Company Law in Accelerated Progress*, ed. S.M. Bartman (Alphen aan den Rijn: Kluwer Law International, 2006), 31-57 (also published in *European Company Law* (2004), 43-56).

director dependence, but the existence of these criteria does not bar a non-executive director from being independent if the board considers her to be so. The *second* is a ruled-based approach where a non-executive director is deemed independent if a number of more or less well-defined criteria on director dependence do not apply to her. This approach is followed in The Dutch Corporate Governance Code. The code contains a number of categorical dependence criteria and does not provide that the supervisory board, apart from testing a non-executive director against these criteria, shall otherwise determine that she is independent. The *third* approach is both principle-based and rule-based. In this approach a non-executive director is independent if the board (or the supervisory board) determines that she has no material relationship with the corporation and has also established that none of a number of more or less well-defined dependence criteria apply to her. The dependence criteria in The Combined Code on Corporate Governance and in The Dutch Corporate Governance code are much alike. Under these criteria (that are non-categorical and categorical respectively) a director is not independent if she:[164]

- 'has been an employee of the company or group within the last five years',[165]
- 'has been an employee or member of the management board of the company (including associated companies [...]) in the five years prior to the appointment',[166]
- 'has, or has had within the last three years, a material business relationship with the company either directly, or as a partner, shareholder, director or senior employee of a body that has such a relationship with the company',[167]
- 'has had an important business relationship with the company, or a company associated with it, in the year prior to the appointment. This includes the case where the supervisory board member, or the firm of which he is a shareholder, partner, associate or adviser, has acted as adviser to the company (consultant, external auditor, civil notary and lawyer) and the case where the supervisory board member is a management board member or an employee of any bank with which the company has a lasting and significant relationship',[168]
- 'has received or receives additional remuneration from the company apart from a director's fee, participates in the company's share option or performance-related pay scheme, or is a member of the company's pension scheme',[169]

---

164. Under The Dutch Corporate Governance Code, best practice provision III.2.2 the dependence criteria shall apply to both the non-executive director and 'his wife, registered partner or other life companion, foster child or relative by blood or marriage up to the second degree'.
165. 'The Combined Code on Corporate Governance', code provision A.3.1, first bullet.
166. 'The Dutch Corporate Governance Code', best practice provision III.2.2, under a.
167. 'The Combined Code on Corporate Governance', code provision A.3.1, second bullet.
168. 'The Dutch Corporate Governance Code', best practice provision III.2.2, under c.
169. 'The Combined Code on Corporate Governance', code provision A.3.1, third bullet.

- 'receives personal financial compensation from the company, or a company associated with it, other than the compensation received for the work performed as a supervisory board member and in so far as this is not in keeping with the normal course of business',[170]
- 'holds cross-directorships or has significant links with other directors through involvement in other companies or bodies',[171]
- 'is a member of the management board of a company in which a member of the management board of the company which he supervises is a supervisory board member',[172]
- 'represents a significant shareholder',[173]
- 'is a member of the management board or supervisory board – or is a representative in some other way – of a legal entity which holds at least ten percent of the shares in the company, unless such entity is a member of the same group as the company',[174]
- 'has close family ties with any of the company's advisors, directors or senior employees',[175]
- 'has served on the board for more than nine years from the date of their first election',[176]
- 'holds at least ten percent of the shares in the company (including the shares held by natural persons or legal entities which cooperate with him under an express or tacit, oral or written agreement',[177] and
- 'has temporarily managed the company during the previous twelve months where management board members have been absent or unable to discharge their duties'.[178]

In accordance with The Combined Code on Corporate Governance '[e]xcept for smaller companies, at least half the board, excluding the chairman, should comprise non-executive directors determined by the board to be independent. A smaller company should have at least two independent non-executive directors' (code provision A.3.2).[179] The chairperson should meet the independence criteria of the code on appointment.[180] In accordance with The Dutch Corporate Governance Code '[a]ll supervisory board members, with the exception of not more than one person, shall be independent' in the sense that the dependence criteria of the code do no not apply to them.[181]

---

170. 'The Dutch Corporate Governance Code', best practice provision III.2.2, under b.
171. 'The Combined Code on Corporate Governance', code provision A.3.1, fifth bullet.
172. 'The Dutch Corporate Governance Code', best practice provision III.2.2, under d.
173. 'The Combined Code on Corporate Governance', code provision A.3.1, sixth bullet.
174. 'The Dutch Corporate Governance Code', best practice provision III.2.2, under f.
175. 'The Combined Code on Corporate Governance', code provision A.3.1, fourth bullet.
176. 'The Combined Code on Corporate Governance', code provision A.3.1, seventh bullet.
177. 'The Dutch Corporate Governance Code', best practice provision III.2.2, under e.
178. 'The Dutch Corporate Governance Code', best practice provision III.2.2, under g.
179. Footnote deleted.
180. 'The Combined Code on Corporate Governance', code provision A.2.2.
181. 'The Dutch Corporate Governance Code', best practice provision III.2.1.

The third approach – that is both principle-based and rule-based – is followed in the New York Stock Exchange Listed Company Manual that applies to corporations that are listed on the New York Stock Exchange.[182] The Manual states in subsection 303A.01 that '[l]isted companies must have a majority of independent directors' (this subsection 303A.01 falls under section 3 ('Corporate responsibility'), Section 303A ('Corporate governance standards')). Under subsection 303A.02 the independence test shall meet the following criteria:

(a) No director qualifies as 'independent' unless the board of directors affirmatively determines that the director has no material relationship with the listed company (either directly or as a partner, shareholder or officer of an organization that has a relationship with the company). Companies must identify which directors are independent and disclose the basis for that determination.

(b) In addition, a director is not independent if:
   (i)   The director is, or has been within the last three years, an employee of the listed company, or an immediate family member is, or has been within the last three years, an executive officer, of the listed company.
   (ii) The director has received, or has an immediate family member who has received, during any twelve-month period within the last three years, more than $100,000 in direct compensation from the listed company, other than director and committee fees and pension or other forms of deferred compensation for prior service (provided such compensation is not contingent in any way on continued service).
   (iii) (A) The director or an immediate family member is a current partner of a firm that is the company's internal or external auditor; (B) the director is a current employee of such a firm; (C) the director has an immediate family member who is a current employee of such a firm and who participates in the firm's audit, assurance or tax compliance (but not tax planning) practice; or (D) the director or an immediate family member was within the last three years (but is no longer) a partner or employee of such a firm and personally worked on the listed company's audit within that time.
   (iv) The director or an immediate family member is, or has been within the last three years, employed as an executive officer of another company where any of the listed company's present executive officers at the same time serves or served on that company's compensation committee.
   (v)   The director is a current employee, or an immediate family member is a current executive officer, of a company that has made payments to, or received payments from, the listed company for property or services in an amount which, in any of the last three fiscal years, exceeds

182.   <www.nyse.com> nyse regulation → listed companies.

the greater of $1 million, or 2% of such other company's consolidated gross revenues (footnote deleted).

The executive directors are sometimes referred to as employee directors; the non-executive directors are sometimes referred to as non-employee directors or non-management directors. The executive directors and the non-independent non-executive directors collectively are sometimes referred to as inside directors; the independent non-executive directors are sometimes referred to as outside directors or simply independent directors.

C.   SCHEDULE 1: THE BOARD AND (SENIOR) MANAGEMENT

Board, or management board and supervisory board	Senior management	Management
non-executive directors (non-employee directors, non-management directors) – 'officers': (1) and (2A): (1) independent non-executive directors (outside directors, independent directors) (inside directors: A and B:) (2A) non-independent non-executive directors (2B) executive directors (employee directors) – 'executive officers'	executive directors (employee directors) – 'executive officers' senior managers – 'executive officers'	executive directors (employee directors) – 'executive officers' senior managers – 'executive officers' managers – 'executives'

D.   RESHAPING SUPERVISION: BOARD COMMITTEES

1.   The Supervisory Gap

[50] The developments which have led the main function of both unitary and dual boards (performed by the executive and the non-executive directors together) to become monitoring management have also had as a result that the supervisory function of the non-executive directors (directed at the executive directors) has been pushed into the background. Therefore, corporations may experience a 'supervisory gap'. A means to redress this supervisory gap is the introduction of committees of the board or the supervisory board that are composed, preferably in the majority or entirely, of independent non-executive directors. By performing their tasks, these board committees may enhance the level of supervision that the non-executive directors as such cannot live up to. Both The Combined Code on

Corporate Governance and The Dutch Corporate Governance Code make three committees mandatory. These mandatory board committees are the audit committee, the nomination committee (the selection and appointment committee) and the remuneration committee.[183]

2. Mandatory Board Committees

[51] In accordance with The Combined Code on Corporate Governance the main role and responsibilities of the audit committee should be inter alia 'to monitor the integrity of the financial statements of the company' (code provision C.3.2, first bullet). The audit committee should consist 'of at least three, or in the case of smaller companies two, independent non-executive directors' (code provision C.3.1).[184] 'The board should satisfy itself that at least one member of the audit committee has recent and relevant financial experience' (code provision C.3.1); 'In smaller companies the company chairman may be a member of, but not chair, the committee in addition to the independent non-executive directors, provided he or she was considered independent on appointment as chairman' (code provision C.3.1). The nomination committee 'should lead the process for board appointments and make recommendations to the board. A majority of members of the nomination committee should be independent non-executive directors' (code provision A.4.1). 'The chairman or an independent non-executive director should chair the committee, but the chairman should not chair the nomination committee when it is dealing with the appointment of a successor to the chairmanship' (code provision A.4.1). 'The remuneration committee should have delegated responsibility for setting remuneration for all executive directors and the chairman, including pension rights and any compensation payments. The committee should also recommend and monitor the level and structure of remuneration for senior management' (code provision B.2.2).[185] The remuneration committee too should consist 'of at least three, or in the case of smaller companies two, independent non-executive directors' (code provision B.2.1).[186] 'In addition the company chairman may also be a member of, but not chair, the

---

183. Cf. also the 'Commission Recommendation of 15 February 2005 on the Role of Non-Executive or Supervisory Directors of Listed Companies and on the Committees of the (Supervisory) Board (2005/162/EC)', OJEU 2005 L 52/51-63 (text with EEA relevance).
184. Footnote deleted. The relevant footnote in The Combined Code on Corporate Governance reads:

    'A smaller company is one that is below the FTSE 350 throughout the year immediately prior to the reporting year'.

185. 'The definition of "senior management" for this purpose should be determined by the board but should normally include the first layer of management below board level'.
186. Footnote deleted. The relevant footnote in The Combined Code on Corporate Governance reads:

    'A smaller company is one that is below the FTSE 350 throughout the year immediately prior to the reporting year'.

committee if he or she was considered independent on appointment as chairman' (code provision B.2.1).

In accordance with The Dutch Corporate Governance Code the supervisory board shall, in case there are more than four non-executive directors, establish three 'key committees' from among the non-executive directors (principle III.5). The task of these committees shall be to prepare the work of the supervisory board (principle III.5). In general, only one member of a committee may be a non-independent non-executive director (best practice provision III.5.1). At least one member of the audit committee shall be a financial expert (best practice provision III.5.7). Neither the audit committee nor the remuneration committee shall be chaired by the chairperson of the supervisory board or by a former executive director of the corporation (best practice provisions III.5.6 and III.5.11). As concerns the remuneration committee the code further prescribes that no more than one member of this committee shall be a non-executive director who serves as an executive director of another Dutch listed corporation (best practice provision III.5.12), and that this committee shall not be chaired by a non-executive director who serves as an executive director of any other listed corporation (best practice provision III.5.11). The amended version of The Dutch Corporate Governance Code adds in best practice provision III.5.13 that, '[i]f the remuneration committee makes use of the services of a remuneration consultant in carrying out its duties, it shall verify that the consultant concerned does not provide advice to the company's management board members'.

Best practice provision III.5.1 of The Dutch Corporate Governance Code requires the supervisory board to 'draw up a set of regulations for each committee'. Likewise, The Combined Code on Corporate Governance states that there shall be 'terms of reference' for the audit committee (code provision C.3.2), the nomination committee (code provision A.4.1) and the remuneration committee (code provision B.2.1).[187]

3.   The Audit Committee[188]

[52] In accordance with The Combined Code on Corporate Governance the main role and responsibilities of the audit committee should include, and in accordance with The Dutch Corporate Governance Code the audit committee shall in any event focus on supervising the activities of the management board with respect to:

   – 'to monitor the integrity of the financial statements of the company, and any formal announcements relating to the company's financial performance, reviewing significant financial reporting judgements contained in them',[189]

---

187. US usage for a committee set of regulations or terms of reference is a committee charter.
188. J.E. Martella, M.R. Paul, T. Philipp & R. James, 'Audit Committee Requirements for Foreign Private Issuers Listed in the United States', *European Company Law* (2004), 62-65; H. Langman, 'De audit-commissie', *Ondernemingsrecht* (2005), 259-263; E. Mouthaan, 'De verantwoordelijkheden van de audit commissie', *Maandblad voor Accountancy en Bedrijfseconomie* (2006), 84-92; E.H.J. Mouthaan, 'The Audit Committee from a European Perspective', *European Company Law* (2007), 10-18.
189. 'The Combined Code on Corporate Governance', code provision C.3.2, first bullet.

- 'the provision of financial information by the company (choice of accounting policies, application and assessment of the effects of new rules, information about the handling of estimated items in the annual accounts, forecasts, work of internal and external auditors, etc.)',[190]
- 'to review the company's internal financial controls and, unless expressly addressed by a separate board risk committee composed of independent directors, or by the board itself, to review the company's internal control and risk management systems',[191]
- 'the operation of the internal risk management and control systems, including supervision of the enforcement of the relevant legislation and regulations, and supervising the operation of codes of conduct',[192]
- 'to monitor and review the effectiveness of the company's internal audit function',[193]
- 'the role and functioning of the internal audit department',[194]
- 'to make recommendations to the board, for it to put to the shareholders for their approval in general meeting, in relation to the appointment, reappointment and removal of the external auditor and to approve the remuneration and terms of engagement of the external auditor',[195]
- 'to review and monitor the external auditor's independence and objectivity and the effectiveness of the audit process',[196]
- 'to develop and implement policy on the engagement of the external auditor to supply non-audit services, taking into account relevant ethical guidance regarding the provision of non-audit services by the external audit firm',[197]
- 'relations with the external auditor, including, in particular, his independence, remuneration and any non-audit services for the company',[198]
- 'compliance with recommendations and observations of internal and external auditors',[199]
- 'the policy of the company on tax planning',[200]
- 'the financing of the company',[201] and
- 'the applications of information and communication technology (ICT)'.[202]

The EC directive on statutory audits of annual accounts and consolidated accounts favors that a 'public-interest entity shall have an audit committee' (Article 41

---

190. 'The Dutch Corporate Governance Code', best practice provision III.5.4, under b.
191. 'The Combined Code on Corporate Governance', code provision C.3.2, second bullet.
192. 'The Dutch Corporate Governance Code', best practice provision III.5.4, under a.
193. 'The Combined Code on Corporate Governance', code provision C.3.2, third bullet.
194. 'The Dutch Corporate Governance Code', best practice provision III.5.4, under d.
195. 'The Combined Code on Corporate Governance', code provision C.3.2, fourth bullet.
196. 'The Combined Code on Corporate Governance', code provision C.3.2, fifth bullet.
197. 'The Combined Code on Corporate Governance', code provision C.3.2, sixth bullet.
198. 'The Dutch Corporate Governance Code', best practice provision III.5.4, under f.
199. 'The Dutch Corporate Governance Code', best practice provision III.5.4, under c.
200. 'The Dutch Corporate Governance Code', best practice provision III.5.4, under e.
201. 'The Dutch Corporate Governance Code', best practice provision III.5.4, under g.
202. 'The Dutch Corporate Governance Code', best practice provision III.5.4, under h.

section 1).[203] Public-interest entities are listed corporations, credit institutions and insurance undertakings (in addition, 'Member States may also designate other entities as public-interest entities, for instance entities that are of significant public relevance because of the nature of their business, their size or the number of their employees') (Article 2 subsection 13). In accordance with Article 41 section 2 the audit committee shall, inter alia:

(a) monitor the financial reporting process;
(b) monitor the effectiveness of the company's internal control, internal audit where applicable, and risk management systems;
(c) monitor the statutory audit of the annual and consolidated accounts;
(d) review and monitor the independence of the statutory auditor or audit firm, and in particular the provision of additional services to the audited entity.

4.   The Nomination Committee (Selection and Appointment Committee)

[53] In accordance with The Dutch Corporate Governance Code the selection and appointment committee shall in any event focus on:

- 'drawing up selection criteria and appointment procedures for supervisory board members and management board members',[204]
- 'periodically assessing the size and composition of the supervisory board and the management board, and making a proposal for a composition profile of the supervisory board',[205]
- 'periodically assessing the functioning of individual supervisory board members and management board members, and reporting on this to the supervisory board',[206]
- 'making proposals for appointments and reappointments',[207] and
- 'supervising the policy of the management board on the selection criteria and appointment procedures for senior management'.[208]

203. 'Directive 2006/43/EC of the European Parliament and of the Council of 17 May 2006 on Statutory Audits of Annual Accounts and Consolidated Accounts, Amending Council Directives 78/660/EEC and 83/349/EEC and Repealing Council Directive 84/253/EEC', OJEU 2006 L 157/87-107 (text with EEA relevance).
204. 'The Dutch Corporate Governance Code', best practice provision III.5.13 (III.5.14 in the amended version of The Dutch Corporate Governance Code), under a.
205. 'The Dutch Corporate Governance Code', best practice provision III.5.13 (III.5.14 in the amended version of The Dutch Corporate Governance Code), under b.
206. 'The Dutch Corporate Governance Code', best practice provision III.5.13 (III.5.14 in the amended version of The Dutch Corporate Governance Code), under c.
207. 'The Dutch Corporate Governance Code', best practice provision III.5.13 (III.5.14 in the amended version of The Dutch Corporate Governance Code), under d.
208. 'The Dutch Corporate Governance Code', best practice provision III.5.13 (III.5.14 in the amended version of The Dutch Corporate Governance Code), under e.

5.   **The Remuneration Committee**[209]

[54] In accordance with The Dutch Corporate Governance Code the remuneration committee shall in any event have the following duties:

- 'drafting a proposal to the supervisory board for the remuneration policy to be pursued',[210]
- 'drafting a proposal for the remuneration of the individual members of the management board, for adoption by the supervisory board',[211] and
- 'preparing the remuneration report'.[212]

II.   CASE STUDY

A.   INTRODUCTION TO THE DISNEY CASE

[55] The *Disney* case deals with the hiring and termination of a President and COO by the US corporation The Walt Disney Company. It is concerned with the functioning of the board of The Walt Disney Company.

[56] In 1994 M.D. Eisner ('Eisner'), the Chairman and CEO of The Walt Disney Company ('Disney'), also temporarily became the President and COO of Disney. However, sooner than foreseen health reasons prompted Eisner and the board of Disney to look for a successor of Eisner as President and COO. Eisner thought that M.S. Ovitz ('Ovitz') would be suited for this position. As a founder and leading partner of Creative Artists Agency ('CAA') Ovitz was well-acquainted with and well-known in the Hollywood entertainment industry, and Eisner had known Ovitz both personally and professionally for about 25 years. On the part of Disney, two directors were primarily involved in the negotiations with Ovitz over an employment agreement: Eisner and I.E. Russell ('Russell', the chairperson of the Disney compensation committee). During these negotiations, Russell sought the assistance of an outside executive compensation consultant and of another member of the compensation committee. Russell had expressed that the remuneration Ovitz would receive under the terms of the agreement as they were being negotiated would – also resulting from the use of share options – be high, even 'at the top level for any corporate officer and significantly above that of the Disney CEO', but 'required to enable Ovitz to adjust to the reduced cash compensation he would receive from a public company, in contrast to the greater cash distributions and other perquisites more typically available from a privately held business'.[213]

209.   J.G. Hill, 'Regulating Executive Remuneration: International Developments in the Post-scandal Era', *European Company Law* (2006), 64-74.
210.   'The Dutch Corporate Governance Code', best practice provision III.5.10, under a.
211.   'The Dutch Corporate Governance Code', best practice provision III.5.10, under b.
212.   'The Dutch Corporate Governance Code', best practice provision III.5.10, under c.
213.   Formulation by the Delaware Supreme Court.

During the negotiations, it also became clear that Eisner and Ovitz did not share the same views on Ovitz's role at Disney – Ovitz hoped to be co-CEO with Eisner but accepted that Eisner wanted him to be President and COO –, and that two members of the board (the CFO and an executive vice president) would continue to report to Eisner rather than to Ovitz. Still, in August 1995 Eisner and Ovitz signed a letter (Ovitz's letter agreement or 'OLA') that contained the outlines of the definitive employment agreement (Ovitz's employment agreement or 'OEA') for a period of time of five years. The agreement of August 1995 was be subject to approval by both the compensation committee and the board of Disney. In September 2005 the compensation committee gave its approval which was followed by the board's decision in executive session to elect Ovitz as president and COO. Ovitz began working for Disney on 1 October 1995. However, the relationship between Ovitz and the other Disney executives did not work out, and eventually in December 1996 Eisner decided to terminate Ovitz. Because Ovitz was terminated 'without cause',[214] under the terms of the employment agreement he became eligible for a severance payment for a non-fault termination ('NFT') totaling to approximately USD 130 million.[215]

B.   THE DECISION OF THE DELAWARE SUPREME COURT

[57] Several shareholders of Disney filed derivative actions on behalf of Disney in the Court of Chancery of the State of Delaware against Ovitz, Eisner and the other members of the board of Disney who had served at the time of the hiring and termination of Ovitz.[216] They claimed that all of these persons had breached their

---

214.   As opposed to 'for cause'.
215.   The Delaware Supreme Court considered:

> '[. . .] Ovitz met with Eisner on December 3, to discuss his termination. Ovitz asked for several concessions, all of which Eisner ultimately rejected. Eisner told Ovitz that all he would receive was what he had contracted for in the OEA. [. . .] On December 11, Eisner met with Ovitz to agree on the wording of a press release to announce the termination, and to inform Ovitz that he would not receive any of the additional items that he requested. By that time it had already been decided that Ovitz would be terminated without cause and that he would receive his contractual NFT payment, but nothing more. Eisner and Ovitz agreed that neither Ovitz nor Disney would disparage each other in the press, and that the separation was to be undertaken with dignity and respect for both sides. After his December 11 meeting with Eisner, Ovitz never returned to Disney. Ovitz's termination was memorialized in a letter, dated December 12, 1996, that Litvack [S.M. Litvack, a member of the board of directors of Disney] signed on Eisner's instruction. The board was not shown the letter, nor did it meet to approve its terms. A press release announcing Ovitz's termination was issued that same day. Before the press release was issued, Eisner attempted to contact each of the board members by telephone to notify them that Ovitz had been officially terminated. None of the board members at that time, or at any other time, objected to Ovitz's termination, and most, if not all, of them thought it was the appropriate step for Eisner to take' (footnote deleted).

216.   Including Ovitz and Eisner eighteen directors in total; S. Parijs, 'De grenzen van aansprakelijk-
        heid van bestuurders in Nederland en de Verenigde Staten', in H. Boschma et al,.

fiduciary duties to Disney. These actions were dismissed by the Court of Chancery. The plaintiffs appealed, but in its judgment of 8 June 2006 the Supreme Court of the State of Delaware affirmed the judgment of the Court of Chancery.[217] The Supreme Court separately went into 'the claims against the Disney defendants' and 'the claims against Ovitz'. The first claims concerned the liability of the directors of Disney in respect of 'approving the OEA, and specifically, its NFT provisions' and 'approving the NFT severance payment to Ovitz upon his termination'. The second claims concerned the liability of Ovitz in respect of 'negotiating for and accepting the NFT severance provisions of the OEA' and 'negotiating a full NFT payout in connection with his termination'. In connection with these claims, the Supreme Court discussed the so-called 'business judgment standard':

> Our law presumes that 'in making a business decision the directors of a corporation acted on an informed basis, in good faith, and in the honest belief that the action taken was in the best interests of the company.' Those presumptions can be rebutted if the plaintiff shows that the directors breached their *fiduciary duty of care* or *of loyalty* or *acted in bad faith*. If that is shown, the burden then shifts to the director defendants to demonstrate that the challenged act or transaction was entirely fair to the corporation and its shareholders (footnotes deleted, emphasis added).

It would thus seem that the business judgment standard which protects a director from liability does not apply in three cases. In these cases a plaintiff must show that a director either breached her fiduciary duty of care to the corporation, or breached her fiduciary duty of loyalty to the corporation, or breached her fiduciary duty to act in good faith to the corporation (i.e. did not act in good faith). In any of these cases 'those breaches of fiduciary duty deprive [. . .] defendants of the protection of business judgment review, and require them to shoulder the burden of establishing that their acts were entirely fair'. There is, however, one more situation in which the 'business judgment presumptions' do not protect a director from liability: that is the case of 'corporate waste'.[218] As concerns the fiduciary duty of care, the Supreme Court stated that 'lack of due care' amounts to 'gross negligence'.

LT: Verzamelde 'Groninger' opstellen aangeboden aan Vino Timmerman (Deventer: Kluwer, 2003), 229-239; B.F. Assink, 'Over vrijheid van ondernemingsbeleid en het enquêterecht: divergentie en convergentie van bestuurlijke gedragsnormen en rechterlijke toetsingsnormen nader bezien', *Ondernemingsrecht* (2006), 307-316; J. Winter, 'Corporate governance handhaving in de VS, EU en Nederland', in *Verantwoording aan Hans Beckman*, eds M.J. Kroeze et al. (Deventer: Kluwer, 2006), 621-645; B.F. Assink, *Rechterlijke toetsing van bestuurlijk gedrag* (Deventer: Kluwer, 2007).

217. Supreme Court of the State of Delaware 8 June 2006 (*In re* The Walt Disney Company Derivative Litigation); <www.courts.delaware.gov> opinions → 2006, 6/8/06 In re The Walt Disney Company et al. v. Eisner et al. 411, 2005.

218. 'Alternatively, the appellants claim that even if the business judgment presumptions apply, the Disney defendants are nonetheless liable, because the NFT payout constituted corporate waste and the Court of Chancery erred in concluding otherwise' (footnote deleted).

In the case under discussion, the 'duty to act in good faith' also played an important role, but the Supreme Court recognized that it was an elusive concept:

> Although the good faith concept has recently been the subject of considerable scholarly writing, which includes articles focused on this specific case, the duty to act in good faith is, up to this point relatively uncharted. Because of the increased recognition of the importance of good faith, some conceptual guidance to the corporate community may be helpful (footnotes deleted).

In the opinion of the Supreme Court, 'as a matter of simple logic, at least three different categories of fiduciary behavior are candidates for the "bad faith" pejorative label':

> The first category involves so-called 'subjective bad faith,' that is, fiduciary conduct motivated by an actual intent to do harm. That such conduct constitutes classic, quintessential bad faith is a proposition so well accepted in the liturgy of fiduciary law that it borders on axiomatic (footnote deleted.),[219]

> The second category of conduct, which is at the opposite end of the spectrum, involves lack of due care – that is, fiduciary action taken solely by reason of gross negligence and without any malevolent intent, and:

> the third category of fiduciary conduct, which falls in between the first two categories of (1) conduct motivated by subjective bad intent and (2) conduct resulting from gross negligence. This third category is what the Chancellor's definition of bad faith – intentional dereliction of duty, a conscious disregard for one's responsibilities – is intended to capture.

In the opinion of the Supreme Court a breach of the fiduciary duty to act in good faith to the corporation would not encompass the second category, but would encompass the third category,[220] as well as the first category. Because in relation to the fiduciary duty of care, the Supreme Court stated that 'lack of due care' amounts to 'gross negligence', the Supreme Court was pressed to 'address the issue of whether gross negligence (including a failure to inform one's self of available material facts), without more, can also constitute bad faith':

> The answer is clearly no. [. . .] [. . .] in the pragmatic, conduct-regulating legal realm which calls for more precise conceptual line drawing, the answer is that grossly negligent conduct, without more, does not and cannot constitute a breach of the fiduciary duty to act in good faith. The conduct that is the subject of due care may overlap with the conduct that comes within the rubric of good faith in a psychological sense, but from a legal standpoint those duties are and must remain quite distinct. Both our legislative history and our common law jurisprudence distinguish sharply between the duties to exercise due care and

---

219. 'We need not dwell further on this category, because no such conduct is claimed to have occurred, or did occur, in this case'.
220. An 'intermediate category of fiduciary misconduct, which ranks between conduct involving subjective bad faith and gross negligence'.

to act in good faith, and highly significant consequences flow from that distinction. [...] There is no basis in policy, precedent or common sense that would justify dismantling the distinction between gross negligence and bad faith (footnotes deleted).

As concerns the first part of the claims against the Disney defendants,[221] the Supreme Court established that:

The Delaware General Corporation Law (DGCL) expressly empowers a board of directors to appoint committees and to delegate to them a broad range of responsibilities, which may include setting executive compensation. Nothing in the DGCL mandates that the entire board must make those decisions. At Disney, the responsibility to consider and approve executive compensation was allocated to the compensation committee, as distinguished from the full board. The Chancellor's ruling – that executive compensation was to be fixed by the compensation committee – is legally correct (footnote deleted).

In the opinion of the Supreme Court, the way the compensation committee had approved the terms of the NFT, although not flawless, did not amount to breach of the fiduciary duty of care. As the Supreme Court considered:

In our view, a helpful approach is to compare what actually happened here to what would have occurred had the committee followed a 'best practices' (or 'best case') scenario, from a process standpoint. In a 'best case' scenario, all committee members would have received, before or at the committee's first meeting on September 26, 1995, a spreadsheet or similar document prepared by (or with the assistance of) a compensation expert [...]. Making different, alternative assumptions, the spreadsheet would disclose the amounts that Ovitz could receive under the OEA in each circumstance that might foreseeably arise. [...] Had that scenario been followed, there would be no dispute (and no basis for litigation) over what information was furnished to the committee members or when it was furnished. Regrettably, the committee's informational and decisionmaking process used here was not so tidy.

But the Supreme Court found that the compensation committee had been aware of the level of the possible severance payment: 'The compensation committee members derived their information about the potential magnitude of an NFT payout from two sources. The first was the value of the [...] options previously granted to Eisner and [F. Wells, the former president and COO] [...]. [...] The committee members knew that by leaving CAA and coming to Disney, Ovitz would be sacrificing "booked" CAA commissions of $150 to $200 million – an amount that Ovitz demanded as protection against the risk that his employment relationship with Disney might not work out'. Thus:

The Court of Chancery noted (and we agree) that although it might have been the better course of action, it was 'not necessary for an expert to make a formal

---

221. '[C]laims arising out of the approval of the OEA and of Ovitz's election as President'.

presentation at the committee meeting in order for the board to rely on that expert's analysis . . . ' (footnote deleted).

Whereas approving the OEA was the responsibility of the compensation committee, selecting Ovitz as president and COO came within he powers of the board. In this, the directors had not breached their fiduciary duty of care:

> The directors thus knew of Ovitz's skills, reputation and experience, all of which they believed would be highly valuable to the Company. The directors also knew that to accept a position at Disney, Ovitz would have to walk away from a very successful business – a reality that would lead a reasonable person to believe that Ovitz would likely succeed in similar pursuits elsewhere in the industry. [. . .] Indeed, Eisner, who had long desired to bring Ovitz within the Disney fold, consistently vouched for Ovitz's qualifications and told the directors that he could work well with Ovitz. The board was also informed of the key terms of the OEA (including Ovitz's salary, bonus and options). Russell reported this information to them at the September 26, 1995 executive session, which was attended by Eisner and all nonexecutive directors. Russell also reported on the compensation committee meeting that had immediately preceded the executive session. [. . .] Relying upon the compensation committee's approval of the OEA and the other information furnished to them, the Disney directors, after further deliberating, unanimously elected Ovitz as President (footnote deleted).

As concerns the second part of the claims against the Disney defendants,[222] the Supreme Court noted that they centered on the assertion 'that even if the OEA approval was legally valid, the NFT severance payout to Ovitz pursuant to the OEA was not'. On the basis of the 'corporate governing instruments' of Disney (in this case: the certificate of incorporation and the bylaws) the Supreme Court concluded that:

> the extrinsic evidence clearly supports the conclusion that the board and Eisner understood that Eisner, as Board Chairman/CEO had concurrent power with the board to terminate Ovitz as President. [. . .] Because Eisner possessed, and exercised, the power to terminate Ovitz unilaterally, we find that the Chancellor correctly concluded that the new board was not required to act in connection with that termination, and, therefore, the board did not violate any fiduciary duty to act with due care or in good faith. As the Chancellor correctly held, the same conclusion is equally applicable to the compensation committee. The only role delegated to the compensation committee was 'to establish and approve compensation for Eisner, Ovitz and other applicable Company executives and high paid employees.' (footnote deleted).

---

222. '[C]laims arising out of the NFT severance payment to Ovitz upon his termination'.

In respect of Eisner's decision to terminate Ovitz, the Supreme Court referred to the judgment of the Court of Chancery:[223]

> With respect to Eisner, the Chancellor found that faced with a situation where he was unable to work well with Ovitz, who required close and constant supervision, Eisner had three options: 1) keep Ovitz as President and continue trying to make things work; 2) keep Ovitz at Disney, but in a role other than as President; or 3) terminate Ovitz. The first option was unacceptable, and the second would have entitled Ovitz to the NFT, or at the very least would have resulted in a costly lawsuit to determine whether Ovitz was so entitled. [. . .] that left only the third option, which was to terminate Ovitz and pay the NFT. The Chancellor found that in choosing this alternative, Eisner had breached no duty and had exercised his business judgment.

These conclusions by the Supreme Court left as a final question whether Ovitz's severance payment constituted corporate waste. In the opinion of the Supreme Court, it did not:

> The claim that the payment of the NFT amount to Ovitz, without more, constituted waste is meritless on its face, because at the time the NFT amounts were paid, Disney was contractually obligated to pay them. The payment of a contractually obligated amount cannot constitute waste, unless the contractual obligation is itself wasteful. Accordingly, the proper focus of a waste analysis must be whether the amounts required to be paid in the event of an NFT were wasteful *ex ante*. [. . .] That claim does not come close to satisfying the high hurdle required to establish waste. The approval of the NFT provisions in the OEA had a rational business purpose: to induce Ovitz to leave CAA, at what would otherwise be a considerable cost to him, in order to join Disney (footnote deleted).

As concerns the first part of the claims against Ovitz,[224] the Court of Chancery had considered 'that Ovitz had breached no fiduciary duty to Disney, because Ovitz did not become a fiduciary until he formally assumed office on October 1, 1995, by which time the essential terms of the NFT provision had been negotiated'.[225] However, on appeal the appellants argued that Ovitz had become a de facto director before 1 October 1995. The Supreme Court dismissed this reasoning:

> the *de facto* officer argument lacks merit, both legally and factually. A *de facto* officer is one who actually assumes possession of an office under the claim and color of an election or appointment and who is actually discharging the

---

223. 'These determinations rest squarely on factual findings that, in turn, are based upon the Chancellor's assessment of the credibility of Eisner and other witnesses. Even though the Chancellor found much to criticize in Eisner's "imperial CEO" style of governance, nothing has been shown to overturn the factual basis for the Court's conclusion that, in the end, Eisner's conduct satisfied the standards required of him as a fiduciary' (footnote deleted).
224. '[N]egotiating and entering into the OEA'.
225. Formulation by the Supreme Court.

duties of that office, but for some legal reason lacks *de jure* legal title to that office. Here, Ovitz did not assume, or purport to assume, the duties of the Disney presidency before October 1, 1995. [. . .] the Chancellor found as fact that all of Ovitz's pre-October 1 conduct upon which appellants rely to establish *de facto* officer status, represented Ovitz's preparations to assume the duties of President after he was formally in office (footnotes deleted).

As concerns the second part of the claims against Ovitz,[226] the appellants argued that Ovitz had played an active part in establishing the level of his severance payment. The Supreme Court dismissed this reasoning too:

The record establishes overwhelmingly that Ovitz did not leave Disney voluntarily. Nor did Ovitz arrange beforehand with Eisner to structure his departure as a termination without cause. To be sure, the evidence upon which the appellants rely does show that Ovitz fought being forced out every step of the way, but in the end, Ovitz had no choice but to accept the inevitable. As the trial court found, 'Ovitz did not "engage" in a transaction with the corporation – rather, the corporation imposed an unwanted transaction upon him.' (footnote deleted).

C.   EVALUATION

[58] *Disney* – in short – dealt with application of the business judgment standard in respect of corporate directors for approving the terms of an employment agreement with a director and for approving severance payment to the director under that agreement in proceedings where the claimants attempted to hold these persons liable.[227] The business judgment standard presumes that the directors of a corporation act on an informed basis, in good faith, and in the honest belief that the action taken was in the best interests of the company, unless a director either breaches her fiduciary duty of care to the corporation, or her fiduciary duty of loyalty to the corporation, or her fiduciary duty to act in good faith to the corporation. In case the plaintiff is able to demonstrate that such a breach of duty did occur the consequence is that the burden of proof shifts to the director: she will be held liable unless she demonstrates that her actions were entirely fair to the corporation and its shareholders. Thus, in *Disney* the Supreme Court of the State of Delaware formulated the central tenet of corporate law that it is presumed that in making a business decision the directors of a corporation acted on an informed basis, in good faith, and in the honest belief that the action taken was in the best interests of the company, and that to rebut these presumptions it is necessary for a plaintiff to show that the directors breached their fiduciary duty of care or of loyalty or acted in bad faith. Under the fiduciary duty of care, lack of due care means acting

226.   '[R]eceiving the NFT payment upon his termination as President of Disney'.
227.   As well as in respect of the director concerned for negotiating the employment agreement and accepting the severance payment.

with gross negligence. An example of this is decision making by a director who fails to inform herself of the available facts. Under the fiduciary duty to act in good faith, lack of good faith means acting with the intent to do harm as well as acting with a conscious disregard for one's responsibilities, but not acting with gross negligence.

Applying the business judgment standard in *Disney* meant that the directors who had approved the terms of the employment agreement and the severance payment were protected by that standard although their actions were not flawless. Although the compensation committee did not hear a compensation expert, it had other sources from which it could conclude the level of severance payment that Disney would have to pay if it came to terminating the director. Relying on that committee and on the qualifications of the director concerned, the board then elected him. When the chairperson and CEO decided to terminate the director, he had other options available (not terminating the director or making changes to the director's position), but he could reasonable discard those options. An interesting element of the *Disney* case is also that the allocation of certain powers of the board of directors to a committee of the board (here the compensation committee) or to an individual director (here the chairperson and CEO) shields the other directors from liability.

III.   (MODEL) CORPORATE GOVERNANCE GUIDELINES

A.   INTRODUCTION

[59] The (model) Corporate Governance Guidelines below offer a cross section of subjects that are dealt with in corporate governance guidelines adopted by the boards of directors of a number of US. listed corporations. These Guidelines are intended to give an overview of many, but not all, subjects, and as these Guidelines offer a cross section, individual corporate governance guidelines may be different in several respects from the overview. The documents that were used to compile the Guidelines are the corporate governance guidelines of the corporations that simultaneously appear in two equity indices: the Standard & Poor's United States 100 and the Standard & Poor's Global 100 indices.[228] The Guidelines offer an overview compiled for academic purposes and do not reflect directly the actual corporate governance guidelines of any of these corporations.[229]

---

228. <www.standardandpoors.com> indices → equity indices → s&p US indices, and <www.standardandpoors.com> indices → equity indices → s&p global indices (the author's selection was made in April 2008).
229. To compile the (model) Corporate Governance Guidelines the corporate governance guidelines of the following thirty-four corporations were used: **American International Group, Inc.**: Corporate Governance Guidelines (<www.aig.com> about aig), **Bristol-Myers Squibb Company**: Corporate Governance Guidelines (<www.bms.com> about us → corporate governance), **Caterpillar Inc.**: Guidelines on Corporate Governance Issues (<www.cat.com> about cat → profile → governance → highlights), **Chevron Corporation**: Corporate

B.   (MODEL) CORPORATE GOVERNANCE GUIDELINES OF THE BOARD OF
                      DIRECTORS OF ABC CORPORATION

[60] The Board of Directors (the 'Board') of ABC Corporation ('ABC' or the
'corporation'), acting on the recommendation of the Governance and Nominating
Committee, has adopted these Corporate Governance Guidelines to assist the
Board in the proper exercise of its responsibilities. These Guidelines reflect the
position of ABC's Board on significant corporate governance issues. The purpose
of the Board, serving as the elected representatives of the ABC's shareholders, is to
enhance the long-term value of the corporation for its shareholders and to ensure

Governance Guidelines (<www.chevron.com> about chevron → company profile),
Citigroup Inc.: Corporate Governance Guidelines (<www.citigroup.com> corporate governance), **The Coca Cola Company**: Corporate Governance Guidelines (<www.thecoca-
colacompany.com> investors → corporate governance), **Colgate-Palmolive Company**:
Board Guidelines on Significant Corporate Governance Issues (<www.colgate.com> our
company → governance), **Covidien Ltd.**: Corporate Governance Guidelines (<www.
covidien.com> investor relations → corporate governance), **Dell Inc.**: Corporate Governance
Principles (<www.dell.com> about dell → investors), **The Dow Chemical Company**: Corporate Governance Guidelines (<www.dow.com> investor relations), **E.I. du Pont de
Nemours and Company**: Corporate Governance Guidelines (<www.dupont.com> investor
center), **EMC Corporation**: Corporate Governance Guidelines (<www.emc.com> about emc
→ investor relations), **Exxon Mobil Corporation**: Corporate Governance Guidelines
(<www.exxonmobil.com> investors), **Ford Motor Company**: Corporate Governance Principles (<www.ford.com> about ford → company information), **General Electric Company**:
Governance Principles (<www.ge.com> our company → governance), **General Motors
Corporation**: Corporate Governance Guidelines (<www.gm.com> investors), **Hewlett-
Packard Company**: Corporate Governance Guidelines (<www.hp.com> company informa-
tion → investor relations), **Intel Corporation**: Guidelines on Significant Corporate Gover-
nance Issues (<www.intel.com> investor relations → corporate governance & responsibility),
International Business Machines Corporation: Corporate Governance Guidelines
(<www.ibm.com> about ibm → investors), **Johnson & Johnson**: Principles of Corporate
Governance (<www.jnj.com> investor relations → corporate governance), **JPMorgan
Chase & Co.**: Corporate Governance Principles (<www.jpmorganchase.com> governance),
3M Company: Corporate Governance Guidelines (<www.3m.com> investor relations),
McDonald's Corporation: Corporate Governance Principles (<www.mcdonalds.com> corporate mcdonald's → investors → corporate governance), **Merck & Co., Inc.**: Policies of
the Board (<www.merck.com> investor relations), **Microsoft Corporation**: Corporate
Governance Guidelines (<www.microsoft.com> about microsoft → investor relations →
corporate information), **Morgan Stanley**: Corporate Governance Policies (<www.morgan-
stanley.com> about morgan stanley → company information), **PepsiCo, Inc.**: Corporate
Governance Guidelines (<www.pepsico.com> investors), **Pfizer Inc.**: Governance of the
Company: Our Corporate Governance Principles (<www.pfizer.com> about pfizer → corporate
governance), **Philip Morris International Inc.**: Corporate Governance Guidelines (<www.
philipmorrisinternational.com> about us), **The Procter & Gamble Company**: Corporate Governance Guidelines (<www.pg.com> company → corporate governance), **Texas Instruments
Incorporated**: Corporate Governance Guidelines (<www.ti.com> investor relations), **Tyco
International Ltd.**: Board Governance Principles (<www.tyco.com> who we are → board of
directors), **United Technologies Corporation**: Corporate Governance Guidelines (<www.utc.
com> governance), **Wal-Mart Stores, Inc.**: Corporate Governance Guidelines (<www.
walmartstores.com> investors).

the continuity and vitality of ABC's business, consistent with the Board's fiduciary duties. Because the Board recognizes that the long-term interests of the shareholders are advanced by responsibly addressing the concerns of other stakeholders, the Board, in discharging this function, considers the concerns of other constituencies and interested parties, including employees, customers, suppliers, partners, local communities, governments, and the public at large. The Board is committed to ensuring that ABC operates in an effective, legal and ethically responsible manner. The Board had adopted these Guidelines to provide an effective corporate governance framework that provides the foundation for ABC's governance. These Guidelines are an evolving set of corporate governance standards and practices, subject to review and change as circumstances warrant, and establish a set of expectations as to how the Board, its committees and ABC's directors and management should perform their functions. At the same time, the Board believes that good corporate governance requires not only an effective set of standards and practices but also a culture of integrity and responsibility throughout the organization.

1. Ethics

[61] The Board and management are jointly responsible for operating ABC's business with the highest standards of ethics. The Board expects each director and each member of senior management to lead by example, emphasizing integrity and responsibility. The Board also expects each director and each member of senior management to adhere at all times to ABC's code of conduct. The Board will not allow any waiver of any ethics policy for any director or any member of senior management.

2. Roles of the Board and Management

[62] **Director responsibilities** Directors must exercise their business judgment to act in what they reasonably believe to be the best interest of the corporation and therefore its shareholders, and must perform their duties of care and loyalty to ABC. In discharging this obligation, directors may reasonably rely on the corporation's senior management, its outside advisors and consultants and internal and external auditors to the fullest extent permitted by law. Directors are expected to expend sufficient attention, energy and time to assure diligent performance of their responsibilities. Directors are expected to attend and participate in the meetings of the Board and of committees on which they serve as well as to attend the annual and special meetings of shareholders. Directors are also expected to make themselves available outside of Board meetings for advice and consultation.

Board oversight The business of ABC is conducted under the direction and oversight of the Board. The Board has responsibility for establishing broad corporate policies and for the overall performance of the corporation. The Board selects the chairperson, the chief executive officer ('CEO'), as well as senior management, and delegates to the CEO the authority and responsibility to manage the ABC's operations. ABC's business is conducted by its management under the direction and leadership of the CEO. Because ABC's business will be conducted under the direction and oversight of the Board, rather than managed by the Board, the roles of the Board and management are related but distinct.

Mix of executive and independent directors Because the purpose of the Board is to enhance long-term shareholder value and to ensure the continuity and vitality of ABC's business, the Board believes that these interests are best served by having a substantial number of objective members on the Board. Therefore, it is the policy of the Board that at all times, except during periods of temporary vacancies, a substantial majority of the members of the Board and all of the members of the Audit Committee, the Compensation Committee and the Governance and Nominating Committee shall qualify as independent directors. The independent directors as a group shall determine the independence of each director. The Board shall annually disclose the independence of each director.

The Board also believes that it is useful and appropriate to have members of senior management, in addition to the CEO, as executive directors. The Board feels that management should encourage senior managers to understand that Board membership is not necessary or a prerequisite to any higher management position in the corporation.

Role of the Board The Board is the ultimate decision-making body of the corporation, except for those matters reserved to or shared with the shareholders. It is the responsibility of the Board to direct and oversee the conduct of ABC's business and to ensure that the interests of the shareholders are being served. In order to carry out this responsibility, the Board considers that its functions include the following:

- *Guidelines* Establishing these Corporate Governance Guidelines and other broad policies for guidance of the organization, such as those contained in ABC's code of conduct.
- *Oversight* Overseeing the conduct of the corporation's business so that it is effectively managed in the long-term interest of shareholders.
- *Ethics* Establishing a high ethical tone at the top that emphasizes a culture of integrity and responsibility that promotes compliance with all applicable laws and regulations.
- *Laws and regulations* Ensuring the corporation's compliance with applicable laws and regulations.
- *Management planning and oversight* Selecting, evaluating and compensating the CEO and planning for CEO succession as well as selecting, evaluating and compensating the other members of senior management (both executive directors and senior managers) and planning for their succession.
- *Strategic and operational planning* Reviewing and approving strategic plans and annual operating plans as well as monitoring the execution and implementation of these plans.

- *Corporate assets* Overseeing that the assets of the corporation are properly safeguarded.
- *Major corporate actions* Reviewing and approving major corporate actions including significant business and financial transactions.
- *Significant events, issues and risks* Reviewing and discussing reports regularly submitted to the Board by management with respect to ABC's performance, as well as significant events, issues and risks that may affect ABC's business or financial performance.
- *Financial reporting and risk management* Reviewing and approving financial reports and statements as well as overseeing the establishment and maintenance of controls to ensure the accuracy and integrity of financial and other disclosures.
- *Management performance* Overseeing the performance of management, and
- *Advice to management* Providing advice and counsel to the CEO and to senior management.

The culture of the Board is such that the Board can operate effectively and swiftly in making key decisions and facing major challenges. Board meetings are conducted in an environment of constructive commentary, open dialogue, mutual respect and trust.

The CEO shall present the corporation's strategy to the Board for discussion by the Board on an ongoing basis.

Role of the CEO and of Management It is the responsibility of the CEO and of management to conduct ABC's business in an effective, legal and ethically responsible manner. The CEO and senior management are accountable to the Board. In order to carry out its responsibility, the functions of management include the following:

- *Operation of business* Conducting the day-to-day operation of the corporation's business;
- *Strategic and operational planning* Developing strategic and operating plans, presenting these plans to the Board as well as executing and implementing these plans;
- *Risk management* Identifying and managing the risks that ABC undertakes in operating its business; and
- *Financial reporting* Ensuring the accuracy and integrity of financial reports and statements and other disclosures as well as establishing and maintaining controls that allow ABC's shareholders to understand ABC's business and risks.

3.   Board Size, Composition and Structure

[63] **Board size** The number of directors should not exceed a number that can function efficiently. Therefore, the number of directors that constitute the full Board shall be no less than six and no more than twenty-one. The number shall

be determined from time to time by the Board, taking into account the nature of ABC's business and the need for diversity of experience and thought without hindering effective discussions. At present, given the size and complexity of the business in which ABC is engaged, as well as the value of diversity of experience and thought among Board members, the Board believes that it will be desirable over time to have a Board of between 14 and 16 members with 3 to 4 executive directors and 11 to 12 non-management directors. The Governance and Nominating Committee shall make recommendations to the Board for changes in the size and composition of the Board where necessary.

Board membership criteria and selection of directors Directors should possess demonstrated abilities, experience and individual skills that help meet the current needs of the Board. It is the intention of the Board to maintain a balance of directors who have longer terms of service and directors who have joined more recently.

Minimum qualifications that directors should possess include high ethical standards, independence of thought, experience and knowledge that the Governance and Nominating Committee deems relevant, ability to work together as part of an effective, collegial group, commitment to representing the long-term interests of ABC as well as a commitment to full participation on the Board and its committees over an extended period of time. Other factors include a demonstrated ability to think strategically and make decisions with a forward-looking focus, a proven record of accomplishments, demonstrated strength of character and mature judgment, a commitment to diversity of age, ethnicity, experience, gender and race, business acumen, educational achievement, experience at the policy-making level in business, education, government or public interest or being accustomed to dealing with complex problems, international experience, personal qualities of leadership, successful leadership experience and stature in the individual's primary field, an inquiring mind, understanding of the corporation's or other related industries, understanding of the various disciplines relevant to the success of a large publicly-traded company in today's global business environment, vision, willingness to challenge management while working constructively as part of an effective, collegial group, practical wisdom.

The Board has delegated to the Governance and Nominating Committee the responsibility for reviewing and recommending nominations and renominations for election to the Board.[230] The Governance and Nominating Committee will recommend nominees to the Board with the goal of creating a balance of age, background, diversity, experience, and knowledge. The Board shall set a slate of nominees for election or re-election at the annual meeting of shareholders. Between annual meetings, the Board may elect directors to serve until the next annual meeting.

Chairperson and CEO The Board shall elect from among its members the chairperson and the CEO. The Board has the authority to decide whether the positions of chairperson and CEO should be held by the same person in light of all relevant and

---

230.   In Dutch usage: appointment.

changing circumstances. The Board currently believes that the same individual should hold the positions of chairperson and CEO, as combining these positions provides unified direction and leadership, serves the best interest of ABC and therefore its shareholders, and has served the corporation well.

The responsibilities of the chairperson shall include:

- Setting the schedule of Board meetings, calling Board meetings, setting the Board agenda and determining the appropriate materials to be provided to the Board;
- Presiding at the meetings of the Board as well as presiding at general meetings of shareholders;
- Facilitating communications between the Board and management; and
- Performing such other responsibilities as may be directed from time to time by the Board or the Governance and Nominating Committee.

All directors shall have complete access to the CEO to discuss at any time any aspects of ABC's business.

Former CEO No individual who has served but is not currently serving as CEO of ABC shall serve as a director.

Director independence standards (including categorical disqualifying factors)
No director qualifies as independent unless the Board affirmatively determines that the director does not have any direct or indirect material relationship with the corporation (other than as a director) that may impair, or appear to impair, the director's ability to make independent judgments, and that the director otherwise satisfies the standards of independence established by applicable laws and regulations. In determining independence the Board will consider all relevant facts and circumstances.

For purposes of applying the following, 'immediate family member' includes spouse, parents, step-parents, children, step-children, brothers, sisters, mothers-in-law, fathers-in-law, sons-in-law, daughters-in-law, brothers-in-law, sisters-in-law as well as anyone living in the director's home (other than as a domestic employee).

For purposes of applying the following, 'corporation' refers to ABC and its direct and indirect subsidiaries.

A director shall not be considered independent if any of the following conditions exist at the time of determination or existed at any time during the immediately preceding 5-year period or, in the case of an immediate family member, at any time during the immediately preceding 3-year period:

- The director is employed by the corporation;
- An immediate family member of the director is employed as an executive officer of the corporation;
- The director receives any direct remuneration (other than compensation received for serving as a director) from the corporation;
- An immediate family member receives any direct remuneration from the corporation in excess of USD 100,000 per year;

- The director is a partner of, is employed by or affiliated with a firm that is the corporation's internal or external auditor;
- An immediate family member of the director is employed as a partner, principal or manager of a firm that is the corporation's internal or external auditor; or
- An executive officer of the corporation serves on the board of directors of a company that employs the director, or employs an immediate family member of the director as an executive officer ('interlocking directorate'/'interlocking directorship').

For the purposes of applying the foregoing, the following conditions shall not in themselves prevent the director from being considered independent if they exist at the time of determination or existed at any time during the immediately preceding 5-year period or, in the case of an immediate family member, at any time during the immediately preceding 3-year period:

- The director or an immediate family member owns 10 percent or less of the equity interests on the corporation;
- The director or an immediate family member owns 10 percent or less of the equity interests of a company that has a relationship with the corporation;
- The director or an immediate family member is an executive officer of a company that does business with the corporation and the other company's annual sales to or purchases from the corporation are both not in excess of USD 1 million and are less than 2 percent of the corporation's (consolidated) annual gross revenues and less than 2 percent of the (consolidated) annual gross revenues of the other company;
- The director or an immediate family member is an executive officer of a company that is indebted to the corporation or is an executive officer of a company to which the corporation is indebted and the aggregate amount of such debt is both not in excess of USD 1 million and less than 2 percent of the corporation's total (consolidated) assets and less than 2 percent of the total (consolidated) assets of the other company; and
- The director or an immediate family member serves as a director, executive officer or trustee of a charitable organization to which the corporation or any of its executive officers contributes and the combined annual contributions to such organization by the corporation and its executive officers are both not in excess of USD 1 million and less than 2 percent of that organization's total annual charitable receipts.

Lead director (presiding director) If the chairperson of the Board is the CEO of the corporation, the independent directors shall elect one director from among their membership as lead director (presiding director). Responsibilities of the lead director (presiding director) shall include:

- Working with the chairperson to set the Board schedule, call Board meetings, set the Board agenda and determine the appropriate materials to be provided to the Board;

- Presiding at all meetings of the Board at which the chairperson is not present and presiding at general meetings of shareholders at which the chairperson is not present;
- Acting as a key liaison between the non-management directors and the executive directors;
- Facilitating communications between the Board and management;
- Leadership of executive sessions of the non-management and independent directors;
- Providing feedback to the chairperson following executive sessions of the non-management and independent directors;
- Serving as focal point for shareholder communications addressed to the non-management or independent directors as a group;
- Recommending to the chairperson the retention of outside advisors or consultants who report directly to the Board; and
- Performing such other responsibilities as may be directed from time to time by the Board or the Governance and Nominating Committee.

4.   Director Tenure and Retirement Policy

[64] No term limits Although directors are expected to serve for at least five years, all directors shall stand for election at each annual meeting of shareholders.

In light of the complexities of ABC's business and the time it takes for a director to become familiar with them and because term limits hold the disadvantage of losing the contribution of directors who have been able to develop over time a unique insight into the corporation and its business, the Board has not established arbitrary term limits for Board service. However, the Board believes that directors should serve only so long as they add value to the Board. A director's contributions to the Board will be considered by the Governance and Nominating Committee each time a director is considered for renomination.

Executive directors will not be nominated or renominated for election after their 70th birthday and must retire from the Board when they reach the age of 70. Non-executive directors will not be nominated or renominated for election after their 72nd birthday and must retire from the Board when they reach the age of 72. However, a director may continue to serve on the Board until the first annual meeting of shareholders following his or her 70th respectively 72nd birthday.

Change in status When (other than as a result of retirement) a non-management director's principal occupation or business or professional affiliation changes substantially during his or her tenure as a director, or when other circumstances arise which may raise questions about the director's continuing qualifications in relation to the board membership criteria, the director shall tender his or her resignation for consideration by the Governance and Nominating Committee, or the Governance and Nominating Committee will ask for this tender. The Governance and Nominating Committee will consider the tendered resignation and recommend to the Board whether to accept the resignation or to ask that the director continues to serve on the Board.

Executive directors are expected to submit their resignation from the Board at the time they resign from ABC.

Approval of a majority of the independent directors No director will be asked to resign from the Board without the approval of a majority of the (remaining) independent directors.

5.   Conduct of Board Meetings

[65] Number of Board meetings The Board shall be responsible for determining the appropriate number and schedule of regular meetings to hold each year. Currently, the Board holds 6 regular meetings each year. The frequency of committee meetings shall be set forth in each committee's charter. Committee meetings are normally held in conjunction with board meetings. Additional meetings of the Board and its committees shall be held in circumstances that create the need for a special meeting. Special meetings may be held in person, or by telephone or other form of interactive electronic communication.

Executive sessions of non-management and independent directors The non-management directors shall meet in executive sessions in connection with each regularly scheduled meeting of the Board. Additional executive sessions of the non-management directors may be called at any time by the lead director (presiding director) or at the request of a majority of the non-management directors. If the Board includes non-management directors who are not independent, the independent directors shall meet in executive session at least once per year. Additional executive sessions of the independent directors may be called at any time by the lead director (presiding director) or at the request of a majority of the independent directors.

Agenda The Board shall be responsible for its agenda, and each director is encouraged to suggest agenda items to the chairperson or the lead director (presiding director) at any time. Directors are free to raise subjects at a Board meeting that are not on the agenda for that meeting.

Pre-meeting materials The Board shall be provided with appropriate written materials in advance of each meeting so that the directors may prepare to discuss the items at the meeting. Materials shall be as concise as possible while giving the directors sufficient information to make informed decisions. Prior to each Board meeting, the chairperson shall distribute appropriate written materials relating to the agenda items to be discussed at the meeting (unless confidentiality or sensitivity concerns suggest that materials not be distributed or be distributed only at the meeting).

Information regarding the corporation's business and performance shall be distributed to all directors on a monthly basis.

Attendance All directors are expected to attend Board meetings. The chairperson may request other members of management to attend part or all of a Board meeting in order to make presentations, respond to questions, provide additional insight into items that are discussed or participate in discussions, or are members of managements with future potential that the chairperson believes should be given exposure to the Board.

Confidentiality In order to facilitate open discussion, all materials distributed to directors and all discussions of the Board and its committees or otherwise between directors are confidential. Directors are expected to maintain this confidentiality.

6.   Committees of the Board

[66] The Board currently maintains the following required standing committees: the *Audit Committee*,[231] the *Compensation Committee*,[232] and the *Governance and Nominating Committee*.[233] The Board shall have the discretion to convene other standing or special committees as it deems appropriate or to dissolve such optional committees. The Audit Committee, the Compensation Committee and the Governance and Nominating Committee shall be composed of at least 3 directors and shall be comprised entirely of directors who qualify as independent and satisfy additional standards established by applicable laws and regulations. Other standing committees will in any event be comprised of a majority of directors who qualify as independent. Generally, a director will be a member of no more than 2 required committees.

The prime duties of the *Audit Committee* shall be:

– To assist the Board in reviewing and approving financial reports and statements.
– To assist the Board in overseeing the establishment and maintenance of controls to ensure the accuracy and integrity of financial and other disclosures.
– To assist the Board in overseeing the performance of the ABC's internal audit function.
– To assist the Board in overseeing ABC's compliance with legal and regulatory requirements.
– To evaluate the performance of ABC's external auditor, including to recommend whether to engage or dismiss the external auditor.

The prime duty of the *Compensation Committee* shall be to approve director compensation.

---

231. Also: Audit and Risk Management Committee.
232. Also: Compensation and Benefits Committee, Committee on Compensation and Executive Development, Compensation and Human Resources Committee, Compensation and Leadership Development Committee, Compensation and Management Development Committee, Compensation and Management Resources Committee, HR and Compensation Committee, Leadership Development and Compensation Committee, Management Compensation Committee, Management Development and Compensation Committee, Personnel and Compensation Committee.
233. Also: Board Affairs Committee, Committee on Corporate Governance, Corporate Governance and Nominating Committee, Committee on Directors and Corporate Governance, Governance Committee, Governance and Stockholder Relations Committee, Nominating and Governance Committee, Nominating and Corporate Governance Committee, Nomination and Governance Committee, Committee on Nominations and Governance.

The prime duty of the *Governance and Nominating Committee* shall be to review and recommend nominations and renominations for election to Board membership. The Governance and Nominating Committee will give appropriate consideration to candidates for Board membership proposed by shareholders and will evaluate such candidates in the same manner as other candidates identified by the committee.

Other committees may include:

- The *Executive Committee* The Executive Committee may during the interval between meetings of the Board, when the Board is not in session, exercise the powers of the Board to act upon any matters that should not be postponed until the next scheduled meeting of the Board. This Committee shall include the CEO.
- The *Finance Committee*[234] The Finance Committee oversees all areas of corporate finance, including capital structure, equity and debt financings, investments, banking relationships, foreign exchange activities and share repurchase activities.
- The *Public Policy Committee*[235] The Public Policy Committee makes recommendations to the Board on public and social policy issues impacting the corporation.
- The *Science and Technology Committee*[236] The Science and Technology Committee shall periodically review and advise the Board on the ABC's direction and investments in technology as well as in research and development.

Each committee is governed by a written charter describing its duties, adopted by the committee and approved by the Board. At the beginning of each year, each committee shall establish to the extent that can be foreseen a schedule of major topics to be discussed during the year. Each committee will keep the Board apprised of its activities on a regular basis through written and oral reports. Whenever a committee, pursuant to its charter, makes a decision or takes an action on behalf of the Board, the chairperson of the committee shall promptly make a report to, or otherwise notify, the Board of such decision or action.

The membership (including the chair) of each committee shall be determined by the Board, acting on the recommendation of the Governance and Nominating Committee and taking into account the desires of individual directors. The membership of the committees shall be rotated on a periodic basis.

---

234. Also: Finance and Investment Committee.
235. Also: Environmental and Public Policy Committee, Public Affairs Committee, Public Issues and Diversity Review Committee, Public Issues Review Committee, Committee on Public Policy and Social Responsibility, Public Policy Advisory Committee, Public Responsibility Committee, Public Responsibilities Committee.
236. Also: Innovation and Technology Committee, Research Committee, Science and Technology Advisory Committee.

7.   Other Board Operations

[67] Access to management The Board, its committees and each director shall have complete access to management and to the corporation's employees. The Board, its committees and each director shall have complete access to the books and records of the corporation.

Access to independent advisors The Board, its committees and each director shall have the right to consult and retain independent financial, legal and other advisors or consultants at the expense of ABC. The Board shall have sole authority to approve related fees and retention terms. Any contact with such advisors or consultants shall be handled in a manner that would not be disruptive to the operations of the corporation.

Director orientation and continuing education The corporation shall have a comprehensive orientation program designed to familiarize new directors with the corporation and its business, with key financial, legal and operational issues, with corporate governance standards and practices as well with sector trends. This program contains written material, oral presentations and site visits. The corporation encourages directors to attend internal and external continuing director education programs on these and other matters. The corporation encourages directors to spend at least one day each year at ABC's headquarters or other facilities.

Director compensation (Executive and non-management) director compensation shall be approved by the Compensation Committee and then submitted to the Board for its decision. ABC's policy shall be to ensure that director compensation is appropriate and competitive to ensure ABC's ability to attract and retain highly-qualified directors, and consistent with market practice. The Board believes that the type of director compensation should align directors' interests with the long-term interests of ABC's shareholders, that the amount of director compensation should be fair and competitive in relation to director compensation at other companies with businesses similar in business, complexity, scope and size to ABC's, and that the structure of the director compensation program should be simple, transparent and easy to understand for shareholders.

Only non-management directors will receive compensation for their services as director and will receive a combination of cash and equity compensation for their services. Non-management directors also receive a one time grant of common shares of the corporation on joining the Board. Non-management director compensation shall not be at a level or in a form that would call into question the Board's objectivity. Therefore, the Compensation Committee shall be sensitive to questions of independence that may be raised when non-management director compensation exceed customary levels for companies with businesses similar in business, complexity, scope and size to ABC's. The corporation does not have a retirement plan for non-management directors. Executive directors receive no compensation for serving as a director in addition to their regular employee compensation as approved by the Compensation Committee and determined by the Board.

Compensation of members of senior management (other than executive directors) shall be determined by the Compensation Committee which reviews its decisions with the Board.

Director share ownership requirements Because requiring directors and other members of senior management to have an appropriate equity ownership in the corporation helps to align their interests with the long-term interests of ABC's other shareholders, and because the Board expects all directors and executive officers to display confidence in the corporation, each director shall at all times own common shares of the corporation. As a guideline, the CEO shall own common shares of the corporation equal in value to at least 5 times the amount of his or her annual compensation, other executive directors shall own common shares of the corporation equal in value to at least 4 times the amount of annual executive compensation, and non-management directors shall own common shares of the corporation equal in value to at least 3 times the amount of the annual compensation received for serving as a director (with 5-year, 4-year and 3-year time periods respectively after their first election to achieve these levels). Also, other members of senior management shall own common shares of the corporation equal in value to at least 3 times the amount of their annual compensation. Because the Board recognizes that exceptions to this policy may be appropriate or necessary in individual situations, the Governance and Nominating Committee may approve such exceptions from time to time.

Non-management directors are prohibited during their term of service from selling any ABC equity instruments.

IPO allocations Directors and their immediate family members shall not be eligible to receive allocations of initial public offerings underwritten by the corporation.

Insurance The corporation provides reasonable directors' and executive officers' insurance for directors and executive officers.

Succession planning The Compensation Committee shall have as its duty to review CEO and senior management succession plans. To assist the Compensation Committee, the CEO annually assesses senior managers and their succession potential and provides the Compensation Committee with an assessment of persons considered potential successors to senior management positions.

Self-evaluation (self-assessment) and evaluation of the CEO The Board will conduct an annual self-evaluation to identify areas of concern or potential issues relating to the Board and its committees and to determine whether it and its committees function effectively as well as to evaluate the effectiveness of individual directors. These evaluations will be administered by the Governance and Nominating Committee.

The non-management directors will conduct the annual evaluation to evaluate the effectiveness of the CEO. This evaluation will be administered by the Compensation Committee. To that end, the Compensation Committee, in consultation with the CEO, sets annual and long-term performance goals for the CEO. The CEO may not attend Board meetings discussing his or her evaluation. The Compensation Committee will use the evaluation when determining the compensation of the CEO.

Other directorships Each director must be able and willing to devote sufficient time and attention to carrying out his or her duties and responsibilities effectively. While the Board acknowledges the value in having directors with significant experience in other businesses and activities, it also understands that effective service requires substantial commitment. Therefore, the Board encourages non-management directors to evaluate carefully the time required to serve on other boards, taking into account board attendance, effectiveness, participation and preparation on these boards. Generally, a non-management director should not serve on more than 5 boards of publicly-traded companies, including ABC's. A non-management director who also serves as executive director of a public company should not serve on more than 3 boards of public companies, including ABC's. An executive director should not serve on more than 3 boards of public companies, including ABC's. Because serving on several Boards may present conflicts of interests directors shall inform the Governance and Nominating Committee before accepting membership on any other board.

It is expected that a director will refrain from serving as a director, officer, employee, advisor or consultant with any competitive business during service with the corporation and for three years (or for a reasonable period of time as determined by the Board) after service with the corporation ends.

Conflicts of interests Directors are expected to avoid any action, position or situation that conflicts with the interests of the corporation. All directors are required to deal at arm's length with the corporation and disclose to the Governance and Nominating Committee circumstances material to the director that might be perceived as an actual or potential conflict of interests. All directors shall recuse themselves from any discussion or decision affecting their personal, business or professional interests. If a material conflict arises that cannot be resolved, the director shall resign. The corporation will not make any personal loans or extensions of credit to directors.

Other members of senior management are subject to these same requirements.

Confidential voting It is the corporation's policy to protect the confidentiality of shareholder votes throughout the voting process. Therefore, the Board acknowledges that proxy cards, ballots and voting tabulations that identify shareholders normally will be kept confidential. Both the tabulators and inspectors of the election, who are appointed by the Board, are independent of the corporation.

Shareholder communication with directors Shareholders may communicate directly with the Board or, if they so wish, with the lead director (presiding director), the non-management or independent directors as a group, or with individual non-management directors.

Shareholder proposals It is the policy of the Board to provide a response to a shareholder proposal that receives a majority vote at a general meeting of shareholders. If a shareholder proposal that is not supported by the Board receives a majority vote the proposal will be reconsidered by the Board.

Interaction with third parties Because the Board feels that it is important that ABC speaks to employees and outside constituencies and interested parties with a single voice the Board believes that management should speak for the corporation. Therefore, management is responsible for establishing effective communications with the corporation's other stakeholders. This policy does not preclude non-management directors from meeting with third parties, but management should be present at such meetings where appropriate. If in exceptional cases a situation arises where a non-management director should serve as a spokesperson for the corporation, the director should first consult with the CEO where possible.

Reporting concerns to the independent directors or the Audit Committee Anyone who has a concern about ABC's conduct, ABC's financial reporting, financial statements or other disclosures, or ABC's controls that ensure the accuracy and integrity of financial and other disclosures may communicate that concern directly to the independent directors or to the Audit Committee. Such communications may be confidential or anonymous.

Review of the Guidelines These Guidelines shall be reviewed periodically by the Board. This review will be administered by the Governance and Nominating Committee. The Governance and Nominating Committee may grant waivers from these Guidelines in exceptional circumstances. The Board shall immediately disclose such waivers.

Chapter 5

The 'Mandatory Organizational Arrangement' in the Netherlands

I. THE 'MANDATORY ORGANIZATIONAL
    ARRANGEMENT'

[68] In accordance with the Dutch Civil Code a corporation (and a private limited company) may be subject to a specific 'mandatory organizational arrangement' that is laid down in Title 4: Corporations, Section 6, Articles 2:152 through 2:164 (and in Title 5: Private limited companies, Section 6, Articles 2:262 through 2:274) of the Dutch Civil Code.[237] In a corporation that is not subject to this arrangement, establishing a supervisory board is optional: under Article 2:140 section 1 of the Dutch Civil Code the articles of association may provide for a supervisory board. If the articles do so, the functions of the supervisory board shall be to supervise the policy of the management board and the general course of affair of the corporation and its affiliated enterprise, and to advise the management board (Article 2:140 section 2). In a corporation that is not subject to the arrangement, the general meeting of shareholders has the power to appoint and dismiss the members of the management board,[238] and in principle[239] also has the power to appoint and dismiss the members of the supervisory board.[240] In a corporation that is subject to the arrangement, establishing a supervisory board is mandatory (and there shall be at

---

237. The 'mandatory organizational arrangement' may also be applicable to cooperative societies and mutual insurance societies.
238. Article 2:132 section 1 and 134 section 1 of the Dutch Civil Code.
239. In accordance with Article 2:143 of the Dutch Civil Code the articles of association of a corporation that is not subject to the 'mandatory organizational arrangement' may provide that one third of the non-executive directors at most shall not be appointed by the general meeting of shareholders.
240. Article 2:142 section 1 and 144 section 1 of the Dutch Civil Code.

least three non-executive directors), appointment and dismissal of the non-executive directors take place in a different way, and the supervisory board has some additional mandatory functions. A corporation is – in principle – subject to the 'mandatory organizational arrangement' if it is a 'large' corporation within the meaning of Article 2:153 section 2 of the Dutch Civil Code. Part A of this chapter consists of the following paragraphs: the *criteria, content* and *exemptions* of the 'mandatory organizational arrangement'.

A.   CRITERIA

[69] In accordance with Article 2:153 section 2 of the Dutch Civil Code a corporation is – in principle – 'large' and thereby subject to the 'mandatory organizational arrangement' if it meets three criteria. These criteria are that the combination of the issued share capital of the corporation and the reserves must be at least EUR 16 million according to the balance sheet and the notes thereon, that the corporation together with its dependent undertakings must employ at least 100 employees in the Netherlands, and that the corporation and/or its dependent undertakings must have established at least one works council in accordance with their obligations under the Works Councils Act. For the purpose of applying this provision dependent undertakings of a corporation shall be either other corporations or private limited companies of which the first-mentioned corporation holds at least 50% of the issued share capital (either directly or indirectly), or partnerships of which the corporation is a full partner (either directly or indirectly). Therefore, when a corporation has an issued share capital that together with the reserves according to the balance sheet and the notes thereon amounts to EUR 20 million, the total number of employees employed by the corporation and its dependent undertakings in the Netherlands is 500, and the number of works councils established by the corporation together with its dependent undertakings in accordance with their obligations under the Works Councils Act is one, that corporation is subject to the 'mandatory organizational arrangement'. But when a corporation has an issued share capital that together with the reserves according to the balance sheet and the notes thereon amounts to EUR 15 million, the total number of employees employed by the corporation and its dependent undertakings in the Netherlands is 2.000, and the number of works councils established by the corporation together with its dependent undertakings in accordance with their obligations under the Works Councils Act is five, that corporation is not subject to the 'mandatory organizational arrangement'.

B.   CONTENT

[70] When a corporation meets the criteria of Article 2:153 section 2 of the Dutch Civil Code it shall – in principle – be organized along the following lines. *First*, in accordance with Article 2:162 of the Dutch Civil Code the supervisory board shall

have the power to appoint and dismiss the executive directors of the corporation. *Second*, although under Article 2:158 of the Dutch Civil Code the general meeting of shareholders of the corporation has the power to appoint the corporation's non-executive directors, the supervisory board itself shall take the lead in the appointment process. In case of a vacancy in the supervisory board, the board shall nominate a candidate to the general meeting of shareholders for appointment (section 4). The general meeting may only appoint a person who was nominated by the supervisory board, and may only reject the nomination by a majority that represents at least one third of the issued share capital of the corporation (sections 4 and 9). Before nomination can take place, the supervisory board shall consult with both the general meeting of shareholders and the works council. Both the general meeting and the works council may recommend persons to the supervisory board for nomination (section 5). Even more, as concerns one third of the members of the supervisory board, the works council has a reinforced recommendation right, which means that the supervisory board must nominate the candidate recommended by the works council to the general meeting of shareholders for appointment (section 6). The supervisory board may only oppose the candidate recommended on the basis of this reinforced recommendation right on the grounds that either the board expects this person not to be suited to carry out the duties of a member of a board of supervisors or that the board expects that following appointment the board of supervisors would not be composed properly (section 6). When the supervisory board and the works council do not come to terms on the recommendation in accordance with this reinforced recommendation right, the board may refer the matter to the Chamber of Business Affairs of the Court of Appeals at Amsterdam for its decision (section 7). *Third*, the general meeting of shareholders does not have the power to dismiss individual non-executive directors of the corporation, but it may under Article 2:161a section 1 of the Dutch Civil Code by a resolution adopted by a majority that represents at least one third of the issued share capital of the corporation vote against the supervisory board as a whole. Such a resolution automatically effects the immediate dismissal of all non-executive directors (section 3).[241] *Fourth*, in accordance with Article 2:164 section 1 of the Dutch Civil Code the management board shall submit to the supervisory board for approval a number of decisions it either takes itself or is a party to when the decision is taken by a dependent undertaking. These are decisions concerning inter alia: issuing shares of the corporation, applying for the listing or de-listing of shares of the corporation, entering into or terminating permanent and major cooperation with another legal person or partnership by either the corporation or a dependent undertaking, taking a participating interest in another corporation or private limited company to the amount of one fourth or more of the combination of the issued share capital of the corporation and the reserves according to the

---

241. O.G. Trojan, 'Het collectief ontslag van de raad van commissarissen: theorie en praktijk', in *Geschriften vanwege de vereniging Corporate Litigation 2006-2007*, eds H. Holtzer et al. (Deventer: Kluwer, 2007), 191-210.

balance sheet and the notes thereon by either the corporation of a dependent undertaking or significantly increasing or decreasing such a participating interest, making investments to the amount of one fourth or more of the combination of the issued share capital of the corporation and the reserves according to the balance sheet and the notes thereon, making a proposal to amend the articles of association of the corporation, termination of the contracts of employment of a significant number of employees by either the corporation or a dependent undertaking, and making significant changes to the conditions of employment of a significant number of employees of either the corporation or a dependent undertaking.

The 'mandatory organizational arrangement' that may apply to a corporation was instigated by two considerations.[242] The first consideration is connected to the agency problem, and especially to the case where a corporation has numerous and dispersed shareholders who as individual shareholders are unable to exert influence over the way the directors and managers of the corporation handle the affairs of the corporation and come across practical difficulties when they want to exert such influence together with fellow shareholders. These practical difficulties include the fact that shareholders may not know who their fellow shareholders are ('shareholder anonymity') and the fact that many shareholders do not attend general meetings ('shareholder absenteeism'). Under these circumstances the general meeting of shareholders does not function properly as a controlling and decision-making mechanism that can bring countervailing power against the management board of the corporation. Under the 'mandatory organizational arrangement' the lack of countervailing power of the general meeting of shareholders is compensated by the countervailing power that the supervisory board can bring against the management board. The second consideration is connected to stakeholder-oriented model of corporate law as opposed to the shareholder-oriented model. The stakeholder-oriented model is based on the idea that a corporation is not just run in the interest of the shareholders but in the interests of a variety of stakeholders. The latter include the corporation's employees. The 'mandatory organizational arrangement' gives the employees of the corporation, represented by the works council, the right to have influence on the composition of the supervisory board of the corporation that under the arrangement has a central role as a countervailing power against the management board.

C.   EXEMPTIONS

[71] A corporation that is 'large' within the meaning of Article 2:153 section 2 of the Dutch Civil Code is *in principle* subject to the 'mandatory organizational arrangement'. However, some corporations are wholly exempted from the

---

242. C. de Groot, *Facetten van ondernemingsrecht* (Amsterdam: Rozenberg Publishers, 2002), at 316.

arrangement and some corporations are partially exempted. When a corporation is wholly exempt it need not be organized along the lines of the 'mandatory organizational arrangement' at all, and when a corporation is partially exempt it must for the most part be organized along those lines but it need not apply the provision that the supervisory board shall have the power to appoint and dismiss the executive directors of the corporation.

Corporations that are wholly exempt include the following:

- Dependent undertakings of a corporation subject to the 'mandatory organizational arrangement' (Article 2:153 section 3, subsection a of the Dutch Civil Code). This exemption is embedded in the working of the arrangement.[243] First, employees of dependent undertakings and works councils established by dependent undertaking are counted on the level of the corporation, making that corporation meet the criteria of Article 2:153 section 2 of the Dutch Civil Code more easily. Second, application of the 'mandatory organizational arrangement' at the level of dependent undertakings would make it difficult for the corporation to integrate these undertakings into its group policy. Third, all works councils – that is a works council that may be established by the corporation and works councils that may be established by dependent undertakings – have the recommendation right and the reinforced recommendation right as concerns the appointment of the non-executive directors of the corporation.[244] Therefore all employees – that is employees of the corporation as well as employees of dependent undertakings –, represented by their respective works councils, have the right to influence the composition of the supervisory board of the corporation.
- A corporation that operates as a holding corporation of an internationally oriented group (Article 2:153 section 3, subsection b of the Dutch Civil Code). A corporation qualifies as a holding corporation if it is a parent company of a group and does not operate an enterprise of its own. The international orientation of the group is measured by the test that the majority of the employees of the group must be employed outside the Netherlands. This exemption was instigated by the consideration that application of the 'mandatory organizational arrangement' would give the right to influence the composition of the supervisory board of the holding corporation only to the minority of the employees of the group, represented by the works council(s), who are employed in the Netherlands to the exclusion of the majority of the employees of the group who are employed outside the Netherlands.[245]

---

243. C. de Groot (2002), at 321-322.
244. In case there is more than one works council, each works council has the recommendation right, but the reinforced recommendation right must be exercised by the works councils collectively (Article 2:158 section 11 of the Dutch Civil Code).
245. C. de Groot (2002), at 324.

Corporations that are partially exempt include the following:

- A corporation that is the subsidiary company of a wholly exempted holding corporation of an internationally oriented group (Article 2:155 section 1, subsection a of the Dutch Civil Code). The reason for this partial exemption is that the 'mandatory organizational arrangement' is not being applied at the level of the holding corporation (because that corporation is exempted) but at the level of the subsidiary corporation (if it meets the criteria of Article 2:153 section 2 of the Dutch Civil Code). Application at this subsidiary level of the 'mandatory organizational arrangement' in all its aspects would make it difficult for the parent corporation to integrate the subsidiary corporation into its group policy.[246] Under the partial exemption, the provision that the supervisory board shall have the power to appoint and dismiss the executive directors of the corporation does not apply. Therefore, the general meeting of shareholders (composed entirely or in the majority of the parent corporation) retains the power to appoint and dismiss the executive directors of its subsidiary corporation.
- A corporation that is a subsidiary company of a foreign parent company, provided that the majority of the employees of the group are employed outside the Netherlands (Article 2:155 section 1, subsection a of the Dutch Civil Code). The reason for partial exemption is also that application of the 'mandatory organizational arrangement' in all its aspects at level of the subsidiary corporation would make it difficult for the parent company to integrate the subsidiary corporation into its group policy.[247] In this situation, however, the foreign parent company will still have to come to terms with the fact that its Dutch subsidiary is subject to the 'mandatory organizational arrangement', albeit in the form of the partial exemption. An example of the kind of conflicts this situation may create is the Corus case.

II.   CASE STUDY

A.   INTRODUCTION TO THE CORUS CASE

[72] Corus Nederland BV, a Dutch private limited company, was a subsidiary company of Corus Group Plc, established in the United Kingdom. Corus Nederland BV was subject to the partial 'mandatory organizational arrangement'. This case was decided before Article 2:161a (and the similar provision for private limited

---

246. C. de Groot (2002), at 325-326.
247. C. de Groot (2002), at 325-326.

companies that are subject to the 'mandatory organizational arrangement') of the Dutch Civil Code came into force.

[73] Corus Group Plc ('Corus Group') was a listed corporation established in the United Kingdom. Two subsidiary companies of Corus Group, Corus Property Ltd. and Corus SPV Ltd. held 81% and 19% respectively of the capital of Corus Nederland BV ('Corus Nederland', formerly Koninklijke Hoogovens NV) that was established in the Netherlands. Corus Nederland had become part of the Corus group in 1999. At the beginning of 2002, Corus Group changed its corporate strategy from a so-called 'multi metal strategy' into a strategy that would concentrate the group's activities on steel production. This strategy change implied that Corus Nederland would have to divest itself of a number of subsidiary companies that were engaged in so-called downstream aluminum activities. To this end, Corus Group and the French corporation Pechiney SA ('Pechiney') had reached an agreement on 23 October 2003 that was intended to result in Corus Nederland selling its downstream aluminum activities to Pechiney in accordance with a Sale and Purchase Agreement ('SPA') to be concluded between Corus Nederland and Pechiney ultimately on 13 March 2003. The management board of Corus Nederland went along with the agreement between Corus Group and Pechiney and put the SPA before the supervisory board of Corus Nederland for its approval. However, the supervisory board of Corus Nederland declined to approve the SPA because it felt that the SPA could endanger the continuity of Corus Nederland as the financial returns of the sale of the subsidiary companies of Corus Nederland might be used to solve losses incurred by the Corus group in its activities in the United Kingdom. Following discussions between Corus Group, the management board of Corus Nederland and the supervisory board of Corus Nederland, the supervisory board came up with a second agreement that was to be concluded between Corus Group and Corus Nederland (in addition to the SPA between Corus Nederland and Pechiney). This second agreement centered on guarantees to be given by Corus Group to Corus Nederland, reinforced by a penalty clause. This was unacceptable for Corus Group because the agreement on the one hand would detach Corus Nederland from the Corus group and on the other hand would allow the supervisory board of Corus Nederland to become involved in the affairs of Corus Group and its subsidiary company Corus UK Limited. Then – as an alternative to the proposal of the supervisory board – Corus Group and the management board of Corus Nederland drafted a so-called 'ringfencing agreement' to be concluded between Corus Group and Corus Nederland. This ringfencing agreement contained commitments on the part of Corus Group that were intended to meet the fears of the supervisory board of Corus Nederland. On 10 March 2003, the management board of Corus Nederland put both the SPA and the ringfencing agreement before the supervisory board of Corus Nederland for its approval. Corus Group, however, did not feel sure that the supervisory board

of Corus Nederland would approve the package of the SPA and the ringfencing agreement.

B.   THE DECISION OF THE CHAMBER OF BUSINESS AFFAIRS TO DISMISS
            THE APPLICATION FOR INTERIM MEASURES

[74] On 11 March 2003, Corus Property Ltd. and Corus SPV Ltd. filed an application with the Chamber of Business Affairs under the provisions on the 'right of inquiry' in Book 2 of the Dutch Civil Code. They asked the Chamber of Business Affairs to find well-founded reasons to doubt good policy on the part of Corus Nederland and appoint persons to investigate the policy and the course of affairs of Corus Nederland, and in particular to order interim measures. They asked the Chamber of Business Affairs to suspend three of the four serving members of the supervisory board of Corus Nederland until exactly 24.00 hours on 13 March 2003. If the Chamber of Business Affairs would order this interim measure, the fourth remaining member of the supervisory board of Corus Nederland – at the same time the CEO of Corus Group – would be in a position to approve the SPA together with the ringfencing agreement. In its judgment of 13 March 2003 the Chamber of Business Affairs dismissed the application for interim measures.[248] The court considered that the question put before it in essence was:

> whether the supervisory board, taking into account all circumstances, including the interests of Corus Nederland, and – as this company is part of the Corus group – the interests and strategy of the Corus group, can reasonably be expected not – or no longer – to withhold its approval.

The Chamber of Business Affairs referred to the fact that the change in the new corporate strategy 'not only is fairly recent, but has also been decided without involvement (or with no more than minimal involvement) of Corus Nederland', and that 'the aluminum activities are financially important for Corus Nederland'. Added to that, 'at first neither the supervisory board nor the management board of Corus Nederland were involved in the transaction concluded between Corus Group Plc and Pechiney (or only to a minimal extent)', and 'it is now known that the proceeds of the transaction will in part be used as a means to refinance the Corus group, in the light of the losses incurred in its activities in the United Kingdom', while 'the very existence of the Corus group in its present form is the result of a fairly recent merger between British Steel Plc and Koninklijke Hoogovens NV'. The Chamber of Business Affairs considered that 'the centralized administration of

---

248. Chamber of Business Affairs 13 March 2003, JOR 2003, 85 (*Corus*), translation of considerations of the court by the author.

a group is not allowed to always, just like that, and without stating proper grounds, put the interests of one company in the group behind those of the group as perceived by the administration'. In this respect, the supervisory board has an important part to play. On the one hand:

> the supervisory board of a company may not, certainly not just like that and without stating proper grounds, pursue a policy that in incompatible with (or disregards) the group strategy, and will have to accept that given the circumstances of a case the interests of the company where the board is established will have to be put behind those of the group as a whole.

On the other hand:

> it is the duty of the supervisory board of a company that is part of group and it is especially the duty of the supervisory board of a company that is subject to the 'mandatory organizational arrangement' (also as a partially exempted company) – more than can be expected of the management board – to consider the question whether the interests of the company were adequately taken into consideration and were properly assessed by the centralized administration of the group, and whether the measures that were taken or the decisions that were made to safeguard those interests are both adequate and effective.

On these ground the court considered that it was:

> not unacceptable that the supervisory board, before approving the sale [. . .] to Pechiney – as agreed upon by the centralized administration of the group –, wishes to discuss intensively whether the interests of the group in having this sale go through are so consequential that the interests of the company where the board is established as perceived by it must be put behind the former interests, and whether the latter interests are properly taken into account,

and it was:

> acceptable that not just the management board, but the supervisory board of Corus Nederland too, wishes to be informed on the question whether [the] refinancing [of the Corus group] will succeed, and if and to what extent and how provisions have been made to guarantee that the interests of Corus Nederland will not be hurt disproportionately and that its interests are also being taken into account.

The foregoing implied that the supervisory board could wield a certain amount of negotiating power in relation to the ringfencing agreement. The Chamber of Business Affairs concluded that the supervisory board had not acted unreasonably by demanding more certainty that the commitments laid down in the ringfencing agreement would indeed be met by Corus Group.

C.   EVALUATION

[75] The key features of the 'mandatory organizational arrangement' are surprisingly in line with 'good' corporate governance. The fact that the supervisory board takes the lead in the appointment of the non-executive directors (Article 2:158 of the Dutch Civil Code) and itself appoints the executive directors (Article 2:162 of the Dutch Civil Code) may be compared to the prime duty of the governance and nominating committee of US corporations which shall be to review and recommend nominations and renominations for election to board membership. And the fact that the management board shall submit to the supervisory board for approval a number of decisions (Article 2:164 section 1 of the Dutch Civil Code) is not far away from the requirement that reviewing and approving major corporate actions including significant business and financial transactions is a function of the full board of US corporations. Thus, on the one hand the role of the supervisory board under the 'mandatory organizational arrangement' is not unlike that of a board committee in a one tier board, and on the other hand the 'mandatory organizational arrangement' serves to bring together the management board and the supervisory board to function in a way that resembles the functioning of a full unitary board.

     Corus – in short – dealt with the question whether Article 2:164 section 1 of the Dutch Civil Code may be applied by the supervisory board of a Dutch subsidiary company to block the implementation of group policy at the level of the subsidiary company. When a corporation either is a subsidiary company of a Dutch holding corporation of an internationally oriented group (that is itself wholly exempted) or is a subsidiary company of a foreign parent company (provided that the majority of the employees of the group are employed outside the Netherlands), the subsidiary company – provided it meets the criteria of Article 2:153 section 2 of the Dutch Civil Code – is subject to the partial 'mandatory organizational arrangement'. In the past, this might lead to difficulties as under Article 2:164 section 1 the management board of the corporation shall still submit to the supervisory board a number of decisions for its approval. In case the management board was inclined to adhere to the group policy, but the supervisory board was not, the supervisory board was in a position to obstruct the implementation of the group policy at the level of the subsidiary. This issue is now resolved because under Article 2:161a of the Dutch Civil Code the general meeting of shareholder can effect the immediate dismissal of all non-executive directors.

III.   SCHEDULES

A.   SCHEDULE 2: ARTICLE 2:158 OF THE DUTCH CIVIL CODE

[76] In a corporation that is subject to the 'mandatory organizational arrangement' establishing a supervisory board of at least three non-executive directors

is mandatory (Article 2:158 sections 1 and 2). In case of a vacancy in the supervisory board, the board shall take measures forthwith to make good the required number of non-executive directors (section 2). This means that the supervisory board shall nominate a candidate to the general meeting of shareholders for appointment (section 4). However, before nomination can take place the board must give both the general meeting of shareholders and the works council the opportunity to recommend persons to the board for nomination (section 5). In general, these recommendations are not binding upon the supervisory board.

However, as concerns one third of the members of the supervisory board, the works council has a reinforced recommendation right (section 6). This means that the supervisory board must nominate the candidate recommended by the works council to the general meeting of shareholders for appointment, unless the board opposes the candidate. The supervisory board may only oppose such a candidate on two grounds: either that the board expects that this person is not suited to carry out the duties of a member of a board of supervisors or that the board expects that following appointment the board of supervisors would not be composed properly. In case the supervisory board opposes the candidate, and the board and the works council do not come to terms, the board may refer the matter to the Chamber of Business Affairs of the Court of Appeals at Amsterdam for its decision (section 7). In case the Chamber of Business Affairs finds for the works council, the supervisory board must nominate the candidate for appointment. In case the Chamber of Business Affairs finds for the supervisory board, the board must give the works council again the opportunity to recommend a person to the board for nomination.

When voting on the nominated candidate, the general meeting of shareholders can either appoint the nominee as non-executive director or reject the nominated candidate. The general meeting cannot appoint a non-executive director who was not nominated. In case the general meeting rejects the nominee by a majority vote that represents at least one third of the issued share capital of the corporation, the supervisory board must nominate a new candidate taking into account the whole procedure described above (section 9). In case the general meeting rejects the nominee by a majority vote that represents less than one third of the issued share capital of the corporation, a new general meeting may be convened to vote on the nominated candidate (section 9). In this second vote, the general meeting of shareholders can by a simple majority vote either appoint the nominee as non-executive director or reject the nominated candidate. The majority vote to reject the nominee now does not need to represent at least one third of the issued share capital of the corporation. In case the general meeting of shareholders rejects the nominee again in the second vote the supervisory board must nominate a new candidate taking into account the whole procedure described above.

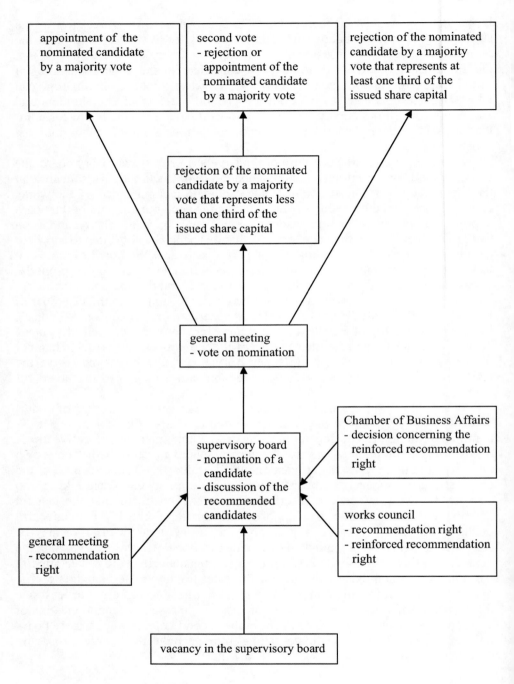

B.   SCHEDULE 3: ARTICLE 2:153 SECTION 3, SUBSECTION A OF
      THE DUTCH CIVIL CODE

[77] A NV has an issued share capital that together with the reserves according to the balance sheet and the notes thereon amounts to EUR 150 million. A NV employs 15 employees in the Netherlands. B NV is a dependent undertaking of A NV because A NV directly holds 50% of the issued share capital of B NV. B NV employs 25 employees in the Netherlands. C NV is a dependent undertaking of A NV because A NV directly holds 60% of the issued share capital of C NV. C NV employs 40 employees in the Netherlands. D NV is also a dependent undertaking of A NV because two of A NV's dependent undertakings (B NV and C NV) together hold 65% of the issued share capital of D NV (B NV holds 35% and C NV holds 30%). D NV employs 120 employees in the Netherlands and has established a works council in accordance with its obligations under the Works Councils Act.

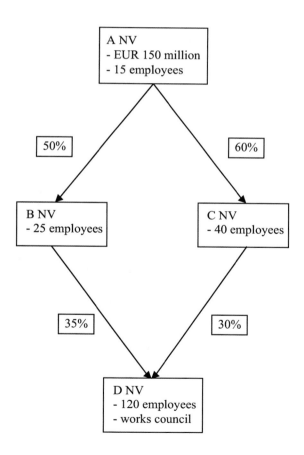

A NV has an issued share capital that together with the reserves according to the balance sheet and the notes thereon amounts to EUR 150 million, together with its dependent undertakings B NV, C NV and D NV employs 200 employees in the Netherlands, and A NV's dependent undertaking D NV has established a works council in accordance with its obligations under the Works Councils Act. A NV meets the criteria of Article 2:153 section 2 of the Dutch Civil Code. A NV is subject to the 'mandatory organizational arrangement'.

Under Article 2:153 section 3, subsection a B NV, C NV and D NV are outside the scope of the 'mandatory organizational arrangement' and are wholly exempt from the arrangement even if they meet the criteria of Article 2:153 section 2.

C.   SCHEDULE 4: ARTICLE 2:153 SECTION 3, SUBSECTION B
                           AND ARTICLE 2:155 SECTION 1, SUBSECTION A OF
                           THE DUTCH CIVIL CODE

[78] A NV has an issued share capital that together with the reserves according to the balance sheet and the notes thereon amounts to EUR 200 million, together with its dependent undertakings B NV and C NV employs 180 employees in the Netherlands, and A NV's dependent undertaking C NV has established a works council in accordance with its obligations under the Works Councils Act. A NV operates as a holding corporation (a corporation that is a parent company of a group and does not operate an enterprise of its own) of an internationally oriented group. The international orientation of the group headed by A NV is measured by the test that the majority of the employees of the group are employed outside the Netherlands. A NV meets the criteria of Article 2:153 section 2 of the Dutch Civil Code. Y Company is a subsidiary company of A NV that employs 250 employees outside the Netherlands.

Under Article 2:153 section 3, subsection b A NV is wholly exempt from the 'mandatory organizational arrangement'.

B NV has an issued share capital that together with the reserves according to the balance sheet and the notes thereon amounts to EUR 80 million, together with its dependent undertaking C NV employs 170 employees in the Netherlands, and B NV's dependent undertaking C NV has established a works council in accordance with its obligations under the Works Councils Act. B NV meets the criteria of Article 2:153 section 2 of the Dutch Civil Code.

B NV is a the subsidiary company of a wholly exempted holding corporation of an internationally oriented group. Under Article 2:155 section 1, subsection a B NV is partially exempt from the 'mandatory organizational arrangement'.

Under Article 2:153 section 3, subsection a D NV is outside the scope of the 'mandatory organizational arrangement' and is wholly exempt from the arrangement even if it meets the criteria of Article 2:153 section 2.

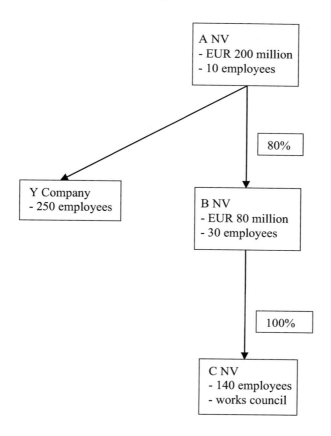

D.   SCHEDULE 5: ARTICLE 2:155 SECTION 1, SUBSECTION A OF THE
DUTCH CIVIL CODE

[79] B NV has an issued share capital that together with the reserves according to the balance sheet and the notes thereon amounts to EUR 80 million,
together with its dependent undertaking C NV employs 150 employees in
the Netherlands, and B NV's dependent undertaking C NV has established a
works council in accordance with its obligations under the Works Councils
Act. B NV meets the criteria of Article 2:153 section 2 of the Dutch Civil
Code. B NV is a subsidiary company of X Corporation. X Corporation
employs 25 employees outside the Netherlands. Y Company is also a
subsidiary company of X Corporation. Y Company employs 250 employees
outside the Netherlands.

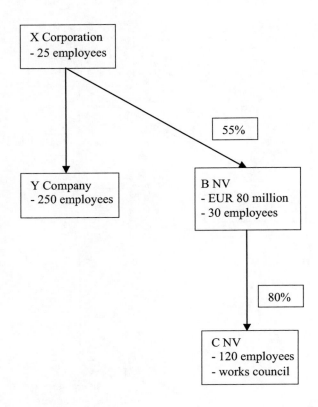

B NV is a subsidiary company of a foreign parent company, and the majority of the employees of the group are employed outside the Netherlands. Under Article 2:155 section 1, subsection a B NV is partially exempt from the 'mandatory organizational arrangement'.

Under Article 2:153 section 3, subsection a C NV is outside the scope of the 'mandatory organizational arrangement' and is wholly exempt from the arrangement even if it meets the criteria of Article 2:153 section 2.

Chapter 6

Risks

I.   RISK MANAGEMENT AND RISK REPORTING

[80] The activities of a corporation are influenced by many risks. Convenient ways to categorize these risks are distinguishing between 'internal' and 'external' risks, 'non-material' and 'material' risks, and 'operational', 'financial' risks and 'other' risks. Corporations may deal with these risks by employing risk management and control systems and by reporting on the concrete risks that influence their activities as well as on the functioning of the risk management and control systems they employ. Part A of this chapter deals with *risk categories, provisions on risk management*, and *provisions on risk reporting*.

A.   RISK CATEGORIES

[81] There are several ways to describe the risks that influence a corporation's activities.[249] *First*, the risks that can affect corporate activities may be divided into risks that a corporation may be able to control ('internal risks') and risks that a corporation is less likely to be able to control ('external risks'). When applying these categories it should be noted that internal risks are not necessarily risks that are coming from within the corporation or its affiliated enterprise and that external

---

249. S. Asaf, *Executive Corporate Finance: The Business of Enhancing Shareholder Value* (Harlow: Pearson Education Limited, 2004); C. de Groot, 'Risicomanagement en risicover-slaggeving tegen de achtergrond van corporate governance', *Maandblad voor Accountancy en Bedrijfseconomie* (2006), 64-71; W.P de Ridder, 'Operationeel risicomanagement: meer dan alleen compliance', *Maandblad voor Accountancy en Bedrijfseconomie* (2007), 138-145.

risks are not necessarily risks that are coming from outside the corporation or its affiliated enterprise. Take the use of information technology ('IT') in the form of computers. This involves risks from within, such as interface failure, and risks from outside, such as hacking. But because a corporation could take measures to prevent both interface failure and hacking, IT risks are internal risks. Likewise, theft of money or goods may be committed by employees of the corporation and hence come from within. But when it is committed by customers it comes from outside. Here too, a corporation can take measures to prevent both, hence these are internal risks. Compare these risks with industrial action. Industrial action is certainly a risk as it can seriously disrupt the activities of a corporation. Industrial action may come from within, because of a strike organized by labor unions to put pressure on the corporation when negotiating a collective labor agreement. Industrial action may also come from outside, as when labor unions organize a nationwide strike during a broader conflict with government over social security legislation. Because a corporation can hardly take measures to prevent any of these strikes happening, industrial action is an external risk. *Second*, the occurrence of risks may influence the activities of a corporation to a smaller or bigger degree. Thus, risks may be divided into risks that in most cases will not lead to serious disruption of corporate activities ('non-material risks') and risks that can seriously disrupt the activities of the corporation ('material risks'). An example of the first category would be employees of the corporation getting sick. Employees are likely to get sick from time to time and in most case this will not put the corporation in jeopardy. Therefore this can be considered a non-material risk. Opposite this are changes in interest rates and currency exchange rates. When a corporation is in part dependent on money lenders that it has to pay back the resources it has borrowed, changes in interest rates may seriously affect the corporation's financial position. And they may do so with negative consequences. Therefore changes in interest rates are a material risk. When the activities of a corporation stretch across several currency zones, changes in currency exchange rates may also have serious consequences for the financial position of the corporation. And these consequences may be detrimental too. So currency exchange rates are also material risks. *Third*, the risks that can affect corporate activities may be categorized according to their nature. A convenient way of dividing risks is distinguishing operational risks from financial risks and considering 'other' risks as a residual category. Operational risks are those that can impair the production process of a corporation. Industrial accidents such as pipeline bursts and fires are examples of this type of risks. Other operational risks are supply failures and losing an important customer. Financial risks pose a threat to the financial continuity of the corporation. Examples are fraud and changes in interest rates and currency exchange rates as already mentioned. Some risks cannot be easily categorized as either operational risks or financial risks. They fall in the residual category. Among these 'other' risks are the failure of an advertising campaign to promote a new product and the failure of a corporation's policy to acquire other businesses or to integrate acquired businesses into the existing business, major changes in regulation and government policies on fiscal or anti-trust matters, and changing consumer preferences.[250] Because of their long term horizon, the 'other' risks that fall into this residual category may also be called strategic risks. Next operational, financial and other (i.e. strategic) risks, IT risks, compliance risks and project risks may be considered as categories in their own right. As concerns IT risks this is a consequence of the fact that the uninterrupted functioning of IT, especially in the form of computers, is so important that IT failure is likely to bring most of the activities of a corporation to a halt.[251] As far as compliance is concerned, corporations need to comply with an ever increasing amount of regulation. This regulation may concern the corporation's corporate governance framework, financial reporting standards, and issues that relate to the personal ethics of directors. Also, project risks may be considered a category in their own right. They would seem to fall somewhere between operational (or financial) risks and strategic risks.

B.   PROVISIONS ON RISK MANAGEMENT

[82] Risk management could be regarded as a subset of the larger subject of management information. Thus risk management and control systems are related to or part of management information systems.[252] Management information systems are intended to provide management with the information its needs to perform its functions. One of these functions is risk management. Risk management and control systems are distinct from management information systems in general as they have a specific object (risks) which may also affect their working. Risk management and control systems concentrate on the identification of the risks that influence the activities of a corporation as well as their description ('risk identification' and 'risk description'), they give management the tools to assess the possible impact of those risks and to formulate adequate responses ('risk assessment' and 'risk response'), and they must allow management to make sure that the formulated responses are in fact implement throughout the organization ('risk

250.   Cf. 'Restoring Trust: Report to the Hon. Jed S. Rakoff, the United States District Court for the Southern District of New York on Corporate Governance for the Future of MCI, Inc.', prepared by Richard C. Breeden, Corporate Monitor ('Restoring trust', August 2003):
       'Long range assessment of risks and review of management's plans for controlling risk did not seem to exist in either traditional telephony or data markets. Internet planning in particular appears to have failed to address cost issues or the possibility of slower than expected growth, though the Company was betting tens of billions in investment predicated on executives' wild guesses about internet growth. [. . .] Though wireless substitution was then and is today one of the most serious risks for WorldCom, even this was not the subject of serious risk analysis by the board', <www.ecgi.org> codes & principles: index of all codes.
251.   S. van Bommel, L. Peek & J. Winterink, 'De betekenis van IT-auditing voor risicobeheersing en IT-governance', *Maandblad voor Accountancy en Bedrijfseconomie* (2008), 43-50.
252.   On these issues: F. de Koning, 'Methoden voor wetenschappelijk onderzoek op het gebied van bestuurlijke informatieverzorging', *Maandblad voor Accountancy en Bedrijfseconomie* (2006), 100-107; F. de Koning, 'Visies op interne beheersing', *Maandblad voor Accountancy en Bedrijfseconomie* (2008), 170-177.

control').[253] Both The Dutch Corporate Governance Code and The Combined Code on Corporate Governance hold provisions on risk management.[254] In accordance with principle II.1 of The Dutch Corporate Governance Code responsibility 'for managing the risks associated with the company activities' shall lie with the management board. This implies not only that the corporation 'shall have an internal risk management and control system that is suitable for the company' (best practice provision II.1.3), but also that such a system shall be assessed and tested in terms of its adequacy and effectiveness. In respect of the latter, according to the code, the internal auditor of the corporation (who 'shall operate under the responsibility of the management board') 'can play an important role in assessing and testing the internal risk management and control systems' (principle V.3).[255] Supporting principle A.1 of The Combined Code on Corporate Governance states that the corporation's board shall perform its functions 'within a framework of prudent and effective controls which enables risk to be assessed and managed'. Main principle C.2 of the code states that '[t]he board should maintain a sound system of internal control to safeguard shareholders' investment and the company's assets'. Also, '[t]he board should, at least annually, conduct a review of the effectiveness of the group's system of internal controls' (code provision C.2.1). The Dutch Corporate Governance Code requires under best practice provision III.1.6 that the supervisory function of the supervisory board shall specifically include 'the structure and operation of the internal risk management and control systems'. To that end, best practice provision III.1.8 states that the supervisory board 'shall discuss at least once a year the corporate strategy and the risks of the business, and the result of the assessment by the management board of the structure and operation of the internal risk management and control systems'.

As concerns the question of maintaining an adequate and effective internal risk management and control system, as well as assessing and testing such a system (and reporting thereon) The Dutch Corporate Governance Code mentions as an example 'the COSO framework for internal control'.[256] The Combined Code on

253. S. Asaf 2004; J. Renard, *Théorie et pratique de l'audit interne* (Paris: Éditions d'Organisation, 2004); M. Kaptein, R. Rozekrans & R. de Groot, 'Integriteitsklimaat als auditobject', *Maandblad voor Accountancy en Bedrijfseconomie* (2005), 466-474; O.C. van Leeuwen, 'Sarbanes Oxley en Tabaksblat: dat valt tegen!', *Maandblad voor Accountancy en Bedrijfseconomie* (2005), 324-325; C. de Groot (2006), 64-71.

254. 'The Dutch Corporate Governance Code: Principles of Good Corporate Governance and Best Practice Provisions', drawn up by the Corporate Governance Committee (December 2003, by the name of the committee's chairperson this committee is also called the Tabaksblat Committee), <www.commissiecorporategovernance.nl> corporate governance code; cf. B. Bier, 'Het risico van de risicobeheersing- en interne controlesystemen: de "in control" verklaring van de code Tabaksblat', *Ondernemingsrecht* (2005), 539-545; 'The Combined Code on Corporate Governance', drawn up by the Financial Reporting Council (version of June 2008, originally July 2003), <www.frc.org.uk> corporate governance.

255. But the latter words are deleted in the amended version of the Dutch Corporate Governance Code.

256. 'The Dutch Corporate Governance Code', Explanation of and notes to certain terms used in the code, under II.1.4.

Corporate Governance refers to the 'Turnbull guidance' as a way of applying main principle C.2 and code provision C.2.1.[257] COSO stands for The Committee of Sponsoring Organizations of the Treadway Commission.[258] This Committee was set up in 1985 to sponsor the work of the National Commission on Fraudulent Financial Reporting (by the name of the commission's first chairperson this commission is also called the Treadway Commission). COSO published 'Internal Control – Integrated Framework' and its successor 'Enterprise Risk Management – Integrated Framework'.[259] The Financial Reporting Council published 'Internal Control: Guidance for Directors on the Combined Code' and its successor 'Internal Control: Revised Guidance for Directors on the Combined Code' (known as the Turnbull guidance and the Revised Turnbull guidance respectively).[260] The Revised Turnbull Guidance 'is based on the adoption by a company's board of a risk-based approach to establishing a sound system of internal control and reviewing its effectiveness. This should be incorporated by the company within its normal management and governance processes. It should not be treated as a separate exercise undertaken to meet regulatory requirements' (paragraph 6).[261]

---

257. 'The Combined Code on Corporate Governance', C.2 Internal Control, footnote.
258. <www.coso.org>.
259. COSO defines internal control as:

'a process, effected by an entity's board of directors, management and other personnel, designed to provide reasonable assurance regarding the achievement of objectives in the following categories:

Effectiveness and efficiency of operations
Reliability of financial reporting
Compliance with applicable laws and regulations'.

J. Emanuels & W. de Munnik, 'Enterprise risk management: een risicobeheersingssysteem voor organisaties', *Maandblad voor Accountancy en Bedrijfseconomie* (2006), 294-299.
260. <www.frc.org.uk> corporate governance → internal control.
261. 'In determining its policies with regard to internal control, and thereby assessing what constitutes a sound system of internal control in the particular circumstances of the company, the board's deliberations should include consideration of the following factors:

the nature and extent of the risks facing the company;
the extent and categories of risk which it regards as acceptable for the company to bear;
the likelihood of the risks concerned materialising;
the company's ability to reduce the incidence and impact on the business of risks that do materialise; and
the costs of operating particular controls relative to the benefit thereby obtained in managing the related risks' (paragraph 16);

'A sound system of internal control reduces, but cannot eliminate, the possibility of poor judgement in decision-making; human error; control processes being deliberately circumvented by employees and others; management overriding controls; and the occurrence of unforeseeable circumstances' (paragraph 22);
    'A sound system of internal control therefore provides reasonable, but not absolute, assurance that a company will not be hindered in achieving its business objectives, or in the orderly and legitimate conduct of its business, by circumstances which may reasonably be foreseen. A system of internal control cannot, however, provide protection with certainty

C.   PROVISIONS ON RISK REPORTING

[83] As concerns risk reporting Article 2:391 section 1 of the Dutch Civil Code states as a general rule that the annual report of a corporation shall contain inter alia 'a description of the main risks and uncertainties that [it] is confronted with'. To this Article 2:391 section 3 adds more specifically that the corporation shall in the annual report also inter alia 'go into the details of its aims and policy concerning the risk management in respect of the use of financial instruments to the extent that this influences the assessment of its assets, liabilities, financial position and results'. Furthermore, best practice provision II.1.4 of The Dutch Corporate Governance

---

against a company failing to meet its business objectives or all material errors, losses, fraud, or breaches of laws or regulations' (paragraph 23);

cf. the (Dutch) Corporate Governance Code Monitoring Committee, 'Third Report on Compliance with the Dutch Corporate Governance Code' (over 2006), at 72-73, <www.commissiecorporategovernance.nl> jaarrapport 2007 (for the English summary: nieuwberichten):

'III. Internal risk management and control systems

The Monitoring Committee notes that compliance and application in the area of internal risk management has improved slightly. Nonetheless, the Committee would make a number of observations about risk reporting in the annual report. It considers that the description of the strategic, operational and financial risks as well as the legislative and regulatory risks can be improved. The Committee therefore makes a number of recommendations for describing the risk profile and the internal risk management and control system.

Description of the risk profile

The description of its risk profile outlines the risks the company encounters in implementing its strategy. The company also states what risks it is prepared to take in order to achieve its objective and if possible quantifies them by means of a sensitivity analysis.

The description should in any event:

- explain the main risks related to the company's strategic objectives and its appetite for risks;
- describe the main strategic, operational, financial, legislative/regulatory and financial reporting risks of the company, including in any event the qualitative impact of these risks;
- contain a sensitivity analysis of the identified risks if it is reasonable to expect such an analysis in the light of the best practices in the sector concerned.

Description of the internal risk management and control system

The description of the internal risk management and control system should indicate what measures the company has taken to control the identified risks. It should deal not only with the system itself but also how it is embedded in the organisation. It is recommended that the following points be discussed:

- the risks which are managed by the internal risk management and control system and, if necessary, the reference model used to configure the system;
- the organisation of the internal risk management and control system and how it is embedded in the organisation;
- the results of a periodic evaluation of the internal risk management and control system and, in so far as applicable, the improvement measures taken as a result' (from the English summary, emphasis deleted).

Code lays down that the management board shall declare in the corporation's annual report 'that the internal risk management and control systems are adequate and effective and shall provide clear substantiation of this'. Under code provision C.2.1 of The Combined Code on Corporate Governance '[t]he board should, at least annually, conduct a review of the effectiveness of the group's system of internal controls and should report to shareholders that they have done so': this review 'should cover all *material* controls, including financial, operational and compliance controls and risk management systems'.[262] The declaration that best practice provision II.1.4 and code provision C.2.1 require the (management) board to make each year is called the 'in control statement'. The Dutch code also deals with risk reporting as concerns external risks. Best practice provision II.1.5 requires that the management board shall 'set out the sensitivity of the results of the company to external factors and variables' in the annual report of the corporation. Risk reporting is also dealt with in the US Sarbanes-Oxley Act of 2002.[263] Title III of the Sarbanes-Oxley Act of 2002 deals with 'Corporate responsibility', Title IV deals with 'Enhanced financial disclosures'. Under Section 404 ('Management assessment of internal controls') a listed corporation shall include in each annual report 'an internal control report' that shall inter alia 'state the responsibility of management for establishing and maintaining an adequate internal control structure and procedures for financial reporting'. Section 302 ('Corporate responsibility for financial reports') requires 'the principal executive officer or officers and the principal financial officer or officers'[264] to certify in each annual (or quarterly) report inter alia not only that 'the signing officer has reviewed the report' and that 'based on the officer's knowledge, the report does not contain any untrue statement of a *material* fact or omit to state a *material* fact', but also more specifically that the signing officers 'are responsible for establishing and maintaining internal controls' and 'have designed such internal controls to ensure that *material information* relating to the issuer and its consolidated subsidiaries is made known to such officers by others within those entities', and that 'based on such officer's knowledge, the financial statements, and other financial information included in the report, fairly present *in all material respects* the financial condition and results of operations of the issuer'.[265]

When comparing the provisions on risk reporting in The Dutch Corporate Governance Code, The Combined Code on Corporate Governance and the Sarbanes-Oxley Act of 2002, it appears that the Dutch Corporate Governance

---

262. Emphasis added.
263. Public Law 107-204 – July 30, 2002, 116 Stat. 745 (107th Congress):

   'An Act To protect investors by improving the accuracy and reliability of corporate disclosures made pursuant to the securities laws, and for other purposes'.

   B.J. Schoordijk, 'Risk management als hoeksteen van corporate governance', in *Tussen Themis en Mercurius*, eds S.H.M.A. Dumoulin et al. (Deventer: Kluwer, 2005), 309-329.
264. '[O]r persons performing similar functions'.
265. Emphasis added.

Code goes further than the other two instruments.[266] The annual review of the internal risk management and control system required under code provision C.2.1 of The Combined Code on Corporate Governance must relate to 'all *material* controls, including financial, operational and compliance controls'.[267] And under Section 302 of the Sarbanes-Oxley Act of 2002 reporting shall include that the internal risk management and control system is designed to ensure that '*material* information' is brought to the attention of the CEO and the CFO and that the financial information provided by the corporation presents the condition and results of the corporation 'in all *material* respects'.[268] However, under best practice provision II.1.4 the in control statement shall imply 'that the internal risk management and control systems are adequate and effective'. In accordance with this provision, risk reporting is not confined to material risks but shall include both non-material and material risks, and shall not be confined to financial risks especially. The (Dutch) Monitoring Committee Corporate Governance Code found in its Report on Compliance with The Dutch Corporate Governance Code (over 2004) that best practice provision II.1.4 is difficult to apply.[269] To meet this situation, the Monitoring Committee formulated a recommendation that is referred to as 'good practice'.[270] Under this good practice, a corporation may interpret best practice provisions II.1.4 as implying that:

– in respect of financial reporting the corporation shall declare that the internal risk management and control systems give a reasonable measure of certainty that the financial reporting by the corporation does not contain material inaccuracies; and
– in respect of other risks the corporation must identity the main risks and describe the internal risk management and control systems that it applies in respect of those risks.

This 'good practice' recommendation limits the scope of the in control statement to *financial reporting risks*.[271] In this respect it is worth noting that the Monitoring

---

266. B.C.J.M. van Beurden, 'De raad van bestuur verklaart: de onderneming is "in control"', *Tijdschrift voor Ondernemingsbestuur* (2004), 159-164.
267. Emphasis added.
268. Emphasis added. For developments in the US: <www.sec.gov > internal control reporting provisions.
269. Corporate Governance Code Monitoring Committee, 'Report on Compliance with The Dutch Corporate Governance Code' (over 2004), at 39, 51, <www.commissiecorporategovernance. nl> information in English.
270. Corporate Governance Code Monitoring Committee, 'Report on Compliance with The Dutch Corporate Governance Code' (over 2004), at 64. J. de Groot & B. Koolstra, 'De "in-control" good practice van de Commissie Frijns lost slechts een deel van de puzzel op', *Maandblad voor Accountancy en Bedrijfseconomie* (2006), 392-400.
271. Corporate Governance Code Monitoring Committee, 'Third Report on Compliance with the Dutch Corporate Governance Code' (over 2006), at 71, <www.commissiecorporategovernance. nl> information in English.

Committee in its Third Report on Compliance with the Dutch Corporate Governance Code (over 2006) stressed that *financial reporting risks* and *financial risks* are not the same thing.[272]

The 'good practice' advocated by the (Dutch) Monitoring Committee Corporate Governance Code is in line with the requirements on the level of the European Union:[273]

> 1. A company whose securities are admitted to trading on a regulated market [. . .] shall include a corporate governance statement in its annual report. That statement shall be included as a specific section of the annual report and shall contain at least the following information:
> [. . .]
> (c) a description of the main features of the company's internal control and risk management systems in relation to the financial reporting process.

In accordance with the amended version of The Dutch Corporate Governance Code, best practice provision II.1.4 is replaced by best practice provisions II.1.4 and II.1.5, and best practice provision II.1.5. is replaced by best practive provision II.1.6. These new provisions read:

> II.1.4 In the annual report the management board shall provide:
>
> a) a description of main risks related to the strategy of the company;
> b) a description of the design and effectiveness of the internal risk management and control systems for the main risks during the financial year; and
> c) a description of any major failings in the internal risk management and control systems which have been discovered in the financial year, any significant changes made to these systems and any major improvements planned, and a confirmation that these issues have been discussed with the audit committee and the supervisory board.
>
> II.1.5 As regards financial reporting risks the management board states in the annual report that the internal risk management and control systems provide a reasonable assurance that the financial reporting does not contain any errors of material importance and that the risk management and control systems worked

---

272. Corporate Governance Code Monitoring Committee, 'Third Report on Compliance with the Dutch Corporate Governance Code' (over 2006), at 71, <www.commissiecorporategovernance. nl> information in English).
273. 'Directive 2006/46/EC of the European Parliament and of the Council of 14 June 2006 Amending Council Directives 78/660/EEC on the Annual Accounts of Certain Types of Companies, 83/349/EEC on Consolidated Accounts, 86/635/EEC on the Annual Accounts and Consolidated Accounts of Banks and Other Financial Institutions and 91/674/EEC on the Annual Accounts and Consolidated Accounts of Insurance Undertakings', OJEU 2006 L 224/1-7 (text with EEA relevance): Article 1 ('Amendments to Directive 78/660/EEC'): Directive 78/660/EEC is hereby amended as follows: 7. the following Article shall be inserted: Article 46a.

properly in the year under review. The management board shall provide clear substantiation of this.

II.1.6 In the annual report, the management board shall describe the sensitivity of the results of the company to external factors and variables.

II.   CASE STUDIES

A.   INTRODUCTION TO THE BAKER PANEL REPORT

[84] The *Baker Panel Report* is a document that underlines the importance of risk management, in this case operational process safety risk management.

[85] In 2005, the BP group (BP p.l.c. and its subsidiary companies, 'BP') operated five refineries in the United States. On 23 March 2005 an industrial accident took place at the BP Texas City refinery that left 15 persons dead and more than 170 injured. The event began when a raffinate splitter tower incurred a high liquid level and high pressure. This started a chain of events that ended in a blowdown drum venting a vapor cloud of highly flammable gasoline components into the air. When this cloud ignited, it caused a number of explosions and fires. The accident was investigated by the US Chemical Safety and Hazard Investigation Board ('CSB'), by BP itself and by an independent panel set up by BP on a recommendation by the CSB. This panel was the BP US Refineries Independent Safety Review Panel (chaired by J.A. Baker). The remit of the panel was 'to make a thorough, independent and credible assessment of the effectiveness of BP Products North America Inc.'s (BP Products) corporate oversight of safety management systems at its refineries [...] and its corporate safety culture'.[274] This assessment was to include both conducting an examination and making recommendations. The authority of the panel did not include determining the exact causes of the accident or establishing responsibilities. The work of the panel resulted in The Report of the BP US Refineries Independent Safety Review Panel ('Baker Panel Report', January 2007).[275] Although the *Baker Panel Report* was directed to BP, the panel felt that its findings could be of wider importance for those concerned with corporate safety oversight, corporate safety culture and process safety management systems.[276] In this respect, by process safety hazards the panel understood hazards that can lead to major accidents, as opposed to personal (sometimes called occupational) safety hazards that can lead to incidents that mostly effect only

---

274. Baker Panel Report, Executive Summary and Appendix A: BP US Refineries Independent Safety Review Panel Charter.
275. <www.csb.gov> completed investigations → March 20, 2007 BP America Refinery Explosion, Texas City, TX, Report of the BP Independent Refineries Safety Review Panel (Baker Panel Report).
276. Baker Panel Report, Panel Statement and Executive Summary.

the employees involved.[277] The *Baker Panel Report* consisted of seven chapters: I. The panel's review, II. Precipitating events for the panel's assessment and report, III. Overview of process safety, personal safety, and corporate safety culture, IV. Overview of BP's organizational structure and its five US refineries, V. BP's health, safety, security, and environment ('HSSE') management framework and process safety-related standards, VI. Findings, and VII. Panel's recommendations. Following the accident of 23 March 2005, BP made a number of changes to its organization and took many other measures.[278]

B.   THE PANEL'S REVIEW

[86] In this chapter, the panel outlined the 'plan of review' it had followed. In comparing its investigation with the investigation of CSB, the panel on the one hand underlined that its investigation was not a thorough investigation of the causes of the accident in the way undertaken by the CSB, as the authority of the panel did not include determining the exact causes of the accident or establishing responsibilities. On the other hand, the investigation by the panel had a broader scope than the investigation by the CSB, as the panel looked into the underlying causes of the accident. In this respect, the panel focused on process safety. The panel faced the particular difficulty that there is no data tracking or benchmarking of process safety accidents. It could, however, draw on general principles of industry best practices and other standards for reducing process risks. The panel's plan of review included visits to BP's US refineries, public meetings, interviews of both refinery personnel and corporate management, investigations by technical consultants, interaction with BP representatives who briefed the panel on issues it had selected, and investigation of documents. During the interviews of both refinery personnel and corporate management, interviewees were not under oath, transcripts were not made, and the panel had to rely on voluntary cooperation. On worker level, the panel made sure to communicate that it would make every possible effort to guarantee anonymity and confidentiality. From the level of refinery managers upward, on the part of BP an attorney or company counsel was present. Also, the panel conducted an anonymous survey for statistical evaluation of approximately 7.500 people by use of a questionnaire. As concerns the investigations by technical consultants, the panel had made clear that these investigations should not just be directed at the process safety management systems in each of BP's five refineries, but also at 'actual performance and documentation of performance' so as to conclude 'whether these systems were followed in practice or were merely "paper systems."'. At one occasion, the technical consultants identified and communicated to BP an immanent hazard in the operation of one of its

---

277.   Baker Panel Report, Executive Summary.
278.   Cf. throughout the Baker Panel Report and Appendix F: BP post-Texas City measures.

refineries, that BP was able to correct. The documents reviewed by the panel totaled more than 340.000 pages. Where BP could not hand over certain documents because of their privileged or sensitive nature, it could sometimes go into their substance in oral briefings.

C.   PRECIPITATING EVENTS FOR THE PANEL'S
          ASSESSMENT AND REPORT

[87] The panel recalled that three events at the refinery precipitated the panel's report: the explosion and fire of 23 March 2005, a hydrogen fire on 28 July 2005, and a gas oil hydrotreater incident on 10 August 2005. All these events were process-related. Following the last event, the CSB – concerned with the effectiveness of safety management systems at the Texas City refinery and the effectiveness of corporate safety oversight, and concerned with corporate safety culture – recommended BP to establish an independent panel.

D.   OVERVIEW OF PROCESS SAFETY, PERSONAL SAFETY,
          AND CORPORATE SAFETY CULTURE

[88] For the purpose of refining operations, the panel understood process safety as 'the prevention and mitigation of unintentional releases of potentially dangerous materials or energy from the refining process'. Process safety management is a form of risk management intended to identity and control process safety hazards. Controlling process safety risks takes place by hard and soft controls. Hard controls are physical controls within a plant such as alarm indicators. Soft controls include internal procedures and industry best practices, and the knowledge and experience of operators. In process safety management, safety is often measured by applying 'key performance indicators' as part of safety management systems. These key performance indicators are used to track safety performance and benchmark safety performance against safety performance at others sites. Key performance indicators are either 'lagging' indicators or 'leading' indicators. Lagging indicators are used in reactive monitoring after the fact. They allow correction of deficiencies following a specific event. Leading indicators are used in active monitoring through inspection and testing. Process safety risks result from the large number of controls that form a complex system that is necessary in process safety management. Process safety hazards tend to have their cause in deficiencies in process safety management. Process safety management also depends on a corporation's safety culture. A corporation's safety culture evolves over time, and must necessarily seek a balance between the operational demands of producing goods or services and safety considerations.

E.   OVERVIEW OF BP'S ORGANIZATIONAL STRUCTURE AND
           ITS FIVE US REFINERIES

[89] BP's governance framework was laid down in the BP 'Management Framework'. This Management Framework was based on three foundations: BP operated in a decentralized manner, the central corporate organization assisted and supported the individual business units, and individual performance contracts played an important role. Under the BP concept of decentralized operations, authority was delegated to the lowest possible point, but accountability was not delegated. This meant that accountability always laid with one specific person (not a committee or a group of persons) who reported to the next level above in the organization. Thus, each organizational level monitored the performance of the next level below, and intervened where necessary. As the *Baker Panel Report* puts it: 'This structure reflects BP's philosophy that leadership monitors but does not supervise the business; leadership only supervises the people who report directly to them'. The same applied to the relationship between the board of BP p.l.c. and the BP group CEO: 'The Board establishes goals, makes broad policy decisions, and monitors the Group Chief Executive's performance, but it does not manage BP's businesses. The Board delegates authority and responsibility for the management of BP's businesses to a single point: the Group Chief Executive. [. . .] The Board delegates all executive management authority to the Group Chief Executive [. . .] who is in turn accountable to the Board'. The BP group CEO delegated authority for refining and marketing issues, including safety issues, to the 'Chief Executive, Refining and Marketing'. At the level below, there was the 'Group Vice-President, Refining', and below this level, regional vice-presidents. Refinery plant managers – who reported to a regional vice-president – enjoyed broad latitude in running a refinery. Each refinery was treated as an individual business unit, and the responsibility of refinery plant managers was both operational en commercial. Her accountabilities included HSSE processes. Refineries could have an operations manager, an HSSE manager, and a head of process safety management; also, each refinery had an HSSE committee. Following the accident of 23 March 2005, BP created the function of Senior Group Vice-President, Safety and Operations. This new function was one level below that of Executive Vice-President (the Chief Executive, Refining and Marketing is an executive vice-president).

F.   BP'S HSSE MANAGEMENT FRAMEWORK AND PROCESS
           SAFETY-RELATED STANDARDS

[90] The sources for BP's process safety management were statutory regulation, BP's group requirements, and minimum standards ('minimum expectations') set by BP. BP's requirements were laid down in documents as the BP Code of Conduct, 'Getting HSE right', the BP Golden Rules, a number of BP Group standards, a number of Group engineering technical practices, and process and personal safety

booklets. BP's minimum standards were laid down in 'process safety minimum expectations' documents.

G.   FINDINGS

[91] In this chapter, the panel considered (1) corporate safety culture, (2) process safety management systems, and (3) performance evaluation, corrective action and corporate oversight.

1.   Corporate Safety Culture

[92] The panel made five observations about BP's corporate safety culture in its US refineries. BP had failed to provide process safety leadership, and had relied too much on underlining personal safety. BP had not 'established a positive, trusting, and open environment with effective lines of communication between management and the workforce, including employee representatives'. BP had not always made available adequate resources for process safety management, and had overloaded refinery personnel with initiatives that could have detracted attention from process safety management. By focusing on short-term goals, BP had not made process safety considerations an integral part of operational decision making. BP had not instilled one single corporate safety culture in its refineries, but had allowed them too much discretion.

2.   Process Safety Management Systems

[93] Notwithstanding the importance of safety culture, process safety performance is also dependent on process safety management systems. As the *Baker Panel Report* stated:

> An effective process safety management system identifies, assesses, and prioritizes process hazards so that management can take appropriate measures to reduce the likelihood and/or severity of process-related incidents. [. . .] A management system has design, execution, and monitoring elements. Design elements lay out the structure and requirements for implementing process safety management activities. Execution elements describe the method and quality requirements for doing process safety work under the management system. Monitoring elements lay out the control system for ensuring that management system results meet the designed expectations. [. . .] Additionally, if the management system is to improve over time, the system should include a process for reviewing performance and ensuring the continued suitability, adequacy, and effectiveness of the system.

The panel found that BP's process safety management systems did not adequately identity and analyze process hazards, and could not always ensure compliance with process safety standards and programs, or with good engineering practices.

3. Performance Evaluation, Corrective Action and Corporate Oversight

[94] One issue the panel considered in this chapter is that '[t]he investigation of incidents represents an important method of evaluating the performance of safety management systems. In this context, the term "incidents" includes events that do not result in injury or major damage and are often referred to as "near misses."'. Another issue the panel considered was the role of the (group) board in health and safety matters. The panel referred to a report issued in 2006 on behalf of the U.K. Health and Safety Commission on occupational safety governance that outlined seven principles for best practices for occupational health and safety governance.[279] This report dealt with occupational health and safety, but the panel considered that the principles could also be used to address the role of the (group) board in process safety. The principles are:

'Director competence': directors shall have an understanding of process safety,

'Director roles and responsibilities': directors shall understand their legal responsibilities for process safety,

'Culture, standards and values': the board shall uphold process safety as a core value,

'Strategic implications': the board shall be responsible for process safety,

'Performance management': the board shall enhance process safety management,

'Internal controls': the board shall manage and control process safety risks, and

'Organizational structures': the board shall integrate process safety management in its corporate governance framework.

In this respect, the panel felt that the board of BP p.l.c. could and should have done more ('The Board of Directors of BP p.l.c. has not ensured, as a best practice, that BP's management has implemented an integrated, comprehensive, and effective process safety management system for BP's five US refineries').

H. PANEL'S RECOMMENDATIONS

[95] The panel's ten recommendations referred to a concerted and lasting effort on the part of BP in (1) enhancing process safety leadership by the board of BP p.l.c.

---

279. Referred to in the Baker Panel Report as: 'Jacqui Boardman and Angus Lyon, Health and Safety Executive, Defining Best Practice in Corporate Occupational Health and Safety Governance, (Research Report 506) (2006)'.

and BP's corporate management ('the process safety "tone at the top"'), (2) establishing an integrated and comprehensive process safety management system, developing (3) process safety knowledge and expertise as well as (4) a process safety culture, (5) defining expectations and strengthening accountability for process safety performance, (6) providing process safety support to line management, (7) developing lagging and leading performance indicators for measuring process safety management, (8) implementing process safety auditing, (9) enhancing board monitoring of process safety performance and publicly reporting on that issue, (10) transforming the corporation into an industry leader in process safety management.

I.   Introduction to the Stone, et al. v. Ritter, et al. Case

[96] Under principle I of The Dutch Corporate Governance Code '[t]he management board and the supervisory board are responsible for the corporate governance structure of the company and compliance with this code'. In its judgment of 14 September 2007 the High Court underlined the importance of corporate governance, more specifically The Dutch Corporate Governance code (in this case principle III.6 and the accompanying best practice provisions) in proceedings under the 'right of inquiry' in Book 2 of the Dutch Civil Code.[280] The High Court did so by referring to the fact that '[t]he Chamber of Business affairs in its judgment [. . .] underscored the importance of principle III.6 of the Tabaksblat-code for situations as the one in which Versatel found itself in which also the interests of a minority of shareholders were at stake. Also the Chamber of Business Affairs took into account in its considerations that Versatel had announced its intention to restrict application of this part of the code. Finally the Chamber of Business Affairs made clear that it considered this restriction to be incorrect and it seems that the Chamber was not convinced that Versatel would show much interest in the minority shareholders as far as the Tabaksblat-code is concerned', to which the High Court added that '[u]nder these circumstances it is understandable that the Chamber of Business Affairs considered ordering [an] interim measures necessary'. These considerations of the High Court accentuate that corporate governance is not only a legal concept but is also embedded in organizational theory. As a legal concept, corporate governance is likely to have relevance in legal proceedings, and because it is closely knit with organizational theory the provisions on the 'right of inquiry' are well suited to emphasize that relevance because these proceedings may result in (interim) measures ordered by the Chamber of Business Affairs. At the same time, it would seem that making failure to observe (good) corporate governance the basis of personal liability of directors is much more difficult, as may be derived from the *Stone, et al. v. Ritter, et al.* case.

---

280. High Court 14 September 2007, JOR 2007, 238 (*Versatel II*), translation of considerations of the court by the author.

J.   The Decision of the Delaware Supreme Court

[97] A subsidiary corporation of AmSouth Bancorporation ('Amsouth'), AmSouth Bank, operated around 600 banking offices in the US where it employed over 11.600 employees. In 2004, AmSouth and Amsouth Bank were fined USD 40 million, and had to pay USD 10 million as a results of civil suits, because bank employees had not filed ' "Suspicious Activity Reports" ("SARs"), as required by the federal Bank Secrecy Act ("BSA") and various anti-money-laundering ("AML") regulations'.[281] Two shareholders of AmSouth, William Stone and Sandra Stone, filed derivative actions on behalf of AmSouth in the Court of Chancery of the State of Delaware against fifteen former and present directors of AmSouth on account of 'corporate loss' by reason of 'oversight liability'. The case was characterized by the facts that:

- 'the directors not only discharged their oversight responsibility to establish an information and reporting system, but also proved that the system was designed to permit the directors to periodically monitor AmSouth's compliance with BSA and AML regulations',
- 'AmSouth's Board at various times enacted written policies and procedures designed to ensure compliance with the BSA and AML regulations', and:
- there were no ' "red flags" – "facts showing that the board ever was aware that AmSouth's internal controls were inadequate, that these inadequacies would result in illegal activity, and that the board chose to do nothing about problems it allegedly knew existed." '.[282]

The actions were dismissed by the Court of Chancery. The plaintiffs appealed, but in its judgment of 6 November 2006 the Supreme Court of the State of Delaware affirmed the judgment of the Court of Chancery.[283] As to the right to file a derivative action the Supreme Court considered that '[i]t is a fundamental principle of the Delaware General Corporation Law that "[t]he business and affairs of every corporation [. . .] shall be managed by or under the direction of a board of directors . . . ." Thus, "by its very nature [a] derivative action impinges on the managerial freedom of directors." Therefore, the right of a stockholder to prosecute a derivative suit is limited to situations where either the stockholder has demanded the directors pursue a corporate claim and the directors have wrongfully refused to do so, or where demand is excused because the directors are incapable of making an impartial decision regarding whether to institute such litigation'.[284] Here the second case applied because the plaintiffs had filed the derivative suit 'without making a pre-suit demand on AmSouth's board of directors'. In its judgment, the Supreme Court referred to the existing Delaware case law (in the

281. Formulation by the Delaware Supreme Court, footnotes deleted.
282. Quotation by the Delaware Supreme Court from the judgment of the Court of Chancery.
283. Supreme Court of the State of Delaware 6 November 2006 (Stone, et al. v. Ritter, et al.); <www.courts.delaware.gov> opinions → 2006, 11/6/06 Stone, et al. v. Ritter, et al. 93, 2006.
284. Footnotes deleted.

Graham, Caremark and Disney cases) in connection to the fiduciary duty to act in good faith to the corporation (i.e. to act in good faith). In the Graham case the Supreme Court had considered that ' *"absent cause for suspicion* there is no duty upon the directors to install and operate a corporate system of espionage to ferret out wrongdoing which they have no reason to suspect exists." '.[285] In the Caremark case the Court of Chancery had opined the Graham case as implying that ' "the duty to act in good faith to be informed cannot be thought to require directors to possess detailed information about all aspects of the operation of the enterprise." '.[286] Then the Supreme Court extensively went into the fiduciary duty to act in good faith:

> As evidenced by the language quoted above, the *Caremark* standard for so-called 'oversight' liability draws heavily upon the concept of director failure to act in good faith. That is consistent with the definition(s) of bad faith recently approved by this Court in its recent *Disney* decision, where we held that a failure to act in good faith requires conduct that is qualitatively different from, and more culpable than, the conduct giving rise to a violation of the fiduciary duty of care (i.e., gross negligence) (footnotes deleted),

> although good faith may be described colloquially as part of a 'triad' of fiduciary duties that includes the duties of care and loyalty, the obligation to act in good faith does not establish an independent fiduciary duty that stands on the same footing as the duties of care and loyalty. Only the latter two duties, where violated, may directly result in liability, whereas a failure to act in good faith may do so, but indirectly (footnote deleted),

> The phraseology used in *Caremark* and that we employ here – describing the lack of good faith as a 'necessary condition to liability' – is deliberate. The purpose of that formulation is to communicate that a failure to act in good faith is not conduct that results, *ipso facto*, in the direct imposition of fiduciary liability. The failure to act in good faith may result in liability because the requirement to act in good faith 'is a subsidiary element[,]' i.e., a condition, 'of the fundamental duty of loyalty.' It follows that because a showing of bad faith conduct, in the sense described in *Disney* and *Caremark*, is essential to establish director oversight liability, the fiduciary duty violated by that conduct is the duty of loyalty (footnotes deleted),[287] and:

> We hold that *Caremark* articulates the necessary conditions predicate for director oversight liability: (a) the directors utterly failed to implement any reporting or information system or controls; *or* (b) having implemented such a system or controls, consciously failed to monitor or oversee its operations thus disabling themselves from being informed of risks or problems requiring their

---

285. Footnote deleted.
286. Quotation by the Delaware Supreme Court from the judgment of the Court of Chancery, footnote deleted.
287. Cf. B.F. Assink, 'Kan de Delaware business judgment rule wat betekenen voor het Nederlandse vennootschapsrecht, specifiek het enquêterecht?', *Ondernemingsrecht* (2008), 230-236.

attention. In either case, imposition of liability requires a showing that the directors knew that they were not discharging their fiduciary obligations. Where directors fail to act in the face of a known duty to act, thereby demonstrating a conscious disregard for their responsibilities, they breach their duty of loyalty by failing to discharge that fiduciary obligation in good faith (footnotes deleted).

K.   EVALUATION

[98] The *Baker Panel Report* underlines the importance of corporate safety culture, risk management and control systems, and corporate oversight (including the board's tone at the top) for risk management, in this case operational process safety risk management. However, risk management failure will not easily result is directors' liability, as is evidenced by *Stone, et al. v. Ritter, et al.*. This case – in short – dealt with the question under what circumstances oversight liability constitutes a breach of a director's fiduciary duty to act in good faith to the corporation. Oversight liability would seem to come under the heading of the fiduciary duty to act in good faith to the corporation rather than under the heading of the fiduciary duty of care to the corporation. This means that oversight liability cannot result from (mere) acting with gross negligence but must involve acting with the intent to do harm or acting with a conscious disregard for one's responsibilities. For oversight liability to exist, directors must either have utterly failed to implement risk management and control systems or have failed to monitor the operation of these systems. The reason for this is that directors cannot be required to possess detailed information about all aspects of the operation of the corporation's enterprise.

Also, a breach of the fiduciary duty to act in good faith does not itself result in liability but is a condition (an element) to establish a breach of the fiduciary duty of loyalty to the corporation.

Chapter 7

Remuneration

I. EXECUTIVE DIRECTORS' REMUNERATION

[99] Executive directors' remuneration (also executive remuneration) is an important issue in corporate governance. Executive remuneration may be classified in
several ways.[288] First, *base, also fixed or non-variable, remuneration* is the settled
quantity of compensation that an executive director is entitled to receive.
Expressed in terms of money, the revenue of such remuneration is certain. *Variable
remuneration* is the fluctuating quantity of compensation that an executive director
may receive. Expressed in terms of money, the revenue of such remuneration may
vary. Second, *non-equity compensation* is remuneration that is not related to (the
value of) the corporation's shares. *Equity-based compensation* is remuneration that
is related to (the value of) the corporation's shares. Base remuneration will in many
cases be non-equity compensation, e.g. the 'fixed salary' referred to in best practice
provision II.2.11 of The Dutch Corporate Governance Code.[289] Variable remuneration could e.g. take the form of share options. Third, remuneration may be *per-
formance-decoupled or performance-independent* and *performance based or
performance-conditioned*. Base remuneration is performance-independent compensation, but variable remuneration may be both performance-independent and
performance-conditioned compensation. Part A of this chapter contains paragraphs
on the *provisions on executive remuneration in the Dutch Civil Code* as well as on

---

288. L. Bebchuk & J. Fried, *Pay without Performance: The Unfulfilled Promise of Executive
      Compensation* (Cambridge: Harvard University Press, 2004); C. de Groot, 'Bezoldiging
      van bestuurders van naamloze vennootschappen', *Ondernemingsrecht* (2005), 464-470.
289. 'The Dutch Corporate Governance Code, Principles of Good Corporate Governance and Best
      Practice Provisions', drawn up by the Corporate Governance Committee (December 2003,
      by the name of the committee's chairperson this committee is also called the Tabaksblat
      Committee), <www.commissiecorporategovernance.nl> corporate governance code.

the *additional provisions on executive remuneration in The Dutch Corporate Governance Code.*[290]

A.   PROVISIONS ON EXECUTIVE REMUNERATION IN
                       THE DUTCH CIVIL CODE

[100] Under Article 2:135 of the Dutch Civil Code, a corporation shall develop a policy on executive remuneration. Remuneration as awarded to individual executive directors shall be in conformity with this policy. The general meeting of shareholders has the exclusive power to set the corporation's policy on executive remuneration (section 1), but it has the power to set the remuneration of the individual executive directors only insofar as the articles of association refrain from designating this power to another organ of the corporation (section 3). In case the articles of association have delegated the power to set the individual executive directors' remuneration to another organ, a number of remuneration arrangements shall nonetheless be subject to the approval of the general meeting (section 4). These are arrangements relating to remuneration through shares and through share option schemes that involve the issue of new shares. However, the resolution that is to be put before the general meeting for its decision only needs to cover the total number of shares or share options that can be granted to the executive directors collectively, as well as the criteria that are used for granting these shares or share options and for modifying the conditions regarding these shares or share options.[291]

Under Article 2:383c section 1 of the Dutch Civil Code, a listed corporation shall disclose[292] the amount of remuneration of each individual executive director. This disclosure shall be broken down into four categories. These are the base (fixed or non-variable) remuneration (defined as 'remuneration being paid periodically'), the remuneration that results from profit participation schemes and bonus schemes, the remuneration that becomes payable after the expiration of a term, and severance pay. Disclosure in all these categories relates to the amount of remuneration that was paid in the course the financial year under consideration. Furthermore, under Article 2:383d section 1 of the Dutch Civil Code, a listed corporation shall disclose[293] in relation to each individual executive director a number of elements in respect of share options that it grants the director (regardless whether these options

---

290.   Cf. also the 'Commission Recommendation of 14 December 2004 Fostering an Appropriate Regime for the Remuneration of Directors of Disted Companies (2004/913/EC)', OJEU 2004 L 385/55-59 (text with EEA relevance); *Top Pay and Performance: International and Strategic Approach*, eds S. Tyson & F. Bournois (Oxford: Elsevier Butterworth-Heinemann, 2005); C. de Groot, 'The Level and Composition of Executive Remuneration: A View from the Netherlands', *European Company Law* (2006), 11-17.
291.   J.M. van Slooten & I. Zaal, 'Gebrekkig loon', *Ondernemingsrecht* (2008), 296-301.
292.   In the notes on the annual accounts.
293.   Also in the notes on the annual accounts.

involve the issue of new shares or do not involve the issue of new shares). This is because share options are (next remuneration that results from profit participation schemes and bonus schemes) an important variable remuneration component. Elements to be disclosed are the exercise price (strike price) of share options held by a director that were *out of* the money[294] or *at* the money[295] at the date the options were granted, as well as both the exercise price (strike price) and the share price in the case of options held by a director that were *in* the money[296] at the grant date (so-called discounted share options). Other elements to be disclosed include the number of options granted in the course of the financial year under consideration, the number of options that were exercised in the course of the financial year, the number of options granted earlier that had not been exercised at the beginning of the financial year, and the number of options that have not yet been exercised at the end of the financial year. Also, the company shall disclose the criteria on which granting or exercising share options is dependent. Finally, under Article 2:383e of the Dutch Civil Code, a listed corporation shall disclose[297] all loans and advance payments a director received from the corporation as well as all financial guarantees made by the corporation in favor of a director.

B.   ADDITIONAL PROVISIONS ON EXECUTIVE REMUNERATION
       IN THE DUTCH CORPORATE GOVERNANCE CODE

[101] The Dutch Corporate Governance Code adds some provisions to the arrangement under Article 2:135 of the Dutch Civil Code whereby the general meeting of shareholders has exclusive power to set the corporation's policy on executive remuneration, but has power to set the remuneration of the individual executive directors only insofar as the articles of association refrain from designating this power to another organ. *First*, the code simply assumes that the general meeting of shareholders, when it decides on the corporation's policy on executive remuneration, does so on the basis of a proposal put before it by the non-executive directors (principle II.2-2). *Second*, the code goes on the assumption that the articles of association empower the non-executive directors to set the remuneration of the individual executive directors (principle II.2-2). As to both tasks of the non-executive directors, the code states that the remuneration committee of the supervisory board shall take the lead. In accordance with best practice provision III.5.10

---

294. This means that that the exercise price of the options is fixed at *a higher level* than the price (market value) on the day, or at *a higher level* than a price average (market value average) over the days, preceding the day on which the options are granted.
295. This means that that the exercise price of the options is fixed *at* the price (market value) on the day, or *at* a price average (market value average) over the days, preceding the day on which the options are granted.
296. This means that that the exercise price of the options is fixed at *a lower level* than the price (market value) on the day, or at *a lower level* than a price average (market value average) over the days, preceding the day on which the options are granted.
297. Also in the notes on the annual accounts.

the remuneration committee shall draft both 'a proposal to the supervisory board for the remuneration policy to be pursued' and 'a proposal for the remuneration of the individual members of the management board'. Based thereon, the supervisory board shall draw up a remuneration report that contains both 'an overview of the remuneration policy planned by the supervisory board for the next financial year and subsequent years' and 'an account of the manner in which the remuneration policy has been implemented in the past financial year' (best practice provision II.2.9). As concerns the remuneration policy principle II.2-1 states that '[t]he remuneration policy proposed for the next financial year and subsequent years as specified in the remuneration report shall be submitted to the general meeting of shareholders for adoption', and as concerns the remuneration of the individual directors principle II.2-1 states that '[t]he supervisory board shall determine the remuneration of the individual members of the management board, on a proposal by the remuneration committee'.

Under best practice provision II.2.13 the remuneration report shall be posted on the corporation's website.[298] By this provision a lot of information on executive remuneration becomes publicly available next the notes to the annual account. Especially since best practice provision II.2.10 prescribes in detail what the remuneration report should contain in any event on the remuneration of the individual executive directors.[299]

---

298. Also, the report of the supervisory board that is part of the annual accounts of the corporation 'shall include the principal points of the remuneration report of the supervisory board [. . .], as drawn up by the remuneration committee': The Dutch Corporate Governance Code, principle II.2-2.
299. As follows:

 'a) a statement of the relative importance of the variable and non-variable remuneration components and an explanation of this ratio;
 b) an explanation of any absolute change in the non-variable remuneration component;
 c) if applicable, the composition of the group of companies (peer group) whose remuneration policy determines in part the level and composition of the remuneration of the management board members;
 d) a summary and explanation of the company's policy with regard to the term of the contracts with management board members, the applicable periods of notice and redundancy schemes and an explanation of the extent to which best practice provision II.2.7 is endorsed;
 e) a description of the performance criteria on which any right of the management board members to options, shares or other variable remuneration components is dependent;
 f) an explanation of the chosen performance criteria;
 g) a summary of the methods that will be applied in order to determine whether the performance criteria have been fulfilled and an explanation of the choice of these methods;
 h) if performance criteria are based on a comparison with external factors, a summary should be given of the factors that will be used to make the comparison; if one of the factors relates to the performance of one or more companies (peer group) or of an index, it should be stated which companies or which index has been chosen as the yardstick for comparison;
 i) a description and explanation of each proposed change to the conditions on which a management board member can acquire rights to options, shares or other variable remuneration components;

Unlike the Dutch Civil Code, The Dutch Corporate Governance also contains material provisions that executive remuneration should meet.[300] Principle II.2-1 of the code has it that the level ('amount') and composition ('make-up' or 'structure') of executive remuneration shall be determined by taking into account inter alia the results and share price performance of the corporation, and by any other relevant developments. Although the code is reluctant to go into the appropriate level of executive remuneration, it does contain some provisions on the composition of executive remuneration.[301] In accordance with principle II.2-1, remuneration composition shall be such that it that it:

- promotes the interests of the corporation in the medium and long run,
- does not encourage executive directors to act in their own interests and neglect the interests of the corporation, and
- does not reward executives who fail to perform (particularly in the case of termination of their contract).

This being the case, the level and composition of executive remuneration shall be such that the corporation can recruit and retain qualified executive directors (principle II.2-1). In order to attain this, executive remuneration could be composed of both a base (fixed or non-variable) component as well as a variable component. In accordance with the code, the variable part of executive remuneration shall be designed specifically to strengthen the commitment of the executive directors to the corporation. Therefore, the variable component of executive remuneration shall be linked to performance criteria (or 'targets') that are 'previously-determined, measurable and influenceable', and shall be achieved by the executive directors 'partly in the short term and partly in the long term'. Because share options may form the brunt of variable executive remuneration, the code goes into much detail to regulate this form of remuneration. The code favors *conditionally awarded share options* over *unconditionally awarded share options*. In the opinion of the code, share options should in principle be awarded *conditionally*, that is to say on the condition that the executive directors will fulfill the performance criteria (making the options 'become unconditional only when the management board members have fulfilled [these] predetermined performance criteria' – best practice provision

---

j) if any right of a management board member to options, shares or other variable remuneration components is not performance-related, an explanation of why this is the case;
k) current pension schemes and the related financing costs;
l) agreed arrangements for the early retirement of management board members'.

300. B.T.M. Steins Bisschop, 'Beloningssystemen: de ongerechtvaardigde hypothese van parallelle belangen tussen aandeelhouders en bestuurders', *Tijdschrift voor Ondernemingsbestuur* (2006), 50-59.

301. However, The Dutch Corporate Governance Code, best practice provision II.2.7 states:

'The maximum remuneration in the event of dismissal is one year's salary (the "fixed" remuneration component). If the maximum of one year's salary would be manifestly unreasonable for a management board member who is dismissed during his first term of office, such board member shall be eligible for a severance pay not exceeding twice the annual salary'.

II.2.1). To further consolidate the provision that performance criteria must relate to targets that the executive directors shall achieve partly in the short and partly in the long term, the code specifies that the normal period within which the performance criteria should be met is at least three years from the grant date (best practice provision II.2.1). Furthermore, the code specifies that the options should at the grant date be *out of* the money or *at* the money (best practice provision II.2.4) and requires that neither the exercise price of the options nor any other conditions surrounding them should be modified during their term (best practice provision II.2.5). *Unconditionally* awarded share options are options that are awarded at the pleasure of the person who awards them, or even automatically, e.g. at the end of the corporation's financial year, without testing whether performance criteria were met. It is the opinion of the code (best practice provision II.2.2) that this type of options should not be granted, and should – in the exceptional case that they are granted –, although being 'unconditional', be made dependent on testing whether performance criteria were met nevertheless. Furthermore, the code prohibits the executive directors from exercising share options that were awarded unconditionally within a period of time of three years after the grant date.

The (Dutch) Monitoring Committee Corporate Governance Code identified in its Third Report on Compliance with the Dutch Corporate Governance Code (over 2006) a number of short term and long term performance criteria that are *de facto* being used. Among these are: (short term) revenue, EBIT(D)(A)/operating profit, net income, earnings per share, economic value added/economic profit, cash flow, cost, total shareholder return, return on invested capital, return on capital employed, work capital, profit before taxes, gross margin, customer satisfaction, employee satisfaction, market share, corporate social responsibility/sustainable development, and: (long term) total shareholder return, earnings per share, EBIT/operating profit, personal goals, strategic goals, product development, risk management, knowledge management, successful conclusion of a contract.[302]

II.   CASE STUDY

A.   INTRODUCTION TO THE RODAMCO NORTH AMERICA CASE

[102] The *RNA* case deals with so-called in control-clauses taking the form of 'single trigger' and 'double trigger' clauses.

[103] Rodamco North America NV ('RNA') was a listed corporation established in the Netherlands. RNA was an investment company whose main activities were in the field of real estate in the United States, Canada and Mexico. The Australian

---

302. Corporate Governance Code Monitoring Committee, 'Third Report on Compliance with the Dutch Corporate Governance Code' (over 2006), at 89, <www.commissiecorporategovernance.nl> information in English.

company Westfield European Investments Pty Ltd.[303] ('Westfield') was a subsidiary company of Westfield Holdings Ltd. ('Westfield Holdings', also a listed corporation). Westfield Holdings and its subsidiaries were primarily involved in real estate development and investment in shopping plazas in Australia, New Zealand, the United States and the United Kingdom. In August 2001 Westfield took over approximately 23,9% of the issued share capital of RNA from the Netherlands pension fund Stichting Pensioenfonds ABP (that itself retained somewhat over 6% of the issued share capital of RNA). RNA managed its real estate portfolio though its subsidiary company URBAN Shopping Centers Inc. ('URBAN'). Westfield proposed that RNA and itself integrate their real estate portfolios (in particular) in the United States under the control of a trust (Westfield America Trust) that was affiliated with Westfield. When RNA refused to go along with this proposal, Westfield asked that an extraordinary general meeting of shareholders be held to discuss the strategy of Westfield and to replace the members of Westfield's management and supervisory boards. In reaction RNA took several defensive measures. These included issuing a large number of shares to Stichting RNA to neutralize the influence of Westfield in the general meeting of shareholders of RNA (as well as giving Stichting RNA a call-option to acquire even more shares when necessary) as well as making adjustments to the employment agreements with the executive directors of RNA, to an agreement with Freeland Corporate Advisors NV ('Freeland'), and to the employment agreements of approximately 100 persons working with URBAN. The agreement with Freeland was a services agreement under which Freeland performed legal and financial services and services concerning investor relations. The adjustments related to the amount of the 'completion payments' to be paid by RNA to its executive directors and the other personnel as well as to Freeland in case of a 'change in control'. The employment agreements with the executive directors were amended to include under change in control the situation where the supervisory board of RNA would no longer consist of 75% of the non-executive directors serving at that moment, unless the board itself agreed to a new composition. In such a change of control situation the executive directors of RNA would be entitled to a completion payment to the amount of three times the base salary and additional remuneration components they received per year. Because the executive directors would be entitled to this completion payment even if they were not terminated, this change of control payment is also called a 'single trigger'. The agreement with Freeland was amended in a similar way in relation to the staff of Freeland that performed services for RNA. The employment agreements with the employees of URBAN were amended to the effect that the duration of the agreements was four years, and that these employees in such a change of control situation would be also be entitled a completion sum. Because these employees would be entitled to the completion sum only if they were terminated or employed at another location, this change of control payment is also called a 'double trigger'.

---

303. Also: Westfield Limited ACN 000 317 279.

B.   THE DECISION OF THE CHAMBER OF BUSINESS AFFAIRS
                             TO CONCLUDE MISMANAGEMENT

[104] On 8 October 2001 Westfield filed an application with the Chamber of
Business Affairs under the provisions on the 'right of inquiry' in the Book 2 of
the Dutch Civil Code. Westfield asked the Chamber of Business Affairs to find
well-founded reasons to doubt good policy on the part of RNA and appoint persons
to investigate the policy and the course of affairs of RNA. In its judgment of
16 October 2001 the Chamber of Business Affairs ordered an investigation to
be held.[304] Following the investigation, the Chamber of Business Affairs in its
judgment of 22 March 2002 concluded that there had been mismanagement on the
part of RNA.[305] In the opinion of the Chamber of Business Affairs, the mismanagement resulted inter alia from the adjustments that had been made to the employment agreements of the executive directors of RNA and to the agreement with
Freeland.[306] In general terms, the court considered:

> that so-called in control-clauses [...] appear to be common in American
> employment relationships to protect the employment position of persons
> that are essential for the continuity of the enterprise and thereby for that con-
> tinuity as such, because those key employees are given a strong impetus not to
> prematurely sever relations with the enterprise even in threatening circum-
> stances. [...] In the light of this the Chamber of Business Affairs accepts the
> defense put forward by RNA to the extent that the amendment of the definition
> of the concept of change in control – in the sense that it also came to include a
> dreaded takeover by Westfield – was as such an acceptable measure to protect
> those persons employed in the enterprise who might be (extra) afraid of the
> changes Westfield proposed to the operations (italics deleted).

But then the Chamber of Business Affairs considered that the totality of the amendments made to the employment agreements and the agreement with Freeland had to
be 'proportional' toward both 'Westfield as a raider' and 'the combined shareholders'.[307] In relation to Westfield the court concluded that the amendments were
not to be considered a poison pill that was not proportional:

> It cannot be maintained that the measures (in the sphere of the employment
> positions) would [...] be disproportionately troublesome to a prospective
> bidder.

---

304. Chamber of Business Affairs 16 October 2001, JOR 2001, 251 (*RNA*).
305. Chamber of Business Affairs 22 March 2002, JOR 2002, 82 (*RNA*), translation of considera-
      tions of the court by the author; J.M. van Slooten, 'Loonmatiging aan de top: mogelijkheden en
      beperkingen', in *Geschriften vanwege de vereniging Corporate Litigation 2004-2005*, eds
      G. van Solinge et al. (Deventer: Kluwer, 2005), 261-276.
306. In the opinion of the court the adjustments that had been made to the employment agreements
      of the persons working with URBAN did not constitute mismanagement.
307. Italics deleted.

However, the amendments were disproportional toward the combined shareholders:

> In the opinion of the Chamber of Business Affairs the measures would be disproportional and thereby unacceptable toward the combined shareholders – Westfield included – if, and to the extent that, the amendments (could) lead to financial detriment to RNA and in that case to its shareholders too that cannot be based on reasonable goals attached to the change in control-clauses, but would e.g. be motivated by giving gratuitous advantages to certain employees. [...] Under the original employment agreements an executive involved would in case of a change in control only be entitled to a *severance payment* in case of a – sought or given – termination within a period of twelve months after an event that came within the meaning of the concept of a change in control. Furthermore, she would be required to refund the *severance payment* if she would be hired elsewhere within a period of time of six months after her dismissal. The amended employment agreements state that the executive involved will in case of a change in control be entitled to the *completion payment*, even if she is not terminated. Furthermore, the amended agreement does not stipulate that the executive shall give a refund if she is hired elsewhere after her termination. In the opinion of the Chamber of Business Affairs these adjustments cannot be justified by reasonable goals attached to change in control-clauses (italics deleted in part).

C.   EVALUATION

[105] *RNA* – in short – dealt with the question whether adjustments that had been made to the employment agreements of the executive directors and other employees of RNA as well as similar changes that applied to other personnel (resulting from adjustments to an agreement with Freeland where this personnel was employed) constituted mismanagement on the part of RNA. The adjustments changed the scope of change in control clauses that would entitle the persons concerned to receive a completion payment in two ways: first by including under change in control situations that had not been included before, and second by introducing single trigger clauses under which entitlement to completion payment would arise even if the persons concerned were not terminated (also these clauses were so construed that they did not contain refund provisions). The Chamber of Business Affairs went along with the first adjustment but not with the second. In the opinion of the court the single trigger clauses could not 'be justified by reasonable goals attached to change in control-clauses', namely 'to protect the employment position of persons that are essential for the continuity of the enterprise'. It would seem that the Chamber of Business Affairs in *RNA* condemned the second adjustment because it was simply out of the ordinary.

Chapter 8

Personal Ethics

I.   PERSONAL ETHICS AND CORPORATE
              GOVERNANCE

[106] Best practice provision II.1.3 of The Dutch Corporate Governance Code, which states that a listed corporation must have a suitable internal risk management and control system, refers to a numbers of 'instruments' that the corporation must employ as part of this system.[308] One of these instruments is 'a code of conduct which should, in any event, be published on the company's website'. The Dutch Corporate Governance Code does not elaborate what a code of conduct is and what the issues are that should be addressed in such a code. In fact, there are two types of codes of conduct. Part A of this chapter first deals with *codes of business conduct and codes of personal ethics* and then goes into *personal ethics for directors*.

A.   Codes of Business Conduct and Codes of
              Personal Ethics

[107] The predecessor to the ASX Corporate Governance Principles and Recommendations,[309] the ASX Principles of Good Corporate Governance and Best

---

308. 'The Dutch Corporate Governance Code: Principles of Good Corporate Governance and Best Practice Provisions', drawn up by the Corporate Governance Committee (December 2003, by the name of the committee's chairperson this committee is also called the Tabaksblat Committee), <www.commissiecorporategovernance.nl> corporate governance code.
309. 'Corporate Governance Principles and Recommendations', adopted by the ASX Corporate Governance Council, convened by the Australian Securities Exchange (August 2007, the successor to the 'Principles of Good Corporate Governance and Best Practice Recommendations' (March 2003)), <www.asx.com.au> listed companies → corporate governance.

Practice Recommendations,[310] distinguished between two types of codes of conduct. *First*, in accordance with principle 10 ('Recognise the legitimate interests of stakeholders'), a listed corporation should '[r]ecognise legal and other obligations to all legitimate stakeholders'. According to recommendation 10.1 this meant that the corporation should '[e]stablish and disclose a code of conduct to guide compliance with legal and other obligations to legitimate stakeholders'. The commentary and guidance made it clear that recommendation 10.1 was concerned with issues like 'trade practices and fair dealing laws, consumer protection, respect for privacy, employment law, occupational health and safety, equal employment opportunity, superannuation, environment and pollution controls', in total with '[p]ublic or social accountability by corporations'.[311] *Second*, in accordance with principle 3 ('Promote ethical and responsible decision-making'), a listed corporation should 'clarify the standards of ethical behaviour required of company directors and key executives (that is, officers and employees who have the opportunity to materially influence the integrity, strategy and operation of the business and its financial performance) and encourage the observance of those standards'. According to recommendation 3.1 this meant that the corporation should '[e]stablish a code of conduct to guide the directors, the chief executive officer (or equivalent), the chief financial officer (or equivalent) and any other key executives' concerning 'the practices necessary to maintain confidence in the company's integrity' and 'the responsibility and accountability of individuals for reporting and investigating reports of unethical practices'.[312] The commentary and guidance made it clear that recommendation 3.1 was concerned with '[p]ersonal ethics'. The code could deal with issues like: 'Conflicts of interest', 'Corporate opportunities', 'Confidentiality', 'Fair dealing', 'Protection of and proper use of the company's assets', 'Compliance with laws and regulations', and 'Encouraging the reporting of unlawful/unethical behaviour'. Also, according to recommendation 3.2, a corporation should '[d]isclose the policy concerning trading in company securities by directors, officers and employees'.

---

310. 'Principles of Good Corporate Governance and Best Practice Recommendations', adopted by the ASX Corporate Governance Council, convened by the Australian Securities Exchange (March 2003, succeeded by the Corporate Governance Principles and Recommendations (August 2007)), <www.asx.com.au> listed companies → corporate governance.

311. The code could deal with issues like:

   – 'Clear commitment by board and management to the code of conduct',
   – 'Responsibilities to shareholders and the financial community generally',
   – 'Responsibilities to clients, customers and consumers',
   – 'Employment practices',
   – 'Obligations relative to fair trading and dealing',
   – 'Responsibilities to the community',
   – 'Responsibilities to the individual',
   – 'How the company complies with legislation affecting its operations', and
   – 'How the company monitors and ensures compliance with its code'.

312. Footnote deleted.

The issues mentioned in (the commentary and guidance to) recommendations 3.1 and 3.2 of the ASX Principles of Good Corporate Governance and Best Practice Recommendations are very similar to what is outlined in the New York Stock Exchange Listed Company Manual that applies to corporations that are listed on the New York Stock Exchange.[313] Not only does subsection 303A.09 ('Corporate Governance Guidelines') require that '[l]isted companies must adopt and disclose corporate governance guidelines', but also does subsection 303A.10 ('Code of Business Conduct and Ethics') require that '[l]isted companies must adopt and disclose a code of business conduct and ethics for directors, officers and employees, and promptly disclose any waivers of the code for directors or executive officers' (both subsection 303A.09 and subsection 303A.10 fall under section 3 ('Corporate responsibility'), Section 303A ('Corporate governance standards')). Under subsection 303A.10 the code of business conduct and ethics must address at least the following issues:

- 'Conflicts of interest': 'A "conflict of interest" occurs when an individual's private interest interferes in any way – or even appears to interfere – with the interests of the corporation as a whole',
- 'Corporate opportunities': 'Employees, officers and directors should be prohibited from (a) taking for themselves personally opportunities that are discovered through the use of corporate property, information or position; (b) using corporate property, information, or position for personal gain; and (c) competing with the company',
- 'Confidentiality': 'Employees, officers and directors should maintain the confidentiality of information entrusted to them by the listed company or its customers, except when disclosure is authorized or legally mandated',
- 'Fair dealing': 'Each employee, officer and director should endeavor to deal fairly with the company's customers, suppliers, competitors and employees. None should take unfair advantage of anyone through manipulation, concealment, abuse of privileged information, misrepresentation of material facts, or any other unfair-dealing practice',
- 'Protection and proper use of company assets': 'All employees, officers and directors should protect the company's assets and ensure their efficient use. Theft, carelessness and waste have a direct impact on the listed company's profitability. All company assets should be used for legitimate business purposes',
- 'Compliance with laws, rules and regulations (including insider trading laws)': 'The listed company should proactively promote compliance with laws, rules and regulations, including insider trading laws', and
- 'Encouraging the reporting of any illegal or unethical behavior': 'The listed company should proactively promote ethical behavior. The company should encourage employees to talk to supervisors, managers or other appropriate personnel when in doubt about the best course of action in a

---

313. <www.nyse.com> nyse regulation → listed companies.

particular situation. Additionally, employees should report violations of laws, rules, regulations or the code of business conduct to appropriate personnel. To encourage employees to report such violations, the listed company must ensure that employees know that the company will not allow retaliation for reports made in good faith'.

The two types of codes of conduct referred to in the ASX Principles of Good Corporate Governance and Best Practice Recommendations could – conveniently – be referred to as a *code of business conduct or a code of business ethics* (the code referred to under recommendation 10.1) and a *code of personal ethics* (the code referred to under recommendation 3.1). A code of business conduct would in particular deal with the way a corporation handles its business activities, and a code of personal ethics would in particular deal with the expectations on the part of a corporation as regards the individual behavior of its directors, managers and employees. The ASX Principles of Good Corporate Governance and Best Practice Recommendations recognized that codes of business conduct and codes of personal ethics are interrelated. The principles allowed the code of personal ethics to be part of the code of business conduct.[314] This interrelation is understandable. A corporation that is committed to high standards of integrity and states so in its code of business conduct, will also – as a matter of convenience possibly in the same document – demand of its directors, managers and employees that they observe high standards of integrity themselves. Likewise, a corporation that is committed to equal opportunity and states in its code of business conduct that it will not engage in discrimination on the basis of age, color, disability, national extraction, political opinion, race, religion, sex, social origin or any other basis, will also – and again as a matter of convenience possibly in the same document – demand of its directors, managers and employees that they refrain from any discrimination and harassment.

B.   PERSONAL ETHICS FOR DIRECTORS

[108] No matter whether rules on personal ethics are laid down in a separate code or are integrated in a code of business conduct, most of these rules will logically apply to the corporation's directors, managers and employees alike.[315] As far as corporate governance is concerned, a corporate governance code and corporate

---

314. 'ASX Principles of Good Corporate Governance and Best Practice Recommendations', commentary and guidance to recommendation 3.1. Cf. the 'ASX Corporate Governance Principles and Recommendations', recommendation 3.1, commentary and guidance:

'It is not necessary for companies to establish a separate code for directors and senior executives. Depending on the nature and size of the company's operations, the code of conduct for directors and senior executives may stand alone or be part of the corporate code of conduct'.

315. C. de Groot, 'Tussen corporate governance en arbeidsrecht: de integriteitscode', *Sociaal Maandblad Arbeid* (2005), 418-425.

governance guidelines could concentrate on rules of personal ethics that have special relevance for the directors of the corporation.[316] The code or guidelines could lay down rules that have an enhanced importance when applied to directors, rules that directors have a special responsibility for, and as a reminder rules on issues that directors are more likely to be confronted with than other personnel. This means that not all the issues mentioned in (the commentary and guidance to) recommendations 3.1 and 3.2 of the ASX Principles of Good Corporate Governance and Best Practice Recommendations and in subsection 303A.10 of the New York Stock Exchange Listed Company Manual must necessarily (also) be regulated in corporate governance codes or guidelines. But these corporate governance instruments could go into some issues of personal ethics.

1.   (Apparent) Complexes and Conflicts of Interests

[109] Principles II.3 (on executive directors) and III.6 (on non-executive directors) of The Dutch Corporate Governance Code state in general terms that situations where there is '[a]ny [complex] of interest or apparent [complex] of interest between the company and [a director] shall be avoided'. As concerns decision making in situations where there is a concrete conflict of interests both principles provide that '[d]ecisions to enter into transactions under which [a director] would have conflicts of interest that are of material significance to the company and/or to the relevant [director] require the approval of the supervisory board'.

In furtherance of these principles best practice provisions II.3.2-II.3.4 (on executive directors) and III.6.1-III.6.3 and III.6.5 (on non-executive directors) hold a number of provisions. *First*, a director 'shall not take part in any discussion or decision-making that involves a subject or transaction in relation to which he has a conflict of interest with the company' (best practice provision II.3.3).[317] *Second*, all transactions involving a conflict of interests with a director 'shall be agreed on terms that are customary in the sector concerned' (best practice provisions II.3.4 and III.6.3). *Third*, as concerns conflicts of interests or potential conflicts of interests that are 'of material significance' to the corporation or a director, the director concerned shall immediately report these conflicts of interest to the chairperson of the supervisory board,[318] 'and shall provide all relevant information, including information concerning his wife, registered partner or other life companion, foster child and relatives by blood or marriage up to the second degree' (best practice provisions II.3.2 and III.6.1).[319] In these cases, the supervisory board shall decide

---

316. And possibly also for the senior managers.
317. The Dutch Corporate Governance Code, BP III.6.2 reads:

   'shall not take part in a discussion and/or decision-making on a subject or transaction in relation to which he has a conflict of interest with the company'.

318. And in case of an executive director also to the other executive directors.
319. Under The Dutch Corporate Governance Code, BP III.6.1 '[i]f the chairman of the supervisory board has a conflict of interest or potential conflict of interest that is of material significance to

whether there is indeed a conflict of interests of material significance. The executive director concerned shall not be present in this meeting and the non-executive director concerned shall not take part in it (best practice provisions II.3.2 and III.6.1). *Fourth*, all decisions to enter into a transaction with a director that is 'of material significance' to the corporation or the director concerned 'require the approval of the supervisory board' (best practice provisions II.3.4 and II.6.3).[320] *Fifth*, the supervisory board shall draw up a set of regulations that stipulate which transactions involving executive or non-executive directors 'require the approval of the supervisory board', i.e. are of material significance (best practice provision III.6.5). The following transactions shall in any event be considered to be of material significance: 'if the company intends to enter into a transaction with a legal entity (i) in which a [director] personally has a material financial interest; (ii) which has a management board member who has a relationship under family law with a [director] of the company, or (iii) in which a [director] of the company has a management or supervisory position' (best practice provisions II.3.2 and III.6.1).[321]

2.   Competition, Gifts Et Cetera

[110] Under best practice provision II.3.1 of The Dutch Corporate Governance Code an executive director shall:

a) not enter into competition with the company;
b) not demand or accept (substantial) gifts from the company for himself or for his wife, registered partner or other life companion, foster child or relative by blood or marriage up to the second degree;
c) not provide unjustified advantages to third parties to the detriment of the company;
d) not take advantage of business opportunities to which the company is entitled for himself or for his wife, registered partner or other life

---

the company and/or to him, he shall report this immediately to the vice-chairman of the supervisory board and shall provide all relevant information, including information concerning his wife, registered partner or other life companion, foster child and relatives by blood or marriage up to the second degree'.

320. 'Such transactions shall be published in the annual report, together with a statement of the conflict of interest and a declaration that best practice provisions [II.3.2 to II.3.4 inclusive/ III.6.1 to III.6.3 inclusive] have been complied with'.

321. Apart from the principles and best practice provisions discussed, The Dutch Corporate Governance Code also stipulates in best practice provision III.6.4:

'All transactions between the company and legal or natural persons who hold at least ten percent of the shares in the company shall be agreed on terms that are customary in the sector concerned. Decisions to enter into transactions in which there are conflicts of interest with such persons that are of material significance to the company and/or to such persons require the approval of the supervisory board. Such transactions shall be published in the annual report, together with a declaration that best practice provision III.6.4 has been observed'.

companion, foster child or relative by blood or marriage up to the second degree.

3.   Ownership of Securities

[111] Under best practice provisions II.2.6 and III.7.3 of The Dutch Corporate Governance Code the supervisory board shall draw up 'regulations' concerning 'ownership of and transactions in securities' by executive directors and non-executive directors respectively for securities 'other than securities issued by their "own" company'. These regulations shall be posted on the company's website. Both best practice provisions also state that executive and non-executive directors 'shall give periodic notice, but in any event at least once a quarter, of any changes in [their] holding of securities in Dutch listed companies to the compliance officer or, if the company has not appointed a compliance officer, to the chairman of the supervisory board'.[322] In the amended version of the Dutch Corporate Governance Code these best practice provisions are replaced by an addition to best practice provision III.6.5: 'The company shall draw up regulations governing ownership of and transactions in securities by management or supervisory board members, other than securities issued by their "own" company'.

4.   Personal Loans

[112] In accordance with best practice provisions II.2.8 and III.7.4 of The Dutch Corporate Governance Code,[323] a listed corporation shall grant its executive directors and non-executive directors respectively 'any personal loans, guarantees or the like', only 'in the normal course of business' and 'after approval of the supervisory board'.[324] As concerns loans et cetera granted to executive directors best practice provision II.2.8 formulates as an additional requirement that granting shall only take place 'on terms applicable to the personnel as a whole'.

5.   Whistleblower Arrangements[325]

[113] In accordance with best practice provision II.1.6 of The Dutch Corporate Governance Code the management board shall draw up a 'whistleblower

---

322. However, an executive or non-executive director 'who invests exclusively in listed investment funds or who has transferred the discretionary management of his securities portfolio to an independent third party by means of a written mandate agreement is exempted from compliance with this last provision'.
323. Best practice provisions II.2.9 and III.7.3 in the amended version of The Dutch Corporate Governance Code.
324. And, should a personal loan have been granted, it shall not be remitted.
325. F. Saelens & C. Galand, 'The Case of Whistleblowing Schemes in the European Union', *European Company Law* (2006), 170-176.

arrangement' to 'ensure that employees have the possibility of reporting alleged irregularities of a general, operational and financial nature in the company to the chairman of the management board or to an official designated by him, without jeopardising their legal position'.[326] Because of its relevance to a large number of persons, the whistleblower arrangement 'shall in any event be posted on the company's website'.

II.   CASE STUDIES

[114] In accordance with principles II.3 and III.6 of The Dutch Corporate Governance Code executive directors and non-executive directors shall avoid all situations where there is '[a]ny [complex] of interest or apparent [complex] of interest between the company and [the director]'. The following best practice provisions II.3.2-II.3.4 (on executive directors) and III.6.1-III.6.3 and III.6.5 (on non-executive directors) are concerned with the way in which the decision-making process in relation to situations where there is a concrete conflict of interests between an executive director or a non-executive director and the corporation should be structured. As concerns the executive directors an additional issue may arise out of the fact the in accordance with Article 2:130 of the Dutch Civil Code both the management board (section 1) and each executive director (section 2) have the power to represent the corporation. The issue of representation of the corporation in case of a conflict of interests is not dealt with in The Dutch Corporate Governance but in the Dutch Civil Code. Under Article 2:146 '[u]nless provided otherwise in the articles of association, in all cases where there is a conflict of interest between the corporation and one or more executive directors, the corporation shall be represented by non-executive directors. The general meeting of shareholders may always designate one or more other persons to represent the corporation'. Article 2:146, and Article 2:256 that holds the same provisions for private limited companies, have over the years led to several judgments of the High Court. Among these are the judgments in the legal proceedings concerning BHV Bouwhout BV and BHV Olie BV, and Bruil-Arnhem Beheer BV.

A.   Introduction to the BHV Case

[115] BHV Holding BV ('BHV Holding') was the sole shareholder and only executive director of BHV Duhout BV ('BHV Duhout'), BHV Bouwhout BV ('BHV Bouwhout') and BHV Olie BV ('BHV Olie'). All four companies had

---

326. Best practice provision II.1.7 in the amended version of The Dutch Corporate Governance Code; under the whistleblower arrangement '[a]lleged irregularities concerning the functioning of management board members shall be reported to the chairman of the supervisory board'.

entered into a credit arrangement with ABN AMRO Bank NV ('ABN AMRO'). Under the terms of this credit arrangement, the companies were jointly and severally liable to ABN AMRO for the amount of the obligations incurred by any and all of them under the arrangement. When entering into the arrangement BHV Duhout, BHV Bouwhout and BHV Olie had been represented by their sole executive director, BHV Holding. All four companies were granted suspension of payment by the court in 2000 and were declared bankrupt in 2001. At the time the court declared the companies bankrupt the bank accounts of BHV Holding and BHV Duhout had a deficit but the bank accounts of BHV Bouwhout and BHV Olie had a credit balance. ABN AMRO used the credit balance on the bank accounts of BHV Bouwhout and BHV Olie as repayment of the debts under the credit arrangement. J.B. Dijkema ('Dijkema'), who was appointed as liquidator by the court after the court had declared the companies bankrupt, objected to this way in which ABN AMRO debited the bank accounts of BHV Bouwhout and BHV Olie and filed an action against ABN AMRO. In the opinion of Dijkema, neither BHV Bouwhout nor BHV Olie was bound by the credit arrangement. Dijkema argued that this was the case because when entering into the arrangement BHV Bouwhout and BHV Olie had been not been properly represented by BHV Holding in view of the conflict of interests between BHV Holding as executive director and these companies. After all, BHV Holding had represented BHV Bouwhout and BHV Olie in a situation where it was in her interest, as parent company of the group, that all subsidiary companies entered into the credit arrangement. Dijkema argued furthermore that neither the general meeting of shareholders of BHV Bouwhout nor the general meeting of shareholders of BHV Olie had explicitly designated BHV Holding to represent them in respect of the transaction concerning the credit arrangement. Both the court of first instance and the court of appeals found for Dijkema. ABN AMRO lodged an appeal with the High Court, but the High Court – ruling that the conflict of interests doctrine did apply in this case – affirmed the judgment of the court of appeals.[327]

B.   SCHEDULE 6: THE BHV CASE

[116] In the BHV case the (argued) conflict of interests between BHV Bouwhout BV and BHV Holding BV and between BHV Olie BV and BHV Holding BV led to legal proceedings between (the liquidator of both) BHV Bouwhout BV and BHV Olie BV and ABN AMRO Bank NV.

---

327. High Court 14 July 2006, JOR 2006, 179 (*BHV*), translation of considerations of the court by the author.

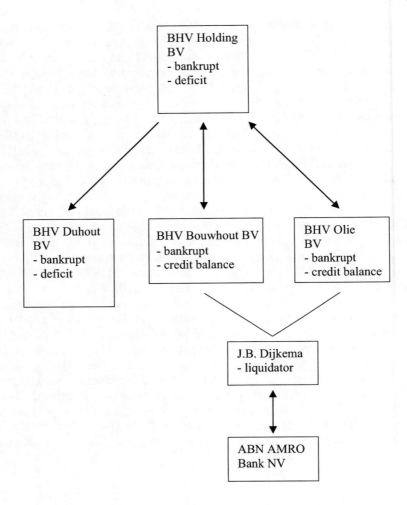

C.   THE JUDGMENT OF THE HIGH COURT

[117] The High Court considered in general terms:

> A well-balanced appraisal of the interest of the company as protected by Article
> 2:256 of the Dutch Civil Code and the legal certainty that must prevail in
> commercial transactions leads to the conclusion that the company can in respect
> of third parties argue that it was not properly represented if the fact that there
> was a conflict of interests between the company and the executive director(s)
> involved was at the time of the transaction either known to the third party or
> should have been known to the third party [. . .]. It follows from the latter that a
> third party, who enters into a transaction with the company and has at that time

reasons to assume that there may be such a conflict of interests, can reasonably be expected to investigate the possibility of improper representation by the executive director of the company. It depends on the concrete circumstances of the case how that investigation should take place and how far-reaching it should be, but that investigation shall in any event be directed at taking away any reasonable doubt as to the existence of a conflict of interests as well as to the question whether the measures were taken that are appropriate in such a case.

The reference by the High Court to 'the question whether the measures were taken that are appropriate in such a case' could be interpreted as the necessity to investigate if the improper representation was undone by the fact that the general meeting of shareholders of the company had designated the executive director to represent the company in respect of the transaction. In this respect the High Court underlined that a decision by the general meeting of shareholders to designate someone to represent the company must be explicit. Therefore, a third party may not infer from the fact that the executive director is also the sole shareholder of the company (the executive director and the sole shareholder being one and the same person) that this person in her capacity as sole shareholder designated herself in her other capacity of executive director to represent the company. The High Court considered that:

> in case of a conflict of interests an explicit decision of the shareholders is required to designate someone to represent the company [...]. The dual capacity of the executive director [...] is not sufficient.

D.   INTRODUCTION TO THE BRUIL CASE

[118] In 1984 Bruil-Arnhem Beheer BV ('Bruil-Arnhem') entered into a contract with Bruil-Kombex-Arnhem BV (Bruil-Kombex'). Bruil-Arnhem sold some industrial grounds to Bruil-Kombex. Also, Bruil-Arnhem allowed Bruil-Kombex an option to have the first right to buy remaining the industrial grounds in case Bruil-Arnhem would want to sell these. With regard to this transaction, both Bruil-Arnhem and Bruil-Kombex were represented by G.B. Bruil ('Bruil'). Bruil was executive director of both companies, shareholder of Bruil-Arnhem and the sole shareholder of Bruil-Kombex. In 1994 all shareholders of Bruil-Arnhem, including Bruil, sold their shares. In 1998 Bruil-Arnhem sold some of the remaining industrial grounds to another party. Bruil-Kombex objected to this because under the contract of 1984 it had the option to buy these grounds. Bruil-Arnhem also indicated that it would not sell what remained of the industrial grounds to Bruil-Kombex. These events prompted Bruil-Kombex to file an action against Bruil-Arnhem. In these proceedings Bruil-Arnhem argued that she was not bound by the option clause in the contract that would force her to sell the remaining industrial grounds to Bruil-Kombex because when the transaction was concluded she had not been properly represented. In her opinion Bruil could not have represented Bruil-Arnhem because of a conflict of interests between Bruil as executive director and Bruil-Arnhem. After all, Bruil

was also involved in Bruil-Kombex that was the other contracting party to the transaction. The court of appeals found for Bruil-Arnhem. Bruil-Kombex lodged an appeal with the High Court. The High Court – ruling that the conflict of interests doctrine did not apply in this case – set aside the judgment of the court of appeals.[328]

E.   SCHEDULE 7: THE BRUIL CASE

[119] In the Bruil case the (argued) conflict of interests between Bruil-Arnhem Beheer BV and G.B. Bruil played a role in legal proceedings between Bruil-Kombex-Arnhem BV and Bruil-Arnhem Beheer BV.

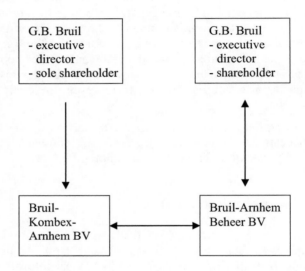

F.   THE JUDGMENT OF THE HIGH COURT

[120] The High Court considered in general terms:

The purpose of Article 2:256 of the Dutch Civil Code is to prevent that the executive director is led (in particular) by her personal interest instead of (solely) by the interest of the company she must serve [. . .]. The purpose if this provision is first and foremost to protect the interest of the company by denying the executive director the power to represent the company if she must be deemed to be unable to safeguard the interest of the company and its affiliated enterprise – because of the existence of a personal interest or because

---

328. High Court 29 June 2007, JOR 2007, 169 (*Bruil*), translation of considerations of the court by the author.

of her involvement with other interests that do not run parallel with the interest of the company – in a way that may be expected of an honest and unbiased executive director.

In respect of the case under consideration the High Court stated that a conflict of interests can 'also occur when the executive director (who is also the sole share-holder) entered into a transaction with another company in which she is also closely involved': 'Also when the capacities of executive director and shareholder in both companies that enter into the transaction come together in one person, the interests of these companies do not necessarily run parallel'. But then the High Court added:

> Especially in cases where a natural person acts in the combined capacity of executive director and shareholder of several companies that form a group, there will not easily be a conflict of interests within the meaning of Article 2:256, because of the intention that – by bringing together the (ultimate) authority in one person – the weighing of the interests of all group companies is concentrated in one person.

Thus, the existence of a conflict of interests depends on 'the concrete circumstances of the case': the conflict of interests doctrine applies only:

> if a personal interest of the executive director in the sense referred to above conflicted with the interest(s) of the company/companies and its (their) affiliated enterprise(s) as construed from circumstances (that are brought to the fore and are being substantiated) that may have influenced the decision making by the executive director involved to such a degree that [. . .] she could not have thought to be able to look after the interest(s) of the company/companies and its (their) affiliated enterprise(s) with the required measure of honesty and objectivity and should have refrained from the transaction.

G.   EVALUATION

[121] The decision of the High Court in *BHV* (as well as earlier decisions)[329] were read as implying that the High Court interpreted Articles 2:146 and 256 of the Dutch Civil Code in an abstract way,[330] meaning that the mere occurrence of a complex of interests between the corporation and an executive director gives rise to the conclusion that there also is a conflict of interests within the meaning of Articles 2:146 and 256.[331] This interpretation was reinforced by considerations like '[the] statutory regulation of conflicts of interests [. . .] is based on the thought that the chance that the executive director in her actions, that should geared to the interest of the company, gives preference to her personal interest, must be

---

329. E.g. High Court 22 March 1996, JOR 1996, 45 (*Mediasafe I*).
330. J. Winter, *Van de BV en de NV* (Deventer: Kluwer, 2006), at 217.
331. W.J.M. van Veen & T.H.M. van Wechem, 'Belangenverstrengeling in het vennootschapsrecht en bij opdracht', *Vermogensrechtelijke Analyses* (2007) issue 3, 43-55.

prevented' in *Joral*,[332] and '[Article] 2:256 does not apply solely if it is certain that the transaction at hand will result in damage' in *Duplicado*.[333] Articles 2:146 and 256 have been much criticized. In particular, these provisions were regarded as impraticable.[334] The reason for this is twofold: first the wide scope of the conflicts of interests doctrine resulting from the abstract interpretation by the High Court, and second that third parties cannot not rely on the supervisory board being competent to represent the corporation in case of a conflict of interests between the corporation and an executive director as they always needed to take into account the possibility that the general meeting of shareholders had designated other persons to represent the corporation. It would seem that the decision of the High Court in *Bruil* represents a shift in the way the High Court interprets Articles 2:146 and 256.[335] It follows from this decision that the existence of a conflict of interests between the corporation and an executive director in general depends on 'the concrete circumstances of the case', which means that the High Court has abandoned its abstract interpretation of these provisions. More specifically, the High Court identifies the situation 'where a natural person acts in the combined capacity of executive director and shareholder of several companies that form a group' where a conflict of interests is unlikely to occur.[336] It follows from the decision that there are more situations where the conflicts of interests doctrine does not apply. Although the decision of the High Court in *Bruil* meets the criticism raised against the earlier case law of the High Court, including *BHV*,[337] it is questionable whether this decision should be welcomed from the point of view of 'good' corporate governance. After all, it limits the number of cases in which corporate decision making in situations that involve conflicts of interests (however apparent) is outside the scope of power of the management board. Instead of abandoning its abstract interpretation of Articles 2:146 and 256, the High Court could also have provided lightening by ruling e.g. that the power of the general meeting of shareholders to designate other persons to represent the corporation is limited to situations where there is no supervisory board. In November 2008 the Dutch government presented a bill to Parliament that inter alia abolishes Articles 2:146 and 256 of the Dutch Civil Code altogether.[338]

---

332. High Court 3 May 2002, JOR 2002, 111 (*Joral*); cf. High Court 22 March 1996, JOR 1996, 45 (*Mediasafe I*).
333. High Court 9 July 2004, JOR 2004, 266 (*Duplicado*).
334. S.M. Bartman, 'De katalyserende werking van het tegenstrijdig belang', *WPNR* 6615 (2005), 237-243; 'M.J.G.C. Raaijmakers, ABN AMRO/Dijkema q.q.: tegenstrijdigheden rond tegenstrijdige belangen in een persoonsgebonden BV', *Ars Aequi* (2007), 148-154.
335. J.M. Blanco Fernández, 'Tegenstrijdig belang en de Hoge Raad', *Ondernemingsrecht* (2008), 416-422; but cf. on this issue L. Timmerman, 'Do Cases Make Bad Law', *Ondernemingsrecht* (2008), 373.
336. C.A. Schwarz, 'Tegenstrijdig belang in beweging: enige actuele ontwikkelingen in rechtspraak en wetgeving', *Tijdschrift voor Ondernemingsbestuur* (2008), 74-82.
337. Ph.A. Ledeboer, 'Tegenstrijdig belang: terug naar de kern!', *Onderneming en Financiering* (2008) issue 2, 64-86.
338. Wijziging van boek 2 van het Burgerlijk Wetboek in verband met de aanpassing van regels over bestuur en toezicht in naamloze en besloten vennootschappen, bill 31 763.

Chapter 9
Public Takeover Bids

I.   THE IMPLEMENTATION OF THE EC DIRECTIVE ON
                     TAKEOVER BIDS IN THE NETHERLANDS

[122] On 21 April 2004 the European Parliament and the Council of the European Union adopted directive 2004/25/EC on takeover bids.[339] This directive has been implemented in the Netherlands mainly in Book 2 of the Dutch Civil Code and in the Financial Supervision Act, but also in secondary legislation. The main implementing provisions in Book 2 of the Dutch Civil Code are Articles 2:359a through 359d and the main implementing provisions in the Financial Supervision Act are Articles 5:70 through 83.[340] The main implementing provisions in the secondary legislation are the Decree of 5 April 2006 implementing Article 10 of Directive 2004/25/EC of the European Parliament and the Council of the European Union of 21 April 2004 on takeover bids ('Decree on Article 10 of the takeover directive'),[341] and the Decree of 12 September 2007 implementing Directive 2004/25/EC of the European Parliament and the Council of the European Union of 21 April 2004 on takeover bids as well as modernizing the rules concerning public takeover bids ('Decree on public takeover bids FSupA').[342] Part A of this chapter consists of the following paragraphs: *aims of the regulation of public takeover bids, defensive tactics in case of a hostile public takeover bid, the*

---

339.   'Directive 2004/25/EC of the European Parliament and of the Council of 21 April 2004 on Takeover Bids', OJEU 2004 L 142/12-23 (text with EEA relevance).
340.   Book 2 of the Dutch Civil Code, Title 8: Dispute resolution by compulsory transfer of shares or compulsory acquisition of shares, and the right of inquiry, Section 3: Public Offers; Financial Supervision Act, Part 5: Financial markets conduct supervision, Chapter 5.5: Rules on public offers in respect of securities.
341.   Staatsblad 2006, 191.
342.   Staatsblad 2007, 329. Z. Tali, 'Nieuwe regels voor openbare biedingen: het Besluit openbare biedingen Wft', *Ondernemingsrecht* (2008), 58-65.

mandatory public takeover bid, the process of public takeover bids, opted in and opted out corporations, and *opted out corporations and the mandatory public takeover bid.*

A.   AIMS OF THE REGULATION OF PUBLIC TAKEOVER BIDS

[123] The general aims of the directive on takeover bids are 'to protect the interests of holders of the securities of companies governed by the law of a Member State when those companies are the subject of takeover bids or of changes of control',[343] and 'to create Community-wide clarity and transparency in respect of legal issues to be settled in the event of takeover bids and to prevent patterns of corporate restructuring within the Community from being distorted by arbitrary differences in governance and management cultures'.[344] To achieve these aims, the directive provides for 'measures coordinating the [national rules], relating to takeover bids for the securities of companies [. . .], where all or some of those securities are admitted to trading on a regulated market' (Article 1 section 1). In short, the directive regulates public takeover bids for the securities of listed corporations. For the purposes of applying the directive, 'securities' are 'transferable securities carrying voting rights in a company' (Article 2 section 1, subsection e),[345] a '[public] takeover' bid is a 'public offer [. . .] made to the holders of the securities of a company to acquire all or some of those securities' (Article 2 section 1, subsection a),[346] the 'offeror' is 'any natural or legal person [. . .] making a bid' (Article 2 section 1, subsection c), and the 'offeree company' is 'a company, the securities of which are the subject of a bid' (Article 2 section 1, subsection b). There are several types of public takeover bids. Takeover bids may be friendly or hostile. A friendly bid is a public takeover bid that is recommended by the unitary or dual board of the offeree company, whereas a hostile takeover bid is not recommended by the unitary or dual board of the offeree company. Takeover bids may be voluntary or mandatory. A voluntary bid is a public takeover bid that the offeror makes of her own free will, whereas a mandatory bid is a public takeover bid that the offeror makes because she is required to do so by law. The concrete aims of regulation of all public takeover bids are 'to ensure market transparency and integrity for the securities of the offeree company, of the offeror or of any other company affected by the bid, in particular in order to prevent the publication or dissemination of false or misleading information'.[347] To achieve these aims, public takeover bids are to a large extent structured around 'the disclosure of [. . .] information and documents' as well as around time periods that must be adhered

---

343.   Preamble of the directive on takeover bids, second recital.
344.   Preamble of the directive on takeover bids, third recital.
345.   Principally shares.
346.   Hence a 'bid' may also be called an 'offer'. Article 5 section 2 of the directive on takeover bids
        uses the phrase 'to launch a bid'.
347.   Article 8 section 1 of the directive on takeover bids.

to.[348] The information and documents that must be disclosed include the decision to make a bid and the offer document[349] (Article 6 of the directive on takeover bids).[350]

B.   DEFENSIVE TACTICS IN CASE OF A HOSTILE PUBLIC TAKEOVER BID

[124] Both voluntary and mandatory public takeover bids may be friendly (recommended by the unitary or dual board of the offeree company) or hostile (not recommended by the unitary or dual board of the offeree company). Especially an 'unsolicited' takeover bid may be considered hostile. A corporation that is the object of a public takeover bid (either voluntary or mandatory) may employ defensive tactics against the bid. These defensive tactics may be divided into pre-bid defensive tactics and post-bid defensive tactics.[351] Pre-bid defensive tactics are structural arrangements (defensive 'constructions') that exist independent of the actual occurrence of a public takeover bid. Post-bid defensive tactics are ad hoc arrangements (defensive 'measures') that are being used when a public takeover bid is immanent or when a public takeover bid has been announced or made. An example of a pre-bid defensive tactic is making use of depository receipts. An example of a post-bid defensive tactic is the issuing of preference shares.

1.   Depository Receipts

[125] When thinking about listed corporations, a listed corporation is usually understood as a corporation whose shares are listed. This however, need not be the case. Instead of the shares of the corporation being listed, depository receipts may be listed. In that case the shares of the corporation are being held by an intermediary. This intermediary is the shareholder that issues to the ultimate investors another kind of securities. These securities are the so-called depository receipts. As part of this arrangement the intermediary is entitled to exercise the voting rights on the shares (for she is the shareholder), but the investors are entitled to receive the dividends handed out by the corporation (because they are the investors of capital). The intermediary functions as a voting trust.[352] Depository receipts may be issued with or without the cooperation of the corporation. When

---

348. Article 8 section 2 of the directive on takeover bids.
349. Also: offer memorandum.
350. The Decree on public takeover bids FSupA uses the phrases *openbaar maken* (make public), that refers to factual situations, *een openbare mededeling doen* (disclose by means of a public announcement), that refers to disclosure requirements under the decree, and *aankondigen door middel van een openbare mededeling* (announce by means of a public statement), that refers to the disclosure requirement in relation to an upcoming public takeover bid under the decree.
351. C. de Groot, *Bescherming en breakthrough bij overname* (Amsterdam: Rozenberg Publishers, 2004), at 5-6.
352. In Dutch: 'administratiekantoor'.

the depository receipts are issued with the cooperation of the corporation, making use of depository receipts is a defensive tactic as the corporation will regard the voting trust as a trusted party.[353]

Under Article 2:118a section 1 of the Dutch Civil Code a holder of listed depository receipts that were issued with the cooperation of the corporation may ask the voting trust that she, as opposed to the voting trust, be entitled to vote on the shares. The voting trust has limited possibilities to deny or restrict such a request or recall the entitlement to vote once it has been given. In accordance with Article 2:118a section 2 the trust can do so in three cases: where a hostile public takeover bid is immanent, has been announced or has been made (subsection a), where a holder of depository receipts or several holders of depository receipts acting in concert hold 25% or more of the issued share capital of the corporation (subsection b), and where in the opinion of the voting trust exercising of voting rights by the holder of depository receipts would seriously contravene the interest of the corporation and its affiliated enterprise (subsection c).[354]

2.   Preference Shares

[126] A corporation may try to counterbalance a hostile takeover bid that is immanent or has been announced or made by issuing shares to a trusted party. Such a trusted part is a so-called white knight. The exercise of voting rights in the general meeting of shareholders by the white knight is intended to neutralize the voting power of the offeror. Although issuing common shares is a possibility, issuing preference shares is a better possibility as preference shares have a specific characteristic. In case common shares are issued, the existing shareholders (possibly including the offeror) enjoy pre-emption rights on the issued shares (relative to the amount of the shares they already hold). But in case preference shares are issued, the existing shareholders (possibly including the offeror) do not enjoy preemption rights on the issued preference shares.[355]

C.   THE MANDATORY PUBLIC TAKEOVER BID

[127] In accordance with Article 5 section 1 of the directive on takeover bids '[w]here a natural or legal person [who], as a result of his/her own acquisition

---

353. On depository receipts: C.A. Schwarz, 'Certificering als beschermingsconstructie: bruikbaarheid in een veranderend tijdsgewricht', *Tijdschrift voor Ondernemingsbestuur* (2004), 220-225; D.F.M.M. Zaman, 'Certificering en modernisering van het ondernemingsrecht- en vennootschapsrecht', *Tijdschrift voor Ondernemingsbestuur* (2004), 215-219.

354. J.G.C.M. Galle, 'Certificering van aandelen: de actuele stand van zaken', *Tijdschrift voor Ondernemingsbestuur* (2005), 135-140.

355. H.J.M.N. Honée, 'Preferente aandelen: financiering of bescherming van de vennootschap?', in P.C. van den Hoek et al., *Corporate governance voor juristen* (Deventer, Kluwer, 1998), 29-41.

or the acquisition by persons acting in concert with him/her, holds securities of a company [. . .] which, added to any existing holdings of those securities of his/hers and the holdings of those securities of persons acting in concert with him/her, directly or indirectly give him/her a specified percentage of voting rights in that company, giving him/her control of that company, [. . .] such a person is required to make a [mandatory] bid'. A mandatory public takeover bid is 'a means of protecting the minority shareholders of that company' and 'shall be addressed at the earliest opportunity to all the holders of those securities for all their holdings at [an] equitable price'. The obligation to make a mandatory bid does not apply '[w]here control has been acquired following a voluntary bid' (Article 5 section 2). Under Article 5 section 3 '[t]he percentage of voting rights which confers control [. . .] and the method of its calculation shall be determined by the rules of the [state] in which the company has its registered office'. The Dutch implementing provisions in the Financial Supervision Act refer to the phrase 'dominant control'. Article 1:1 defines dominant control as 'the ability to exercise at least 30 percent of the voting rights in a general meeting of shareholders of a corporation'. In accordance with Article 5:70 section 1 any person who alone or together with persons acting in concert, acquires dominant control in a listed corporation established in the Netherlands, shall make a public takeover bid for all the listed shares of the corporation.[356] The person who comes to possess 30 percent of the voting rights transgresses the 'bidding threshold'. Until she makes the mandatory public takeover bid, she may be referred as the 'prospective offeror'.[357]

Both Articles 5:71 and 72 of the Financial Supervision Act contain exceptions to the obligation to make a mandatory bid. Under Article 5:71 section 1 the obligation to make a mandatory bid shall not apply inter alia:

- in case a prospective offeror already had dominant control at the time the shares of the corporation were listed for the first time (subsection i),[358] and in case a prospective offeror acquired dominant control:
- as a result of a voluntary bid for all the shares of the corporation (subsection b);[359]
- as part of a transfer of participations within a corporate group (subsection e);
- in a corporation that has been granted suspension of payment by the court or has been declared bankrupt by the court (subsection f);
- through hereditary succession (subsection g); and
- as a result of entering into a marriage or registered partnership, provided that the person she married or entered into the registered partnership with already had dominant control (subsection k).

Under Article 5:72 section 1 the obligation to make a mandatory bid shall not apply if a prospective offeror – upon acquiring dominant control – loses her dominant

---

356. As well as for all the listed depository receipts that were issued with the cooperation of the corporation.
357. H.M. de Mol van Otterloo, 'Het verplicht bod', *Ondernemingsrecht* (2006), 206-210.
358. Or the depository receipts that were issued with the cooperation of the corporation.
359. Or for all the depository receipts that were issued with the cooperation of the corporation.

control within a period of thirty days. This is the so-called pardon period. One the one hand, a prospective offeror may ask the Chamber of Business Affairs to extend the pardon period with a maximum of sixty days (Article 5:72 section 2), but on the other hand Article 5:72 section 1 does not apply to a prospective offeror who exercised her voting rights during the pardon period (Article 5:72 section 1, subsection b).

When a prospective offeror does not make a mandatory public takeover bid, inter alia the offeree company and any shareholder of the offeree company may file an application with the Chamber of Business Affairs and ask it to order the prospective offeror to make the mandatory bid (Article 5:73 section 1 of the Financial Supervision Act).[360] The applicants may also ask the Chamber of Business Affairs to order measures (Article 5:73 section 2) as well as interim measures (Article 5:73 section 4). The measures mentioned in Article 5:73 section 2 are (a) suspension of the exercise of voting rights of the prospective offeror for a period to be determined by the court, (b) temporary exclusion of the prospective offeror from attending the general meeting of shareholders, (c) temporary transfers of shares of the prospective bidder to a trustee, and (d) suspension or annulment of decisions of the general meeting of shareholders of the offeree company.

D.   THE PROCESS OF PUBLIC TAKEOVER BIDS

[128] Article 6 of the directive on takeover bids deals with '[i]nformation concerning bids'. The *first* of the disclosure requirements that this provision details is 'a decision to make a bid', that must be disclosed 'without delay' (section 1). In case of a friendly voluntary bid, in accordance with Article 5 section 1 of the Decree on public takeover bids FSupA, both the offeror and the offeree company shall announce by means of a public statement the upcoming public takeover bid no later than the offeror and the offeree company have reached an understanding on the bid that is to be made, even if that understanding is only conditional. In case of a hostile voluntary bid, in accordance with Article 5 section 2 of the decree, the upcoming public voluntary takeover bid shall be deemed to be announced by means of a public statement when the offeror has made public concrete information on the contents of the upcoming public takeover bid.

In case of a mandatory bid, under Article 5:70 section 1 of the Financial Supervision Act a (prospective) offeror shall announce the mandatory public takeover bid immediately following the pardon period referred to in Article 5:72 section 1. In accordance with Article 5 section 3 of the Decree on public takeover bids FSupA, a mandatory bid shall be deemed to be announced by means of a public statement inter alia when the offeror made an announcement in conformity with Article 5:70 section 1 (subsection a), or when a decision of the Chamber of

---

360. Or any holder of the depository receipts that were issued with the cooperation of the corporation.

Business Affairs on the basis of Article 5:73 section 1 to order the prospective offeror to make the mandatory bid has become irrevocable (subsection b).

The *second* of the disclosure requirements that Article 6 of the directive on takeover bids details is the 'offer document', that must be disclosed 'in good time' (section 2, paragraph 1). In accordance with Article 5:74 section 1 of the Financial Supervision Act an offeror is prohibited from making a public takeover bid for the securities of a corporation that are admitted to trading on a regulated market in the Netherlands unless the offeror makes publicly available an offer document that was approved by the Netherlands Authority for the Financial Markets.[361] In case of a voluntary bid (either friendly or hostile), in accordance with Article 7 section 1 of the Decree on public takeover bids FSupA, the offeror shall – within a period of time of four weeks following the announcement by means of a public statement of the upcoming public takeover bid – disclose by means of a public announcement either that she will apply for approval of the offer document by the Netherlands Authority for the Financial Markets or does not intend to apply for approval. When the offeror discloses that she will apply for approval of the offer document she shall state the period of time within which she will do so; this period of time shall be twelve weeks at most (starting from the announcement by means of a public statement of the upcoming public takeover bid).[362]

In case of a mandatory bid, in accordance with Article 7 section 2 of the Decree on public takeover bids FSupA, the offeror shall – within a period of time of four weeks following the announcement by means of a public statement of the upcoming public takeover bid – disclose by means of a public announcement that she will apply for approval of the offer document by the Netherlands Authority for the Financial Markets. The offeror shall state the period of time within which she will do so; this period of time shall be twelve weeks at most (starting from the announcement by means of a public statement of the upcoming public takeover bid).[363]

The Netherlands Authority for the Financial Markets shall decide on the approval of the offer document within a period of time of ten business days starting from the receipt of the application for approval of the offer document (Article 5:77 section 1 of the Financial Supervision Act). In making its decision, the authority shall consider whether the offer document contains all information that a reasonably informed and careful person who is forming an opinion on the public takeover bid would need in order to reach a responsible judgment (Article 8 section 1 of the Decree on public takeover bids FSupA). When the authority makes it known to the offeror that it approves the offer document, the offeror shall within six business days either make the public takeover bid by making the offer document publicly available or disclose by means of a public announcement that she will not make the bid (Article 5:78 of the Financial Supervision Act).

---

361. Or in some cases approved by the designated competent authority of another state.
362. Article 7 section 3 of the Decree on public takeover bids FSupA.
363. Article 7 section 3 of the Decree on public takeover bids FSupA.

The offeror who makes a public takeover bid shall set an acceptance period (Article 14 section 1 of the Decree on public takeover bids FSupA). The acceptance period shall begin no sooner than on the first business day following the day on which the offeror made the bid (Article 14 section 2). The acceptance period shall have both a minimum duration and a maximum duration.[364] The maximum duration of the acceptance period is ten weeks (Article 14 section 5). However, the offeror has the opportunity to once extend the original acceptance period with at least two and at most ten weeks (Article 15 section 1). The offeror who makes a public takeover bid shall also state any conditions to which the bid is subject (Article 12 section 1). She may not include offer conditions whose fulfillment depends on her will (Article 12 section 2).

The offeror may not make a mandatory public takeover bid subject to conditions (Article 24 of the Decree on public takeover bids FSupA).

Ultimately on the third business day following the acceptance closing date the offeror shall disclose by means of a public announcement whether or not she declares the bid unconditional (Article 16 s 1 of the Decree on public takeover bids FSupA).[365] When the offeror declares the bid unconditional she shall state the total value, the number and the percentage of the shares that were tendered to her pursuant to the public takeover bid as well as the total number and the percentage of the shares that she will hold in the offeree company after the tendered shares are delivered to her (Article 16 section 2).[366]

The (Dutch) Monitoring Committee Corporate Governance Code proposed in its Report on the Evaluation and Updating of the Dutch Corporate Governance Code that the code should be supplemented with a chapter containing a principle and best practice provisions relating to public takeover bids.[367] The proposed text read:

VI. The position of the management board and the supervisory board in the case of takeovers

Principle VI Takeover bid for shares in the company
    In the event of any (proposed) takeover bid for shares in the company the management board and the supervisory board shall carefully weigh all the interests involved. The management board shall be guided in its actions exclusively by the interest of the company and its affiliated enterprise. The supervisory board shall be closely involved in the takeover process.

---

364. Depending on the nature of the bid, the minimum duration is either two weeks or four weeks (Article 14 sections 3 and 4 of the Decree on public takeover bids FSupA).
365. The Dutch phrase *gestanddoening van het bod* is here translated as *declaring the bid unconditional*.
366. Delivering the shares takes place on the so-called settlement date.
367. Corporate Governance Code Monitoring Committee, 'Report on the Evaluation and Updating of the Dutch Corporate Governance Code', at 88-89, <www.commissiecorporategovernance.nl> information in English.

VI.1 The management board and the supervisory board shall discuss the possibility of a takeover bid being made for the shares of the company and shall consider how the supervisory board members should guide a takeover process.

VI.2 If one or more management board members of the company conduct consultations about a takeover bid (proposed or otherwise) with a potential bidder, the supervisory board shall be immediately informed of this.

VI.3 The supervisory board shall ensure that the negotiating process with a bidder or potential bidder proceeds properly. This applies in particular if one or more management board members have a considerable personal (financial) interest in the takeover or potential takeover.

VI.4 If the company arranges for a fairness opinion to be produced in the context of a takeover bid, the person engaged to produce this opinion shall be an expert who has no (financial) interest in the success or failure of the takeover. The management board shall submit the expert's engagement to the supervisory board for approval.

VI.5 In the position taken by the management board on the takeover bid, as referred to in the Public Bids Decree (*Besluit openbare biedingen*),[368] the management board shall outline the consequences of the success of the bid for the company's stakeholders, including the shareholders, employees and creditors.

VI.6 As soon as the management board of a company in respect of which a takeover bid has been announced or issued receives a request from a third party who is a competing bidder (or potentially competing bidder) to inspect the particulars of the company in the same way as the bidder, it shall immediately discuss the request with the supervisory board.

These ideas were not followed in the amended version of The Dutch Corporate Governance Code, that states in best practice provsions II.1.10 and II.1.11:

II.1.10 If a takeover bid for the company's shares or for the depositary receipts for the company's shares is being prepared, the management board shall ensure that the supervisory board is closely involved in the takeover process in good time.

II.1.11 If the management board of a company for which a takeover bid has been announced or made receives a request from a competing bidder to inspect the company's records, the management board shall discuss this request with the supervisory board without delay.

E.   Opted In and Opted Out Corporations

[129] Articles 9, 11 and 12 of the directive on takeover bids hold provisions on a number of defensive tactics that listed corporations may employ. In accordance

---

368.   The Decree on public takeover bids FSupA.

with Article 12 section 1 the substantive provisions of Articles 9 and 11 are optional in the sense that a state has the choice to either make Articles 9 and 11 obligatory for corporations established in that state or 'may reserve the right not to require companies [. . .] to apply [those provisions]'. In the latter case however, a state 'shall nevertheless grant companies [. . .] the option, which shall be reversible, of applying [those provisions]' (Article 12 section 2). The implementing provisions in the Netherlands make use of the possibility laid down in Article 12 section 1 in connection with Article 12 section 2. Thus, a listed corporation established in the Netherlands may by its own choice either be an opted out corporation that reserves the right to employ defensive tactics as referred to in the directive or an opted in corporation that has relinquished the right to employ defensive tactics as referred to in the directive. The relevant provisions are Articles 2:359a and 359b of the Dutch Civil Code. In accordance with Article 2:359a of the Dutch Civil Code Article 2:359b shall apply to listed corporations established in the Netherlands (meaning that all or part of the shares of the corporation are listed).[369] In principle, a listed corporation is opted out. However, in accordance with Article 2:359b the articles of association of a listed corporation may provide that it is an opted in corporation to the effect that it takes on the so-called anti-frustration and breakthrough rules.[370] These rules are laid down in Article 2:359b sections 1 and 2:

First, under Article 2:359 section 1 – following the announcement by means of a public statement of an upcoming (voluntary or mandatory) public takeover bid – the offeree company shall not engage in any operation that could frustrate the bid unless the general meeting of shareholders approves the operation beforehand (subsection a), and in addition shall not execute decisions taken before that announcement that were not yet fully implemented and could frustrate the bid unless the general meeting of shareholders approves those decisions (subsection b). Article 2:359 section 1, subsection a and b are anti-frustration rules. Article 2:359b section 1, subsection a shall apply until the moment of disclosure by means of a public announcement whether or not the offeror declares the offer unconditional, or the bid has lapsed. This provision does not stand of the way of seeking an alternative bid. Article 2:359b section 1, subsection b too shall – probably – apply until the moment of disclosure by means of a public announcement whether or not the offeror declares the offer unconditional, or the bid has lapsed. This provision does not stand in the way of the corporation executing decisions that are part of the normal operation of business, unless such a decision could frustrate the bid.

Under Article 2:359 section 1 the following provisions shall apply to the decision making in the general meeting of shareholders of the offeree company

---

369. Or of the depository receipts that were issued with the cooperation of the corporation.
370. S.M. Bartman, 'Analysis and Consequences of the EC Directive on Takeover Bids', *European Company Law* (2004), 5-8; M.J. van Ginneken, 'Vijandige overnames en het vennootschappelijk belang', *Ondernemingsrecht* (2006), 526-534; M.P. Nieuwe Weme & G. van Solinge, 'Beschermingsmaatregelen tegen vijandige biedingen: beperkingen en nieuwe mogelijkheden', *Ondernemingsrecht* (2006), 211-220; C. de Groot, *Parlementaire geschiedenis het openbaar overnamebod* (Zutphen: Uitgeverij Paris, 2007).

that decides on approving an operation or decision within the meaning of Article 2:359 section 1 subsections a or b: restrictions on the exercise of voting rights shall not be applicable (subsection d) and each share shall carry one vote (subsection e). Article 2:359 section 1, subsections d and e are breakthrough rules that support the anti-frustration rules of Article 2:359 section 1, subsections a and b. Article 2:359 section 1, subsection d shall apply to restrictions on the exercise of voting rights that are laid down in the articles of association of the offeree company, in contracts concluded between the offeree company and shareholders,[371] and in contracts concluded among shareholders.[372] Article 2:359 section 1, subsection e shall apply irrespective of the nominal value shares may have.

Second, under Article 2:359 section 1 – following the announcement by means of a public statement of an upcoming (voluntary or mandatory) public takeover bid – restrictions on the transfer of shares[373] shall not be applicable vis-à-vis the offeror in relation to shares[374] tendered to her during the acceptance period of the bid (subsection c). Article 2:359 section 1, subsection c is a breakthrough rule in its own right. This provision shall apply to restrictions that are laid down in the articles of association of the offeree company, in contracts concluded between the offeree company and shareholders,[375] and in contracts concluded among shareholders.[376]

Third, under Article 2:359 section 2 an offeror who as a result of a public takeover bid holds at east 75% of the issued capital of the offeree company is allowed to convene a general meeting of shareholders of the offeree company within a short period of time after the acceptance closing date. In this general meeting a number of provisions shall apply to the decision making. Restrictions on the exercise of voting rights shall not be applicable (in the way outlined with regard to Article 2:359 section 1, subsection d). Each share shall carry one vote (in the way outlined with regard to Article 2:359 section 1, subsection e). Special rights that shareholders may have in accordance with the articles of association concerning appointment or dismissal of executive directors and non-executive directors shall not be applicable. Article 2:359 section 2 too is a breakthrough rule in its own right.

F. OPTED OUT CORPORATIONS AND THE MANDATORY PUBLIC TAKEOVER BID

[130] When a corporation is opted out, it reserves the rights to employ defensive tactics. These defensive tactics may include making use of depository receipts and

---

371. Or holders of depository receipts that were issued with the cooperation of the corporation.
372. Or holders of depository receipts that were issued with the cooperation of the corporation.
373. And on the transfer of depository receipts that were issued with the cooperation of the corporation.
374. Or depository receipts that were issued with the cooperation of the corporation.
375. Or holders of depository receipts that were issued with the cooperation of the corporation.
376. Or holders of depository receipts that were issued with the cooperation of the corporation.

the issuing of preference shares. Using depository receipts is a structural arrangement, and issuing preference shares is an ad hoc arrangement that will in many
cases be employed following the announcement by means of a public statement of
an upcoming public takeover bid. But these defensive tactics would not be practical
solutions if the voting trust or the white knight would face the obligation to make a
mandatory public takeover bid. However, Article 5:71 of the Financial Supervision
Act – that contains exceptions to the obligation to make a mandatory public takeover bid – comes to the help of both the voting trust and the white knight. Under
Article 5:71 section 1, subsection d the obligation to make a mandatory bid shall
not apply to a legal person that is not affiliated with the offeree company that has
issued to investors depository receipts that were issued with the cooperation of
the offeree company. Under Article 5:71 section 1, subsection c the obligation to
make a mandatory bid shall not apply to a legal person that is not affiliated with
the offeree company that has as its object to promote the interests of the offeree
company and its affiliated enterprise and that starts holding shares following the
announcement by means of a public statement of an upcoming public takeover bid
for a period of two years at most for the protection of the offeree company.

II.   CASE STUDIES

A.   Introduction to the Stork Case

[131] The *Stork* case is another example of the way the Chamber of Business
Affairs and the High Court consider investors' rights and obligations. It is
concerned with the question to what extent shareholders are able to influence
policy lines set by the management board. This case was decided before the legislation to implement the directive on takeover bids in the Netherlands came into
force.

[132] Stork NV ('Stork') was a listed corporation established in the Netherlands. It
was the parent company of a multidivisional group that developed, manufactured
and sold industrial products and systems in five fields: aerospace, poultry and food
processing, technical services, printing and industrial components. The management board of Stork consisted of three persons, its supervisory board consisted of
five persons. Stork employed approximately 12.400 employees, of which around
9.000 were working in the Netherlands. Stork was subject to the 'mandatory organizational arrangement'. Centaurus Capital Limited ('Centaurus') and Paulson &
Co. Inc. ('Paulson') were investment funds that are described as hedge funds. In the
words of the Chamber of Business Affairs they 'attract money from (institutional)
investors and invest this money almost exclusively in listed securities, whilst they
hedge their market- and currency risks'.[377] Both Centaurus and Paulson had
invested in Stork since 2004, Centaurus through an associated fund and Paulson

---

377. Author's translation.

itself as well as through associated funds. From 2002 Stork had begun concentrating on core activities. In 2004 it sold its activities in the field of industrial components, in its annual report on 2005 it announced that it would in the future concentrate on aerospace, poultry and food processing and technical services, and there were ideas to concentrate on two rather than three activities. In December 2005 Paulson informed Stork that it believed that 'Stork's current strategic position' was in need of review because in today's market, '[i]nvestors like to invest in single-industry companies and accordingly value conglomerates at a significant discount to the sum of their parts'.[378] It attributed this to 'the lack of strategic focus, the excess layers of overhead and the stifling of incentive at the operating level'. Paulson made some suggestions that included that Stork should concentrate on aerospace activities and divest itself of all other activities, splitting up the Stork group altogether, or seek a private equity firm that would be prepared to make a takeover bid and de-list Stork after that (it might then restructure the group, and possibly retain Stork's conglomerate status). However, in February 2006 at the presentation of its annual accounts and annual report on 2005 Stork announced that it would keep concentrating on the three activities aerospace, poultry and food processing, and technical services. Following this announcement Centaurus and Paulson sent a letter to Stork's management and supervisory boards. They stated that they owned over 20% of the issued share capital of Stork, referred to the 'substantial undervaluation' of the shares that constituted a 'discount at which the shares trade' that was unacceptable, and proposed the following item to be included in the agenda of the upcoming annual general meeting of shareholders of Stork: that Stork would – preferably – end its conglomerate status by concentrating on aerospace activities and spinning off all other activities, or – in the alternative – go for 'a take-private of the Company as a whole [. . .] by actively investigating and pursuing private third-party interest'. Having discussed the letter with Centaurus and Paulson, Stork announced that it would investigate and further explain at the general meeting the take-private option (which it referred to as a 'public to private' transaction, 'PTP'). At the general meeting in March 2006 Centaurus and Paulson supported this course of action.

In July 2006 Stork communicated to its shareholders that it had concluded from its investigation that a PTP would not be a successful option. In reaction, Centaurus and Paulson sent a letter to Stork in which they stated that although a PTP had not been their first choice, they had supported it 'as we prefer to work together with management to create value rather than insist on our own priorities', that Stork should pursue the PTP option once more with force, or indeed concentrate on its aerospace activities and 'commence a transparent auction sale process [. . .] to sell all of Stork's non-aerospace assets'. Centaurus and Paulson also stated that, to underline their commitment to Stork, they had independently raised their shareholdings. In September 2006 Stork explained its position to its shareholders at an extraordinary general meeting of shareholders. When asked by other shareholders to comment, Centaurus and Paulson declined to do so. Also in

---

378. Paulson referred to a single-industry company as 'pure play'.

September 2006, Centaurus and Paulson informed Stork that they would vote on the now 31,4 % of the issued share capital they held in Stork, representing a voting interest of 32,9%,[379] jointly as concert parties, and requested another extraordinary general meeting to be convened to vote on the following item to be put on the agenda: that the management and supervisory boards of Stork should concentrate on the aerospace activities and that Stork should divest itself of all other activities, to be executed within a year. Centaurus and Paulson also made their request for an extraordinary general meeting to be convened public, adding that '[a]s a matter of clarification, neither Centaurus nor Paulson have any intention of making a public bid for Stork'. In October 2006, at the extraordinary general meeting, where 52,87% of the issued share capital of Stork was represented, the majority of the shareholders accepted the proposal of Centaurus and Paulson. However, already before the extraordinary general meeting Stork had argued that it would not regard the outcome of the voting as binding. After the extraordinary general meeting, Centaurus and Paulson indicated that they were willing to discuss the situation that had arisen with Stork – preferably with just the supervisory board – in order to try to bring the ideas of both parties together. Thereafter a meeting took place in November 2006 that was attended by Centaurus and Paulson and by the CEO and two members of the supervisory board on the part of Stork. Stork proposed that a representative of Centaurus and Paulson would be appointed to the supervisory board of Stork on the provision that Centaurus and Paulson would allow Stork eighteen months to rethink its future. Centaurus and Paulson did not react to this proposal and no solution was reached.

In November 2006 the management and supervisory boards of Stork sent a letter to the shareholders in which they stated that they did not accept the outcome of the voting of the October extraordinary general meeting as binding. Centaurus and Paulson then requested that a new extraordinary general meeting be convened to vote on the following items to be put on the agenda: dismissal of the supervisory board by the general meeting of shareholders deciding on the basis of Article 2:161a of the Dutch Civil Code, and adoption of a provision in the articles of association that would make decisions of the management board on substantial investments and disinvestments (over EUR 100 million) subject to approval of the general meeting. As early as 1977 (elaborated in 1986 and renewed in 1990) Stork had established an anti-takeover arrangement that allowed it to issue preference shares to Stichting Stork ('the Foundation') in case of a hostile takeover. In December 2006 Stork issued preference shares to the Foundation. The extraordinary general meeting of shareholders was scheduled for 18 January 2007.

B.   THE DECISION OF THE CHAMBER OF BUSINESS AFFAIRS
                TO ORDER AN INVESTIGATION

[133] On 5 January 2007 eleven shareholders of Stork – the investment fund associated with Centaurus, Paulson and nine investment funds associated with

---

379.   Because of 'the treasury stock of Stork'.

Paulson – filed an application with the Chamber of Business Affairs under the provisions on the 'right of inquiry' in the Book 2 of the Dutch Civil Code. They asked the Chamber of Business Affairs to find well-founded reasons to doubt good policy on the part of Stork and appoint persons to investigate the policy and the course of affairs of Stork, and to order interim measures in respect of Stork. On its part, Stork argued that the Chamber of Business Affairs should dismiss the lawsuit as unfounded, or – if an investigation was ordered – to include in that investigation the actions of Centaurus and Paulson also. In its judgment of 17 January 2007 the Chamber of Business Affairs ordered an investigation into the policy and the course of affairs of Stork from 1 September 2005 onward and also ordered several interim measures.[380] The Chamber of Business Affairs considered that the relationship between the management and supervisory boards of Stork on the one hand and Centaurus and Paulson on the other hand had developed into 'an atmosphere of reproaching, confrontation, mutual distrust and flawed communications', and that the parties had been unable to solve these 'fouled up relations' themselves. The Chamber of Business Affairs noted that it could not – at this time – conclude which of the parties was to blame. The Chamber of Business Affairs established that each of the parties had behaved in a way that was objectionable. The court was inter alia puzzled by the fact that Centaurus and Paulson had refused to comment at the September 2006 extraordinary general meeting and had not reacted to the proposal that the management and supervisory boards of Stork had made during their November 2006 meeting. As for Stork, it inter alia puzzled the court that the supervisory board of Stork had been reluctant to meet in November 2006 with Centaurus and Paulson without a member of the management board being present. The court considered:

> In this respect it must be taken into account that Centaurus c.s., given their quantitative position as Stork's shareholders, are (a conglomerate of) shareholders (that) who (is) are entitled to play an important role in Stork in the system of checks and balances of corporate governance and that the supervisory board does have a role especially as mediator (too) in conflicts as these between shareholders and the management board.

In general terms, the court stated that:

> anti-takeover arrangements as the one that is now being employed in principle can have as their object only to give to the management and supervisory boards for a period of time space to ascertain themselves of the intentions

---

380. Chamber of Business Affairs 17 January 2007, JOR 2007, 42 (*Stork*), translation of considerations of the court by the author;. J.M. de Jongh, 'Gij zult splitsen! Instructies van aandeelhouders in beursvennootschappen', *Ondernemingsrecht* (2007), 34-43; G.N.H. Kemperink, 'De rol van de raad van commissarissen bij opsplitsingsscenario's in het licht van de Stork-beschikking', in *Geschriften vanwege de vereniging Corporate Litigation 2006-2007*, eds H. Holtzer et al. (Deventer: Kluwer, 2007), 109-125; K. Schwarz & B. Steins Bisschop, 'Piercing the Myth of Management Control: The Ius Commune of the Shareholders' and Stakeholders' Models', *European Company Law* (2007), 58-63.

of a shareholder who seeks dominant control and to be able to discuss with her the views about the policy she advocates and to discuss this with the other shareholder as well as to seek alternatives.

The court also states in general terms that:

> It is, in principle, not for the Chamber of Business Affairs to decide by what strategy a corporation must pursue its policy or what vision is correct in case there are differences of opinion. Discussions on these issues must be held within the framework of company law in the Netherlands as well as prevailing views on corporate governance, that boil down to the fact that strategy setting is in principle a function of the management board, that a supervisory board – if it exists – has a supervisory function in that respect, and that the general meeting of shareholders can forward its opinion by exercising the rights given to it by statutory law and by the articles of association, among which since 1 October 2004 is the right to abandon confidence in the supervisory board of a 'large' corporation.[381]

From these general observations the Chamber of Business Affairs concluded that the use of the anti-takeover measure that allowed Stork to issue preference shares to the Foundation in case of a hostile takeover was at odds with the amendments of 2004 to the 'mandatory organizational arrangement' concerning the board of supervisors in 'large' companies. This was aggravated by the fact that the Chamber of Business Affairs expressed doubt as to whether the intention of Centaurus and Paulson to have the supervisory board dismissed by the general meeting of share-holders deciding on the basis of Article 2:161a of the Dutch Civil Code as such constituted a hostile takeover. But the Chamber of Business Affairs also considered that the strategy pursued by the management board of Stork had been seminal – as evidenced by the price at which shares in Stork traded –, and was supported by inter alia the supervisory board, the central works council, employees, trade unions, business relations and institutional investors. Therefore, the Chamber of Business Affairs concluded that the strategy of Stork was both sound and well-founded. Against this, Centaurus and Paulson had not forwarded convincing arguments that the strategy they sought was preferable. The Chamber of Business Affairs ordered an investigation into the policy and the course of affairs of Stork from 1 September 2005 onward and ordered inter alia the following interim measures:

- that the extraordinary general meeting of shareholders was prohibited to vote on the items put on the agenda by Centaurus and Paulson of the extraordinary general meeting for 18 January 2007 on that or any other date,
- that Stork was obliged to annul the issuing of preference shares to the Foundation, and
- that it appointed three extra members on the supervisory board of Stork to be empowered to 'set the agenda for annual and extraordinary meetings of shareholders and to have a deciding say in matters concerning the strategy

---

381. Article 2:161a of the Dutch Civil Code.

of Stork as well as in matters of dissension between Stork and Centaurus and Paulson, all at the discretion of these persons'.

C.   INTRODUCTION TO THE ABN AMRO CASE

[134] The *ABN AMRO* case concerns the takeover of ABN AMRO Holding NV. This case was decided before the legislation to implement the directive on takeover bids in the Netherlands came into force. It deals with the question to what extent the management board of a corporation shall need the approval of the general meeting of shareholders for major decisions.

[135] ABN AMRO Holding NV ('ABN AMRO Holding') was a listed corporation established in the Netherlands. ABN AMRO Holding was the parent company of a banking group ('ABN AMRO'). Part of the activities of the group was in the field of retail banking in inter alia the Netherlands, the United States, Brazil and Italy. Operating from the Netherlands, ABN AMRO had expanded into the United States in 1979 by acquiring LaSalle Bank Corporation ('LaSalle'), Brazil in 1998 by acquiring Banco Real SA and Italy in 2005 by acquiring Antonveneta Spa. ABN AMRO employed approximately 100.000 employees. ABN AMRO Holding NV held LaSalle through its subsidiary companies ABN AMRO Bank NV ('ABN AMRO Bank') and ABN AMRO North America Holding Company.

    The management board and the supervisory board of ABN AMRO Holding were constantly reviewing the position and strategy of the corporation. In the opinion of these boards, there appeared to be three possible options for a sound future: going further alone (the 'stand alone' scenario), growth by acquiring smaller competitors, and entering into a merger with a bank of the same size or a somewhat larger size. The strategy of ABN AMRO Holding had been a combination of 'stand alone' and growth by making acquisitions, but gradually the management and supervisory boards had come to the conclusion that the most viable option for ABN AMRO was to enter into a merger. In connection with this, ABN AMRO Holding had entered into preliminary talks with Barclays PLC ('Barclays'), established in the United Kingdom. The management and supervisory boards had always considered splitting up ABN AMRO as a fourth option, but had rejected this alternative because selling some valuable parts, like LaSalle, might appear to be profitable but would leave the remainder of ABN AMRO too small to be split up further profitably. However, on 20 February 2007, a shareholder of ABN AMRO Holding, The Children's Investment Fund Management (UK) LLP ('TCI', holding somewhat over 1% of the issued share capital of ABN AMRO Holding), sent a letter to ABN AMRO Holding in which it expressed concerns over the strategy of ABN AMRO and an ensuing undervaluation of the shares of ABN AMRO Holding. TCI argued that ABN AMRO should cease making further acquisitions and be split up itself instead. TCI also put on the agenda of the upcoming annual general meeting of shareholders of ABN AMRO Holding on 26 April 2007 proposals to this effect. This letter by TCI did put the talks with Barclays under pressure. Also, and to add to the growing disarray, Bank of America Corporation ('Bank of America'), established in the United States, expressed an interest to acquire LaSalle.

Shortly after TCI had expressed its concerns, on 19 March 2007 ABN AMRO Holding publicly announced that it was engaged in 'exclusive' discussions with Barclays to merge their operations. This intended merger would result in establishing a new holding corporation in the United Kingdom (also to be called 'Barclays') with its head office in the Netherlands. Then, on 12 April 2007 ABN AMRO Holding received a letter from three banks, The Royal Bank of Scotland Group PLC ('RBS', established in The United Kingdom), Fortis NV and Fortis SA/NV (together 'Fortis', established in the Netherlands and Belgium respectively), and Banco Santander Central Hispano SA ('Santander', established in Spain), that stated that they as a consortium were prepared to make a public takeover bid for ABN AMRO Holding.

After Vereniging van Effectenbezitters ('DIA'), on behalf of the shareholders it represented, had expressed its displeasure with the exclusionary character of the discussions between ABN AMRO Holding and Barclays, ABN AMRO Holding showed willingness to talk to the consortium following the exclusionary period of the talks with Barclays that ended on 20 April 2007.[382] On 22 April 2007 ABN AMRO Bank – as the subsidiary company of ABN AMRO Holding that held the shares in ABN AMRO North America Holding Company – and Bank of America reached an agreement under which ABN AMRO Bank would sell its shares in ABN AMRO North America Holding Company (and with it LaSalle) to Bank of America for USD 21 billion to be paid in cash. Possibly Bank of America insisted on this swift transaction because it feared that after the intended merger between ABN AMRO Holding and Barclays the post-merger Barclays would (have to) sell LaSalle to recoup the costs of the takeover, and wanted to make sure that LaSalle would come into its possession now rather than come into possession of the consortium first. The 'Purchase and Sale Agreement' between ABN AMRO Bank and Bank of America included a so-called 'go shop' arrangement under which ABN AMRO Bank could until 6 May 2007 inform Bank of America in case a third party had expressed interest in acquiring LaSalle and had made a 'superior proposal'. Whether a proposal was indeed superior was to be determined by ABN AMRO Bank itself on the basis of 'all legal, financial, regulatory and other aspects (. . .), including the likelihood of consummation'. The agreement gave Bank of America the opportunity to match a superior proposal within five business days in order to be able to acquire LaSalle anyhow. If Bank of America would not match the proposal, ABN AMRO Bank could terminate the agreement, having to pay USD 200 million to Bank of America.

On 23 April 2007 ABN AMRO Holding and Barclays announced that they had reached an understanding on the intended merger. This merger would take place by a public takeover bid, recommended by the management board of ABN AMRO Holding, to be made by Barclays to the shareholders of ABN AMRO Holding to

---

382. 'Dutch Investors' Association', abbreviated in Dutch 'VEB', <www.veb.net>.

trade their shares in ABN AMRO Holding for shares in Barclays. Following the acquisition, existing shareholders of Barclays would own approximately 52% and existing shareholders of ABN AMRO Holding would own approximately 48% of the shares of the post-merger Barclays. Also following the acquisition, the board of the post-merger Barclays would consist of 10 members from the pre-merger Barclays and nine members from the pre-merger ABN AMRO Holding. The bid would entail the sum of EUR 67 billion. The earlier Purchase and Sale Agreement between ABN AMRO Bank and Bank of America was related to the intended merger between ABN AMRO Holding and Barclays because the understanding on the public takeover bid stated that the bid by Barclays was conditional on ABN AMRO Bank divesting itself of LaSalle, and also because ABN AMRO Holding announced on 23 April 2007 that after the merger a large part of the sum that Bank of America would pay for acquiring ABN AMRO North America Holding Company would be handed out to the shareholders of the post-merger Barclays (the shareholders of the pre-merger Barclays and the pre-merger ABN AMRO Holding). These events led to reactions from several parties.

First, DIA argued that ABN AMRO Bank could not sell the shares in ABN AMRO North America Holding Company (and with it LaSalle) to Bank of America without the prior approval of the general meeting of shareholders of ABN AMRO Holding. Second, the three banks that acted as a consortium repeated their offer to make a public takeover bid for ABN AMRO Holding, for approximately EUR 72,2 billion. Any such bid would however be conditional on ABN AMRO Bank not divesting itself of LaSalle.

On 26 April 2007 a majority of the shareholders that attended the annual general meeting of ABN AMRO Holding voted in favor of (some of) the proposals put on the agenda by TCI. These included the proposal that ABN AMRO Holding should seek maximum shareholder value by being split up or entering into a merger. During the general meeting the management board and the supervisory board stated that on 20 February 2007 the management board had – approved by the supervisory board on 13 March 2007 – decided to embark on a strategy that would result in a merger of ABN AMRO Holding. The management and supervisory boards also stated that the agreement with Bank of America was not the result of any request on the part of Barclays.[383]

D.   THE DECISION OF THE CHAMBER OF BUSINESS AFFAIRS TO ORDER INTERIM MEASURES

[136] On 27 April 2007 DIA together with five shareholders (DIA et al.) filed an application with the Chamber of Business Affairs under the provisions on the 'right of inquiry' in the Book 2 of the Dutch Civil Code. They asked the Chamber of

---

383. The events surrounding ABN AMRO are also discussed in P. Battes & P. Elshout, *De val van ABN Amro* (Amsterdam: Uitgeverij Business Contact, 2008) and in J. Smit, *De prooi: blinde trots breekt ABN Amro* (Amsterdam: Prometheus, 2008).

Business Affairs to find well-founded reasons to doubt good policy on the part of ABN AMRO Holding and ABN AMRO Bank and appoint persons to investigate the policy and the course of affairs of these companies from 1 January 2006 onward, and to order interim measures. In its judgment of the 3 May 2007 the Chamber of Business Affairs ordered interim measures.[384] DIA et al. basically repeated their view that ABN AMRO Bank could not sell its shares in ABN AMRO North America Holding Company (and with it LaSalle) to Bank of America without the prior approval of the general meeting of shareholders of ABN AMRO Holding. They took the position that the Purchase and Sale Agreement between ABN AMRO Bank and Bank of America constituted well-founded reasons to doubt good policy because it prevented the shareholders of ABN AMRO Holding from seriously deciding between a public takeover bid by Barclays and a better bid by the consortium of banks or any other party. In their opinion the Purchase and Sale Agreement showed favor to Barclays over others because it could in effect only discourage others from making a public takeover bid for ABN AMRO Holding as such parties would be not willing to bid for ABN AMRO Holding without being able to acquire LaSalle also. In fact, as DIA et al. argued, of the three banks that formed the consortium, Fortis was mainly interested in taking over the activities of ABN AMRO in the Netherlands, Santander the activities in Brazil and Italy, and RBS those in the United States. DIA et al. felt that the Purchase and Sale Agreement had a direct link with the intended public takeover bid by Barclays, if only because the understanding on the bid stated that the bid by Barclays was conditional on ABN AMRO Bank divesting itself of LaSalle. DIA et al. supposed that the Purchase and Sale Agreement had been framed during the negotiations between ABN AMRO Holding and Barclays as a 'reversed poison pill' when the consortium of banks had announced that it was prepared to make a public takeover bid for ABN AMRO Holding. This would have been a consequence of the fact that the management board of ABN AMRO Holding recommended the intended public takeover bid by Barclays, but did not recommend the intended bid by the consortium. On their part, ABN AMRO Holding and ABN AMRO Bank stated that they did not understand why the consortium would not be willing to make a public takeover bid for ABN AMRO Holding without being able to acquire LaSalle, and moreover that the Purchase and Sale Agreement had yielded USD 21 billion which was too good an offer not to accept. In the alternative, the 'go shop' arrangement in the Purchase and Sale Agreement would allow RBS to make a separate offer for LaSalle, that could then be followed by a public takeover bid for ABN AMRO Holding by the consortium or some of its members. As concerns these diverging opinions the court concluded that:

> in respect of the sale of LaSalle it has not been established for a fact that ABN AMRO Holding and ABN AMRO Bank, Barclays and Bank of America have

---

384. Chamber of Business Affairs 3 May 2007, JOR 2007, 143 (*ABN AMRO*), translation of considerations of the court by the author; C. de Groot, A. van Nood & F. Lambert, 'The ABN AMRO Ruling: Some Commentaries', *European Company Law* (2007), 168-176.

engaged in a coordinated effort to frustrate the Consortium in its efforts. Rather than that, it may be assumed, as ABN AMRO Holding and ABN AMRO Bank have stated, that this represented a 'good opportunity' and a windfall, that they themselves connected to the public takeover bid by Barclays.

With respect to the principal question whether selling the shares in ABN AMRO North America Holding Company (and with it LaSalle) to Bank of America required the prior approval of the general meeting of shareholders of ABN AMRO Holding the Chamber of Business Affairs referred to its earlier case law that discussions on the strategy of a corporation must be held within the framework of company law in the Netherlands as well as prevailing views on corporate governance, that boil down to the fact that strategy setting is in principle a function of the management board, that a supervisory board – if it exists – has a supervisory function in that respect, and that the general meeting of shareholders can forward its opinion by exercising the rights given to it by statutory law and by the articles of association.[385] To this the court added:

> Within that framework the decision making on (the ownership of) shares and the rights attached to them is the exclusive right of the shareholder. Although she, in certain circumstances, may be required to take into account other interests than hers alone, the decision making on this issue as such and in principle falls within her realm. Differences of opinion that may occur between shareholders of the same company will have to be resolved in the adequate arena, the general meeting of shareholders.

On the basis of these two starting points the Chamber of Business Affairs concluded in the first place that the decision to sell LaSalle was as such a decision that fell to the management boards of ABN AMRO Holding and ABN AMRO Bank, under the supervision of the supervisory board. But the Chamber of Business Affairs referred to a number of circumstances in the second place. As the court considered:

> The present case is characterized [. . .] by a concurrence of, on the one hand, a decision that in principle falls within the competence of the management board (selling LaSalle) and, on the other hand, a decision that falls within the competence of the shareholders (selling the shares they have in ABN AMRO Holding). This poses the question to what extent in view of the circumstances of the present case (only) the matter of strategy setting by (the management of) ABN AMRO Holding is at stake, or (also) the matter of (decision making about the) ownership of the shares in ABN AMRO Holding.

The Chamber of Business Affairs came to the conclusion that the latter was the case. It did so on the basis of an intricate reasoning. The court considered that the decision of the management and supervisory boards of ABN AMRO Holding to no

---

385. Chamber of Business Affairs 17 January 2007, JOR 2007, 42 (*Stork*).

longer follow the 'stand alone' strategy but opt for a merger (or seek a public takeover bid by a third party) meant that 'the domain of issues that – within the framework of statutory law and corporate governance rules – fall within the competence of them, i.e. the management board and the supervisory board, has been abandoned, and that the decision making about such a public takeover bid (recommended or not recommended by the management board and the supervisory board of ABN AMRO Holding) falls within the competence of the shareholders'. To this the court added that now that ABN AMRO Holding was 'up for sale' the role of the management and supervisory boards was 'to create for the benefit of the shareholders the best possible conditions and also to refrain from influencing that process in any way (at least to the effect that the shareholders are being deprived of their power to decide)'. In the opinion of the court it had to follow from this that the management board of ABN AMRO Holding could not separate one asset from all others and sell that asset – certainly not an asset as important for ABN AMRO as LaSalle – without giving the shareholders of ABN AMRO Holding the opportunity to express their views on that sale. As the court added: 'not even if the management board thinks that it acts solely in the interests of the shareholders'. In fact, the sale of LaSalle, the conditions of the Purchase and Sale Agreement, and the connection of that transaction with the intended public takeover bid by Barclays had presented the shareholders with a *fait accompli*. The court furthermore considered that the foregoing was true all the more now that there was another party that wished to make a public takeover bid on ABN AMRO also. This bid by the consortium could well prove to be more profitable that the bid by Barclays that had the support of the management board.

The Chamber of Business Affairs found support for its line of reasoning in statutory law. In accordance with Article 2:8 of the Dutch Civil Code a legal person and those who are involved in its organization shall exercise due care in relation to each other's interests. And in accordance with Article 2:107a section 1 of the Dutch Civil Code the management board of a corporation shall need the approval of the general meeting of shareholders for any decision 'in respect of a major change in the identity or the character of the corporation or its enterprise'. Such decisions shall in any event include a decision to transfer the enterprise or most of the enterprise to a third party (subsection a), a decision to enter into or end permanent cooperation of the corporation with another party in case this decision is of far-reaching importance to the corporation (subsection b), and a decision to take a participating interest or to divest the corporation of a participating interest in another company to the amount of at least one third of the assets according to the balance sheet with the notes thereon (or at least one third of the assets according to the consolidated balance sheet with the notes thereon) (subsection c). In this respect the Chamber of Business Affairs considered that even if the decision to sell LaSalle did not literally meet the criteria of Article 2:107a of the Dutch Civil Code, 'there is at least at hand an issue that is so much alike the cases that come within that provision – either generally or specifically – that it must be put on equal footing with those cases, and that the management board and the supervisory board of ABN AMRO Holding should have felt obliged to put the decision to sell LaSalle before the general meeting of shareholders'. Therefore, both Article 2:8 and 'the notion that is the basis of Article 2:107a' preclude that 'the general meeting of shareholders of ABN AMRO Holding – against its will, without having been able to express its views [. . .] – were to accept the sale of LaSalle in connection with the intended merger with Barclays, without being able to become acquainted with and assess other public takeover bids by parties that have expressed an interest in the enterprise of ABN AMRO as a whole with its subsidiary companies'.

Based on the foregoing, the Chamber of Business Affairs considered that it could not rule out the possibility that it would in the further course of the proceedings before it find well-founded reasons to doubt good policy on the part of ABN AMRO Holding and ABN AMRO Bank and appoint persons to investigate the policy and the course of affairs of these companies. It therefore felt free to order interim measures. The Chamber of Business Affairs prohibited ABN AMRO Holding and ABN AMRO Bank from (further) executing or (further) lending assistance to any and all acts that would implement the Purchase and Sale Agreement or to divest themselves in any other way of ABN AMRO North America Holding Company or its subsidiary companies, without the prior approval of the general meeting of shareholders of ABN AMRO Holding. In ordering these interim measures the court was not much convinced by the reasoning of ABN AMRO Holding, ABN AMRO Bank, Barclays and Bank of America that ABN AMRO Bank might expect Bank of America to submit a claim for damages if ABN AMRO Bank could not fulfill the Purchase and Sale Agreement. In the opinion of the Chamber of Business Affairs this would in the first place be the result of ABN AMRO Bank's own doing, and could in the second place be an aspect that the general meeting of shareholders of ABN AMRO Holding could, when discussing whether or not to approve the Purchase and Sale Agreement, take into account.

E.　　　　　THE DECISION OF THE HIGH COURT TO SET ASIDE THE JUDGMENT OF THE CHAMBER OF BUSINESS AFFAIRS

[137] ABN AMRO Holding and ABN AMRO Bank, Bank of America, as well as Barclays lodged an appeal with the High Court against the judgment of the Chamber of Business Affairs. Formally, the appeal concentrated on the question whether the Chamber of Business Affairs could have ordered interim measures the way it had done. Materially, the appeal raised the question whether the Chamber of Business Affairs had correctly considered that ABN AMRO Holding and ABN AMRO Bank could not sell the shares in ABN AMRO North America Holding Company (and with it LaSalle) to Bank of America without the prior approval of the general meeting of shareholders of ABN AMRO Holding. In its judgment of 13 July 2007 the High Court set aside the judgment of the Chamber of Business Affairs and dismissed the application of DIA et al. for interim measures.[386]

---

386. High Court 13 July 2007, JOR 2007, 178 (*ABN AMRO*), translation of considerations of the court by the author; W. Oostwouder, 'Can You Trust the Dutch (Company Law System)?', *European Company Law* (2007), 211-216.

The High Court supported the reasoning of the Chamber of Business Affairs up to and including the point where the Chamber had considered that the decision to sell LaSalle was as such a decision that fell to the management boards of ABN AMRO Holding and ABN AMRO Bank, under the supervision of the supervisory board (above: 'the Chamber of Business Affairs concluded in the first place'), but did not support the reasoning of the Chamber from the point where it had considered that a number of circumstances were at stake that led to a different conclusion in the case at hand (above: 'the Chamber of Business Affairs referred to a number of circumstances in the second place'). In this respect, the High Court referred to The Dutch Corporate Governance Code as a source of generally accepted convictions about the state of the law in the Netherlands. In the opinion of the High Court in the present case principles II and IV were relevant and could be used to interpret Articles 2:8 and 2:9 of the Dutch Civil Code. Under principle II.1 '[t]he role of the management board is to manage the company, which means, among other things, that it is responsible for achieving the company's aims, strategy and policy, and results'.[387] Under principle IV.1 '[t]he general meeting of shareholders should be able to exert such influence on the policy of the management board and the supervisory board of the company that it plays a fully-fledged role in the system of checks and balances in the company'. Principle IV.1 elaborates this by stating that '[a]ny decisions of the management board on a major change in the identity or character of the company or the enterprise shall be subject to the approval of the general meeting of shareholders'. In accordance with Article 2:8 of the Dutch Civil Code a legal person and those who are involved in its organization shall exercise due care in relation to each other's interests, and in accordance with Article 2:9 executive directors are under an obligation to fulfill their duties toward the corporation faithfully. On this basis the High Court concluded that neither Article 2:8 nor Article 2:9 demanded of the management board that it put before the general meeting of shareholders for approval – or even for consultation – an issue that fell within its competence (as the decision to sell an important asset like LaSalle) on sole ground that the shareholders had an interest to sell their shares at the highest possible price (now that a second group of bidders had expressed an interest to acquire the corporation). To this the High Court added that:

> In commercial transactions legal certainty shall be upheld especially, which means that absent statutory provisions or provisions in the articles of association no such far-reaching powers should fell to the general meeting of shareholders on the basis of unwritten rules only that would also apply solely on the basis of the circumstances of the case. Third parties must be able to rely on

---

387. Or – in the words of the amended version of the Dutch Corporate Governance Code – 'that it is responsible for achieving the company's aims, the strategy and associated risk profile, the development of results and corporate social responsibility issues that are relevant to the enterprise'.

transactions made by the management board within the framework of its powers attributed by statutory provisions or provisions in the articles of association being irreversible in principle [...]. This also follows from the measure of decisiveness with which the management board must be able to establish and execute the strategy of the corporation's enterprise.

This emphasis on statutory provisions (and provisions in the articles of association) left the High Court with the question whether the decision of ABN AMRO Holding and ABN AMRO Bank to sell the shares in ABN AMRO North America Holding Company (and with it LaSalle) to Bank of America came within the meaning of Article 2:107a of the Dutch Civil Code. The High Court answered this question in the negative. In general terms, it considered that it followed from the legislative history that the scope of application of Article 2:107a is limited to decisions 'that are so far-reaching that they lead to a transformation of shareholder status in the sense that a shareholder would as it were become an investor in and have a stake in a substantially different corporation'. This, however, was not the case, 'even not though the transaction at stake is sizeable ("major")'. More specifically, the High Court considered that the decision to sell the shares in ABN AMRO North America Holding Company did not meet the criteria of Article 2:107a section 1 under a, b or c because these three cases should be interpreted against the background of the restrictive notion underlying of Article 2:107a. In this case the transaction did not come within the meaning of Article 2:107a section 1, subsection c especially because it did not meet 'the quantitative criterion': 'And this is not changed by the fact that taking into account the total make-up of the balance sheet of ABN AMRO Holding and ABN AMRO Bank, meeting that criterion is practically impossible'. The High Court also noted that Article 2:107a section 2 ('The absence of approval of the general meeting of shareholders of a decision within the meaning of section 1 shall not affect the power of either the management board or the executive directors to represent the corporation') withholds decision making that violates section 1 from having 'external effect', and that the judgment of Chamber of Business Affairs – prohibiting ABN AMRO Holding and ABN AMRO Bank from divesting themselves in any way of ABN AMRO North America Holding Company or its subsidiary companies without the prior approval of the general meeting of shareholders of ABN AMRO Holding – was therefore 'unjustified in respect of both Bank of America and Barclays'.

F.   EVALUATION

[138] In *Stork* the Chamber of Business Affairs formulated as a central tenet of corporate law that strategy setting is in principle a function of the management board of a corporation, that the supervisory board – if it exists – has a supervisory function in that respect, and that the general meeting of shareholders can forward its opinion by exercising the rights given to it by statutory law and by the articles of association. In *ABN AMRO* this tenet was repeated by the Chamber of Business

Affairs and supported by the High Court. *ABN AMRO* – in short – dealt with the question whether the management board and the supervisory board of ABN AMRO Holding should have involved the general meeting of shareholders in the decision making on divesting ABN AMRO North America Holding Company (and with it LaSalle) to Bank of America against the background of two (possible) public takeover bids for ABN AMRO Holding. The first was a bid by Barclays that was supported by the management and supervisory boards of ABN AMRO Holding (Barclays was not interested in acquiring LaSalle). The second was a bid by RBS, Fortis and Santander acting as a consortium that was not supported by the management and supervisory boards of ABN AMRO Holding (the consortium was interested in acquiring LaSalle). Because the decision making on divesting ABN AMRO North America Holding Company (and LaSalle) took place against this background the Chamber of Business Affairs had decided that the management and supervisory boards of ABN AMRO Holding should have put the decision before the general meeting of shareholders for its approval. In the opinion of the Chamber of Business Affairs it was 'unacceptable that a part of the enterprise of ABN AMRO would be split off and sold without that meeting being able to properly assess that split off and sale against other possible (legal forms of) bids by parties for (the shares of) the enterprise of ABN AMRO as a whole and judge all bids on their merits'. In the opinion of the High Court, however, the general meeting of shareholders of ABN AMRO Holding was not entitled to approve the decision as 'no such far-reaching powers should fell to the general meeting of shareholders on the basis of unwritten rules only'.

In *ABN AMRO* there was a clear difference of opinion between the Chamber of Business Affairs and the High Court on the measure of influence that the general meeting of shareholders should be able to exert on the policy of the management board and the supervisory board of a corporation with respect to major issues. This difference of opinion mainly relates to the question whether a right of approval of the general meeting on major issues can be based on the wording of principle IV.1 of The Dutch Corporate Governance Code that '[a]ny decisions of the management board on a major change in the identity or character of the company or the enterprise shall be subject to the approval of the general meeting of shareholders', where necessary by interpreting Article 2:107a of the Dutch Civil Code extensively. As such, both the extensive interpretation by the Chamber of Business Affairs and the restrictive interpretation by the High Court of Article 2:107a are sustainable. But there is something else. First, by adding to its decision that the transaction to divest ABN AMRO North America Holding Company (and LaSalle) did not come within the meaning of Article 2:107a section 1, subsection c the consideration that this was not changed by 'the fact that taking into account the total make-up of the balance sheet of ABN AMRO Holding and ABN AMRO Bank, meeting that criterion is practically impossible', the High Court took away much of the *effet utile* of Article 2:107a. Second, the High Court did not take into account that the transaction took place against a very particular background, consisting of two (possible) public takeover bids for ABN AMRO Holding. This makes the decision of the High Court difficult to reconcile with the basic notion of 'good' corporate governance expressed in principle IV.1 of the code that '[t]he general meeting of shareholders should be able to exert such influence on the policy of the management board and the supervisory board of the company that it plays a fully-fledged role in the system of checks and balances in the company'.

Chapter 10
Investor Relations

I. INVESTORS' RIGHTS AND OBLIGATIONS

[139] In accordance with principle IV.1 of The Dutch Corporate Governance Code '[g]ood corporate governance requires the fully-fledged participation of shareholders in the decision-making in the general meeting of shareholders. It is in the interest of the company that as many shareholders as possible take part in the decision-making in the general meeting of shareholders. The company shall, in so far as possible, give shareholders the opportunity to vote by proxy and to communicate with all other shareholders', and '[t]he general meeting of shareholders should be able to exert such influence on the policy of the management board and the supervisory board of the company that it plays a fully-fledged role in the system of checks and balances in the company'.[388] Under principle IV.4 '[i]nstitutional investors shall act primarily in the interests of the ultimate beneficiaries or investors and have a responsibility to the ultimate beneficiaries or investors and the companies in which they invest, to decide, in a careful and transparent way, whether they wish to exercise their rights as shareholder of listed companies', and '[i]nstitutional investors shall be prepared to enter into a dialogue with the company if they do not accept the company's explanation of non-application of a best practice provision of this code'.[389] The guiding principle

---

388. 'The Dutch Corporate Governance Code: Principles of Good Corporate Governance and Best Practice Provisions', drawn up by the Corporate Governance Committee (December 2003, by the name of the committee's chairperson this committee is also called the Tabaksblat Committee), <www.commissiecorporategovernance.nl> corporate governance code.
389. In the amended version of The Dutch Corporate Governance Code the latter provison is replaced by an amendment of principle I that applies to all shareholders:

    'Shareholders take careful note and make a thorough assessment of the reasons given by the company for any non-application of the best practice provisions of this code. They should

in this connection is the recognition that corporate governance requires a tailor-made approach and that it is perfectly possible for a company to justify instances of non-application of individual provisions'. Likewise, in accordance with main principles D.1 and D.2 of The Combined Code on Corporate Governance '[t]here should be a dialogue with shareholders based on the mutual understanding of objectives.[390] The board as a whole has responsibility for ensuring that a satisfactory dialogue with shareholders takes place', and '[t]he board should use the AGM to communicate with investors and to encourage their participation'. And under main principles E.1 and E.3 of the code '[i]nstitutional shareholders should enter into a dialogue with companies based on the mutual understanding of objectives', and '[i]nstitutional shareholders have a responsibility to make considered use of their votes'. It follows form these provisions that corporate governance gives investors rights but also puts obligations on investors, especially institutional investors. Thus, part A this chapter consists of the following paragraphs: *investors' rights*[391] and *obligations of investors.*[392]

A.   INVESTORS' RIGHTS

1.   **Attending, Participating and Voting in the General Meeting**

[140] The rights of investors will normally include the right to attend the general meeting of shareholders and participate in discussions and the right to vote in the general meeting. Investors' rights may also include the right to put items on the agenda for a general meeting and the right to convene a general meeting. The rights

---

avoid adopting a "box-ticking approach" when assessing the corporate governance structure of the company and should be prepared to engage in a dialogue if they do not accept the company's explanation. There should be a basic recognition that corporate governance must be tailored to the company-specific situation and that non-application of individual provisions by a company may be justified'.

390.   'The Combined Code on Corporate Governance', drawn up by the Financial Reporting Council (version of June 2008, originally July 2003), <www.frc.org.uk> corporate governance.
391.   Cf. also 'Directive 2007/36/EC of the European Parliament and of the Council of 11 July 2007 on the exercise of certain rights of shareholders in listed companies', OJEU 2007 L 184/17-24; H.M. Vletter-van Dort, 'Het stemgedrag van institutionele beleggers', *Tijdschrift voor Ondernemingsbestuur* (2007), 163-170; in October 2008 the Dutch government presented a bill to Parliament to implement the Directive (Wijziging van boek 2 van het Burgerlijk Wetboek en de Wet op het financieel toezicht ter uitvoering van richtlijn nr. 2007/36/EG van het Europees Parlement en de Raad van de Europese Unie van 11 juli 2007 betreffende de uitoefening van bepaalde rechten van aandeelhouders in beursgenoteerde vennootschappen (PbEU L 184), bill 31 746).
392.   J.S.T. Tiemstra & J. de Keijzer, 'Algemene vergadering van aandeelhouders: hoeksteen van corporate governance of niet-representatieve formaliteit', *Ondernemingsrecht* (2008), 192-197; the obligation on the part of investors to make a mandatory public takeover bid is discussed in chapter 9A.

of investors could also include the option that investors do not have to attend the general meeting and participate in discussions in person but may be represented by a person who stands proxy and include the possibility that investors do not have to vote in the general meeting in person but may be represented by a person who stands proxy. As a further development, investors' rights could include the possibility to attend the general meeting of shareholders and participate in discussions and to vote in the general meeting from a distance, i.e. by electronic means of communication. In respect of the foregoing, investors could include both shareholders and holders of depository receipts.[393]

In accordance with Article 2:108 section 1 of the Dutch Civil Code a general meeting of shareholders shall be held at least once a year. This is the annual general meeting ('AGM'). A general meeting held between times may be referred to as an extraordinary general meeting of shareholders ('EGM'); such a general meeting sometimes has the character of a 'consultative' general meeting of shareholders. Both the management board and the supervisory board may convene a general meeting (Article 2:109). Invitations to attend a general meeting shall be extended to all shareholders and to all holders of depository receipts that were issued with the cooperation of the corporation (Article 2:113 section 1). Shareholders are entitled to attend, participate in discussions and vote in the general meeting (Article 2:117 section 1). Holders of depository receipts that were issued with the cooperation of the corporation are entitled to attend and participate in discussions in the general meeting (Article 2:117 section 2). Only holders of *listed* depository receipts that were issued with the cooperation of the corporation may ask the voting trust that they, as opposed to the voting trust, be entitled to vote on the shares (Article 2:118a section 1). A shareholder is entitled to vote proportionate to the total nominal value of the shares she holds (Article 2:118 sections 2 and 3). A holder of listed depository receipts that were issued with the cooperation of the corporation who has voting rights is entitled to vote proportionate to the total nominal value of the shares that correspond to the depository receipts she holds.

Both shareholders and holders of depository receipts that were issued with the cooperation of the corporation that represent at least 1% of the issued capital of the corporation are entitled to request the corporation to put items on the agenda for a general meeting (Article 2:114a sections 1, 2 and 4). In case of a listed corporation they are already entitled to do so if they represent an amount of at least EUR 50 million of the issued capital. However, a corporation may refuse putting proposed items on the agenda on account of a 'consequential interest on the part of the corporation'. Shareholders and holders of depository receipts that were issued with the cooperation of the corporation that represent at least 10% of the issued capital of the corporation are entitled to file an application with the court for authorization to convene a general meeting of shareholders (Article 2:110 sections 1 and 2). The court shall authorize the applicants if it establishes that the

---

393. Holders of depository receipts may be divided into holders of receipts that were issued with the cooperation of the corporation and holders of receipts that were issued without the cooperation of the corporation.

management board and the supervisory board denied a request by the applicants to convene a general meeting, and that the applicants have 'a reasonable interest' that the general meeting be held (Article 2:111 section 1).

The (Dutch) Monitoring Committee Corporate Governance Code proposed in its Advisory Report on the Company-Shareholder Relationship and on the Scope of the Code that shareholders and holders of depository receipts that were issued with the cooperation of the corporation shall exercise their right to request the corporation to put items on the agenda for general meeting and their right to file an application with the court for authorization to convene a general meeting only after having discussed the items they want to raise with the management board. In respect of important items, the Monitoring Committee added that the management board should be allowed a 'response time' of 180 days.[394] Also, the Monitoring Committee proposed that the present criteria for entitlement to request the corporation to put items on the agenda for a general meeting should be changed into a threshold of 3 percent.[395] The ideas of the Monitoring Committee are reflected in an additional principle (principleVI.4[-2] on 'Responsibility of shareholders') and best practice provisions IV.4.4, IV.4.5, IV.4.6 as well as II.1.9 in the amended version of The Dutch Corporate Governance Code, that read:

> principleVI.4[-2] Shareholders shall act in relation to the company, the organs of the company and their fellow shareholders in keeping with the principle of reasonableness and fairness. This includes the willingness to engage in a dialogue with the company and their fellow shareholders.

> IV.4.4 A shareholder shall exercise the right of putting an item on the agenda only after he consulted the management board about this. If one or more shareholders intend to request that an item be put on the agenda that may result in a change in the company's strategy, for example through the dismissal of one or more management or supervisory board members, the management board shall be given the opportunity to stipulate a reasonable period in which to respond (the response time). This shall also apply to an intention as referred to above for judicial leave to call a general meeting pursuant to Article 2:110 of the Netherlands Civil Code. The shareholder shall respect the response time stipulated by the management board within the meaning of best practice provision II.1.9.
> IV.4.5 A shareholder shall vote as he sees fit. A shareholder who makes use of the voting advice of a third party is expected to form his own judgment on the voting policy of this adviser and the voting advice provided by him.
> IV.4.6 If a shareholder has arranged for an item to be put on the agenda, he shall explain this at the meeting and, if necessary, answer questions about it.

---

394. Corporate Governance Code Monitoring Committee, 'Advisory Report on the Company-Shareholder Relationship and on the Scope of the Code', at 15-16, <www.commissiecorporate governance.nl> information in English.
395. Corporate Governance Code Monitoring Committee, 'Advisory Report on the Company-Shareholder Relationship and on the Scope of the Code', at 21-22.

II.1.9 If the management board invokes a response time within the meaning of best practice provision IV.4.4, such period may not exceed 180 days from the moment the management board is informed by one or more shareholders of their intention to put an item on the agenda to the day of the general meeting at which the item is to be dealt with. The management board shall use the response time for further deliberation and constructive consultation. This shall be monitored by the supervisory board. The response time may be invoked only once for any given general meeting and may not apply to an item in respect of which the response time has been previously invoked or meetings where a shareholder holds at least three quarters of the issued capital as a consequence of a successful public bid.

Shareholders are entitled to have a proxy representative attend, participate in discussions and vote on their behalf in the general meeting (Article 2:117 section 1). Holders of depository receipts that were issued with the cooperation of the corporation are entitled to have a proxy representative attend and participate in discussions in the general meeting (Article 2:117 section 2).[396] The power to be represented may be limited in the articles of association of the corporation, but cannot be denied as concerns representation by inter alia an attorney at law, a civil law notary and a registered accountant.

In accordance with Article 2:117a the articles of association may provide that shareholders and holders of depository receipts that were issued with the cooperation of the corporation are entitled to exercise their rights to attend, participate in discussions and vote[397] in the general meeting (either in person or represented by a proxy representative) by using electronic means of communication (sections 1 and 4). Such electronic means of communication must at a minimum allow that the shareholder or holder of depository receipts that uses them can be identified and that she is able to take cognizance of the deliberations passively and cast votes (section 2). The corporation may attach further conditions to the use of electronic means of communication (section 3). These may include that the shareholder or holder of depository receipts that uses them shall be able to participate in the deliberations actively (section 2).[398]

---

396. Presumably holders of *listed* depository receipts that were issued with the cooperation of the corporation who have voting rights on the basis of Article 2:118a section 1 are also entitled to vote represented by a proxy representative.
397. Only holders of *listed* depository receipts that were issued with the cooperation of the corporation may have voting rights on the basis of Article 2:118a section 1.
398. R.G.J. Nowak, 'Het wetsvoorstel elektronische communicatiemiddelen', *Ondernemingsrecht* (2005), 227-231; H.M. Vletter-van Dort, 'De invloed van elektronisch stemmen op de besluitvorming in de vennootschap', in *Verantwoording aan Hans Beckman*, eds M.J. Kroeze et al. (Deventer: Kluwer, 2006), 545-560; A. van der Krans, 'De virtuele aandeelhoudersvergadering', *Ondernemingsrecht* (2007), 277-282; A. van der Krans, *De virtuele aandeelhoudersvergadering* (Deventer: Kluwer, 2009).

2.   Record (Registration) Date

[141] Articles 2:117b and 119 of the Dutch Civil Code provide for a so-called record (or registration) date. A record date is a date set at some time before the general meeting of shareholders is held that fixates which investors may attend, participate in discussions or vote in the general meeting, regardless whether they are investors at the time the general meeting is actually held. This makes it possible that shares and depository receipts are being traded in the build-up to the general meeting, while it remains clear which investors have attending, participation or voting rights (even if they no longer are investors in the corporation at the time of the general meeting). In accordance with Article 2:119 sections 1 and 2 the general meeting of shareholders may authorize the management board to provide that a person shall be deemed[399] to be a shareholder or holder of depository receipts when the general meeting is held if she was a shareholder or holder of depository receipts at a date set at a maximum of 30 days before the general meeting and signed up in a register (as indicated by the management board). In addition, in accordance with Article 2:117b sections 1 through 3 the articles of association may allow a shareholder or holder of depository receipts to vote[400] before the general meeting of shareholders is held by using electronic means of communication during a period of time that begins at a date set at a maximum of 30 days before the general meeting if she was a shareholder or holder of depository receipts at the date set at a maximum of 30 days before the general meeting and signed up in a register (as indicated by the management board).

B.   Obligations of Investors

1.   Notification of Holdings of Shares or Depository Receipts and Voting Rights

[142] In the Netherlands Article 5:38 of the Financial Supervision Act requires persons who acquire or lose disposition of shares or depository receipts (section 1) as well as voting rights (section 2) in a listed corporation established in the Netherlands[401] to notify Netherlands Authority for the Financial Markets immediately in case the percentage of the shares or depository receipts, or voting rights that they have come to hold overpasses or underpasses certain thresholds. The relevant thresholds are 5, 10, 15, 20, 25, 30, 40, 50, 60, 75 and 95 percent (section 3). For the purposes of applying this provision options to acquire shares or depository receipts shall be treated as shares and depository receipts,[402] and voting

---

399. For the purposes of applying Articles 2:117 sections 1 and 2 and 117a sections 1 and 4 of the Dutch Civil Code.
400. Only holders of *listed* depository receipts that were issued with the cooperation of the corporation may have voting rights on the basis of Article 2:118a section 1.
401. Article 5:33 section 1, subsection a of the Financial Supervision Act.
402. Article 5:33 section 1, subsection b of the Financial Supervision Act.

rights shall include voting rights that a person may exercise as a result of an agreement concluded with a third party by which she has acquired voting rights.[403] Also, a person shall be deemed to have voting rights when she has concluded an agreement with a third party by which voting rights have been temporarily transferred to her for a consideration,[404] and when she has concluded an agreement with a third party that stipulates a permanent common policy concerning the exercise of voting rights.[405]

The (Dutch) Monitoring Committee Corporate Governance Code proposed in its Advisory Report on the Company-Shareholder Relationship and on the Scope of the Code that the first threshold should be lowered to 3 percent, followed by ascending thresholds of 1 percent each.[406]

2.　　　　Reporting by Institutional Investors

[143] Article 5:86 of the Financial Supervision Act requires institutional investors established in the Netherlands that have invested in listed shares or listed depository receipts to report on compliance with the principles and best practice provisions of The Dutch Corporate Governance Code that are addressed to institutional investors (section 1). An institutional investor that does not apply or does not fully apply a principle or best practice provision shall explain the reasons for departure. Institutional investors are investment institutions (investment companies and investment funds), life insurers and pension funds.[407] Reporting and explaining may inter alia take place in the annual report or on the website of the institutional investor (2). The provisions in The Dutch Corporate Governance Code that are addressed to institutional investors are laid down in principle IV.4 and the accompanying best practice provisions. In accordance with the best practice provisions institutional investors shall publish 'their policy on the exercise of the voting rights for shares they hold in listed companies' (best practice provision IV.4.1) and report 'on how they have implemented their policy on the exercise of the voting rights' (best practice provision IV.4.2), and 'on whether and, if so, how they have voted as shareholders in the general meeting of shareholders' (best practice provision IV.4.3).

The (Dutch) Monitoring Committee Corporate Governance Code proposed in its Advisory Report on the Company-Shareholder Relationship and on the Scope of the Code that all shareholders (alone or acting in concert) that hold at least five percent of the issued share capital of a corporation should be obliged to disclose their intentions.[408]

403.　Article 5:33 section 1, subsection e of the Financial Supervision Act.
404.　Article 5:45 section 6 of the Financial Supervision Act.
405.　Article 5:45 section 5 of the Financial Supervision Act.
406.　Corporate Governance Code Monitoring Committee, 'Advisory Report on the Company-Shareholder Relationship and on the Scope of the Code', at 19.
407.　Article 1:1 of the Financial Supervision Act.
408.　Corporate Governance Code Monitoring Committee, 'Advisory Report on the Company-Shareholder Relationship and on the Scope of the Code', at 20.

II.   CASE STUDY

A.   Introduction to the DSM Case

[144] The *DSM* case is an example of the way the Chamber of Business Affairs and the High Court consider investors' rights and obligations. It deals with the principle of equality of shares and of shareholders.

[145] Koninklijke DSM NV ('DSM') was a listed corporation established in the Netherlands. Its share capital was divided into a large number (184,849,837) of ordinary shares and a smaller number (44,040,000) of preference shares. The ordinary and preference shares had the same nominal value and carried the same voting rights. On 27 September 2006 DSM issued a press release in which it announced its intention to introduce a so-called loyalty dividend for holders of ordinary shares. Under this arrangement a shareholder could register her shares with DSM and would after a period of three years be entitled to receive a once-only extra dividend to the amount of 30% of the average dividend handed out per share over the three preceding years, and thereafter to receive an annual extra dividend to the amount of 10% of the dividend handed out per share that year. Next the condition that shareholders had to hold on to their shares for at least there years, the proposed arrangement included several other conditions share-holders should meet. A shareholder would be entitled to receive the extra dividends only if she held her shares on her own account and a shareholder who was a legal person could be obliged to reveal the identity of the members of the management board and the supervisory board. Also, a participating shareholder would have to terminate her securities account and hold her shares outside the stock account system, which would render trading her shares on the stock market more difficult. DSM defended the arrangement as a means to reward long-term shareholders and to improve communication with shareholders. DSM put the loyalty dividend on the agenda of the annual meeting of shareholders scheduled for 28 March 2007 for its approval. Already before this general meeting a number of shareholders of DSM made it known that they opposed the arrangement.

B.   The Decision of the Chamber of Business Affairs to Order
            an Interim Measure

[146] On 19 March 2007 twelve shareholders of DSM – all investment funds associated with Franklin Mutual Advisors LLC – ('Franklin et al.') filed an application with the Chamber of Business Affairs under the provisions on the 'right of inquiry' in the Book 2 of the Dutch Civil Code. They asked the Chamber of Business Affairs to find well-founded reasons to doubt good policy on the part of DSM as concerns the proposed loyalty dividend and appoint persons to investigate the policy of DSM in this respect, and to order interim measures. Franklin et al.

argued that the proposed loyalty dividend violated Article 2:92 section 1 of the Dutch Civil Code which states that – unless provided otherwise in the articles of association – all rights and obligations that shares have shall be the same proportionate to their nominal value. In its judgment of 28 March 2007 the Chamber of Business Affairs by way of interim measure prohibited DSM to put the proposal to the vote in the general meeting of shareholders of that day or any later moment.[409] In the opinion of the Chamber of Business affairs the proposed loyalty dividend was to such an extent in violation of Article 2:92 section 1 of the Dutch Civil Code that it could not even be introduced by means of an amendment of the articles of association. The court considered that Article 92 section 1:

> allows a corporation to introduce in its articles of association provisions that have the effect that the corporation has several categories of shares that may have different rights as concerns dividend, entitlement to the residual assets should the corporation be liquidated, voting rights et cetera. Only objective characteristics of shares as described in the articles of association may lead to differentiation of the rights attached to shares. Such a differentiation cannot be allowed to result from a further relationship with the corporation that a shareholder must enter into.

The Chamber of Business Affairs concluded:

> The amendment of the articles of association that is now at issue to introduce the loyalty dividend violates this interpretation. The reason for this is that under the proposed provisions in the articles of association the question to what amount a shareholder is entitled to dividend depends neither on the category of the shares she holds nor on the rights and obligations that are attached to those shares in accordance with the articles of association. Rather, under the proposed provisions in the articles of association the entitlement to dividend is made dependent on the question whether a shareholder has accepted a supplementary arrangement that regulates her relationship with DSM, acceptance of which does not change the nature of the shares she holds.

C.   THE DECISION OF THE HIGH COURT TO SET ASIDE THE JUDGMENT OF THE CHAMBER OF BUSINESS AFFAIRS

[147] On 17 September 2007 the advocate general to the High Court lodged an appeal with the High Court against the judgment of the Chamber of Business Affairs 'in the interest of the law'. This is a procedure under which the advocate general has the possibility to seek a judgment by High Court in cases where the parties to the dispute do not lodge an appeal but the advocate general is of

---

409. Chamber of Business Affairs 28 March 2007, JOR 2007, 118 (*DSM*), translation of considerations of the court by the author.

the opinion that the advancement of the law requires a decision by the High Court on a legal issue. Judgments of the High Court in these proceedings do not affect the position of the original parties. In its judgment of 14 December 2007 the High Court set aside the judgment of the Chamber of Business Affairs.[410] The High Court disagreed with the Chamber of Business Affairs on two issues: the interpretation of Article 2:92 of the Dutch Civil Code and the circumstances in which the Chamber of Business Affairs may order interim measures in the course of proceedings under the 'right of inquiry' in the Book 2 of the Dutch Civil Code. On Article 2:92 section 1 – unless provided otherwise in the articles of association all rights and obligations that shares have shall be the same proportionate to their nominal value – the High Court considered as follows:

> The ground rule contained therein that all rights and obligations that shares have shall be the same proportionate to their nominal value is not mandatory, but may be departed from in the article of association. It follows neither from the wording nor from the purpose of this provision that departure in the articles of association from this ground rule is only possible in relation to shares of a specific category. Especially Article 2:92 section 1 [...] does not require that shares of the same category shall always yield entitlement to dividend in equal amount. For that reason Article 92 section 1 is not at odds with an arrangement in the articles of association that awards shareholders who have registered a financial reward under certain circumstances, e.g. consisting of an additional dividend, provided that this arrangement does not violate the principle of equal treatment laid down in Article 2:92 section 2 of the Dutch Civil Code.

Thus the High Court distinguished Article 2:92 section 1 from Article 2:92 section 2. Section 1 contains the principle of *equal treatment of shares*, Section 2 (the corporation shall treat shareholders, as well as holders of depository receipts, who are in the same position in the same way) contains the principle of *equal treatment of shareholders*. The High Court did not go into the question when an arrangement that is conformity with section 1 would be at odds with section 2.[411]

On the issue under which circumstances the Chamber of Business Affairs may order interim measures the High Court considered that although Article 2:349a section 2 of the Dutch Civil Court allows the Chamber of Business Affairs to order interim measures before it – on the basis of its finding that there are well-founded reasons to doubt good policy – has appointed persons to investigate the policy and the course of affairs of a corporation:

> at that stage this authority must be used with restraint. At that stage the finding that there are well-founded reasons to doubt good policy can only be made on the basis of a limited discussion between the parties to the dispute, and provisionally. [...] In any event, in the exercise of its authority the Chamber of

---

410. High Court 14 December 2007, JOR 2008, 11 (*DSM*), translation of considerations of the court by the author; M.L. Lennarts & M.S. Koppert-van Beek, 'Loyalty Dividend and the EC Principle of Equal Treatment of Shareholders', *European Company Law* (2008), 173-180.
411. J.M.M. Maeijer, note under High Court 14 December 2007, NJ 2008, 105 (*DSM*).

Business Affairs must sufficiently take into account, and carefully weigh, the interests of the parties involved [...]. This leads to the conclusion that the authority to order interim measures before ordering an investigation can only be exercised in case exercising that authority is warranted by reasons of consequential weight concerning the state of affairs of the corporation or the interest of the inquiry. [...] There is no ground to assume why in the present case it was not possible to wait for the outcome of the decision making process in the general meeting of shareholders of DSM.

D.   Evaluation

[148] *DSM* – in short – dealt with the question whether the loyalty dividend arrangement proposed by DSM was compatible with Article 2:92 of the Dutch Civil Code. In the opinion of the Chamber of Business Affairs the arrangement violated Article 2:92 section 1 (the principle of equal treatment of shares). The court considered that Article 2:92 section 1 is 'a fundamental and mandatory rule of Dutch company law' that only allows differentiation in the rights and obligations attached to shares when the shares are of different classes (or, if they are of the same class, when these rights and obligations are outlined in the articles of association without referring to other instruments like contractual arrangements). In the opinion of the High Court, however, Article 2:92 section 1 allows differentiation in the rights and obligations attached to shares of the same class because neither the wording not the purpose of Article 2:92 section 1 prohibit this differentiation. When differentiating in the rights and obligations attached to shares of the same class, a corporation must make sure that it stays within the boundaries of Article 2:92 section 2 (the principle of equal treatment of shareholders).

In *DSM* there was a clear difference of opinion between the Chamber of Business Affairs and the High Court on the extent that the principle of equal treatment of shareholders should have. This difference of opinion mainly relates to the question whether a corporation may differentiate in the rights and obligations that are attached to shares of the same class. As such, both the interpretations by the Chamber of Business Affairs and by the High Court of Article 2:92 are sustainable. But there is something else. First, the distinction the High Court makes between the principle of equal treatment of shares (Article 2:92 section 1) and the principle of equal treatment of shareholders (Article 2:92 section 2) is rather elusive, and the High Court does not explain its meaning. This distinction is not supported by the OECD Principles of Corporate Governance (2004).[412] In accordance with principle III[413] section A '[a]ll shareholders of the same series of a class should

---

412. <www.oecd.org> browse (by topic) → corporate governance.
413. 'The Equitable Treatment of Shareholders: The corporate governance framework should ensure the equitable treatment of all shareholders, including minority and foreign shareholders. All shareholders should have the opportunity to obtain effective redress for violation of their rights'.

be treated equally', to which this principle III section A adds subsection 1 that '[w]ithin any series of a class, all shares should carry the same rights'. Second, under the loyalty dividend arrangement proposed by DSM a participating share-holder would have to hold her shares outside the stock account system, and hold on to her shares for at least three years. This changes the nature of her shareholder status from holding shares that are easily transferable into shares that are almost impossible to transfer. That is difficult to reconcile with shareholder status in a listed corporation.

Concluding Remarks

[149] From the discussion in this book of several corporate governance issues some conclusions on corporate governance may be – tentatively – drawn:

In accordance with the working definition of corporate governance developed in chapter 1 corporate governance is the regulation of the corporate form that – by rethinking corporate law with the purpose of guaranteeing the enhancement of shareholder value in the long term – addresses the roles of the corporation's centralized administration (the unitary or dual board and the managers) and of the corporation's shareholders, by specifically taking into account elements like integrity, transparency, proper supervision and accountability. This definition puts the whole of corporate governance against the background of guaranteeing the enhancement of shareholder value in the long term. Core issues of corporate governance include the role of the corporation's centralized administration (the board and management). the composition and functioning of corporate boards, risk management, executive directors' remuneration, personal ethics for directors, public takeover bids, and investor relations. 'Good' corporate governance on the part of a corporation means that a corporation follows the rules required under these issues. What these rules are can be derived from inter alia corporate governance codes and guidelines, statutory regulation and listing rules, reports like *Restoring Trust* and the *Baker Panel Report*, and court decisions. In this book many of these rules have been identified. Because the purpose of corporate governance in the end is the enhancement of shareholder value in the long term, arguments derived from what amounts to 'good' corporate governance are especially relevant for investors. This explains why those arguments are being forwarded in corporate litigation, including shareholder litigation. Examples of arguments derived from 'good' corporate governance (even if they do not literally go by that name) brought to the fore by investors are found in the *Getronics* (chapter 2), *Versatel* (chapter 2), *Laurus* (chapter 3), *Disney* (chapter 4), *Corus* (chapter 5), *Stone, et al. v. Ritter, et al.*

(chapter 6), *RNA* (chapter 7), *BHV* and *Bruil* (chapter 8), *Stork* (chapter 9), *ABN AMRO* (chapter 9), and *DSM* (chapter 10) cases.

Both the Supreme Court of the State of Delaware and the Dutch Chamber of Business Affairs and High Court have formulated a central tenet of corporate law. In *Disney* the Supreme Court formulated that it is presumed that in making business decisions the directors of a corporation acted on an informed basis, in good faith, and in the honest belief that the action taken was in the best interests of the company, and that to rebut these presumptions it is necessary for a plaintiff to show that the directors breached their fiduciary duty of care or of loyalty or acted in bad faith (the business judgment standard). From the decisions by the Chamber of Business Affairs and the High Court in *Stork* and in *ABN AMRO* it follows that strategy setting in corporate affairs is in principle a function of the management board of a corporation, that the supervisory board – if it exists – has a supervisory function in that respect, and that the general meeting of shareholders can forward its opinion by exercising the rights given to it by statutory law and by the articles of association. These tenets were formulated in very distinct legal proceedings. Whereas *Disney* centered around derivative actions concerning directors' liability, *Stork* and *ABN AMRO* were proceedings under the 'right of inquiry' in Dutch law that allows the court to find well-founded reasons to doubt good policy and to conclude mismanagement on the part of a corporation as well as to order (interim) measures in respect of the corporation. However distinct these proceedings may be, the central tenets formulated have much in common. Both the wording that it is presumed that in making a business decision the directors of a corporation acted on an informed basis, in good faith, and in the honest belief that the action taken was in the best interests of the company, and the phrase that strategy setting in corporate affairs is in principle a function of the management board of a corporation, that the supervisory board has a supervisory function and that the general meeting can give its opinion within the boundaries of statutory law and by the articles of association, stress the role of corporate boards by giving these boards a broad measure of (entrepreneurial) discretion that remains outside the scope of shareholder influence. This would seem to imply that when arguments based on 'good' corporate governance are brought to the fore by investors in a derivative action concerning directors' liability, the executive and non-executive directors will not be easily held liable by the court for their actions. This would seem to imply likewise that in cases where investors argue on the basis of arguments derived from 'good' corporate governance that there are well-founded reasons to doubt good policy and that there is mismanagement on the part of a corporation resulting from the actions of the executive or non-executive directors, the court will not easily follow those arguments. The reason for this is that arguments derived from 'good' corporate governance serve to further the interests of the investors of a corporation by means of curbing the (entrepreneurial) discretion of the directors of the corporation. Or, to put it differently, these are arguments of shareholder protection that are at variance with the central tenets formulated by the Supreme Court and the Chamber of Business Affairs and High Court.

The case law discussed in chapters 2 through 10 neatly illustrates the forego-ing. Although the Supreme Court in *Disney* and *Stone, et al. v. Ritter, et al.* drew attention to the importance of a good corporate governance framework, it did not hold the directors liable in these cases. Although arguments related to 'good' corporate governance were advanced in the *ABN AMRO* and *DSM* cases as well as in the *Bruil* case, the High Court did not go along with those arguments. In *ABN AMRO* and *DSM* the High Court set aside the opposite decisions by the Chamber of Business Affairs, and in *Bruil* the High Court set aside the opposite decision by the court of appeals that had protected shareholder interests. On the whole, shareholder protection by means of invoking 'good' corporate governance seems to have but limited effect. Courts recognize an argument based on 'good' corporate gover-nance only in specific circumstances, e.g. when the corporation has experienced a (near) downfall (*Laurus*),[414] to correct a situation that is out of the ordinary by most standards (*RNA*),[415] or when the investors are able to depend to their advantage on specific legislation (Article 2:161a of the Dutch Civil Code in the *Stork* case).

The 'right of inquiry' in Dutch law is, however, relevant as means of promot-ing shareholder protection because it offers solutions of a procedural nature in the form of measures, especially the interim measures, that the Chamber of Business Affairs may order in respect of a corporation. Cases where shareholders were able to convince the court to do so are *Versatel, Stork, ABN AMRO* and *DSM*. It is all the more regrettable that the High Court in *DSM* curbed the freedom of the Chamber of Business Affairs to order interim measures.

Going back to the question whether rules of 'good' corporate governance are capable of being legally enforced, the foregoing would seem to imply that corpo-rate governance has but limited relevance as a legal concept and represents foremost a set of expectations on how corporations should be organized ideally. On that note, it would also seem that rules of 'good' corporate governance that have developed so far have not been capable of protecting to any significant degree either the financial sector or any sector in the economy from the financial and economic crisis that is now at hand.

---

414. Cf. the opposite outcome in the *Getronics* case (chapter 2).
415. In the *Corus* case (chapter 5) the applicants asked the Chamber of Business Affairs to suspend three of the four members of the supervisory board of Corus Nederland until exactly 24.00 hours on 13 March 2003 by way of interim measure. This would allow the remaining member of the supervisory board to approve an arrangement put before the board. The court dismissed the application. This decision is understandable because the application itself can be regarded as out of the ordinary.

References to the Dutch Corporate Governance Code

(References are to paragraph numbers)

III Supervisory board

IV.1.1 The general meeting of shareholders of a company not having

IV.1.2 The voting right on financing preference shares shall be based

IV.1.3 If a serious private bid is made for a business

IV.1.4 The policy of the company on additions to reserves and

IV.1.5 A resolution to pay a dividend shall be dealt with

IV.1.6 Resolutions to approve the policy of the management board

IV.1.7 The company shall determine a registration date for the exercise

Depositary receipts for shares
principle IV.2 Depositary receipts for shares are a means of preventing a

IV.2.1 The management of the trust office shall enjoy the confidence

IV.2.2 The managers of the trust office shall be appointed by

IV.2.3 A person may be appointed to the management of the

IV.2.4 The management of the trust office shall be present at

IV.2.5 In exercising its voting rights, the trust office shall be

IV.2.6 The trust office shall report periodically, but at least once

IV.2.7 The report referred to in best practice provision IV.2.6 shall

IV.2.8 The trust office shall, without limitation and in all circumstances

Provision of information to and logistics of the general meeting of shareholders
principle IV.3 The management board or, where appropriate, the supervisory board shall

IV.3.1 Meetings with analysts, presentations to analysts, presentations to investors and

IV.3.2 Analysts' reports and valuations shall not be assessed, commented upon

IV.3.3 The company shall not pay any fee(s) to parties for

IV.3.4 Analysts meetings, presentations to institutional or other investors and direct

IV.3.5 The management board and the supervisory board shall provide the

IV.3.6 The company shall place and update all information which it

IV.3.7 If a right of approval is granted to the general

Relationship and communication of the external auditor with
  the organs of the company
principle V.4 The external auditor shall, in any event,
  attend the meeting

V.4.1 The external auditor shall in any event attend the
  meeting
V.4.2 When the need arises, the external auditor may request
  the
V.4.3 The report of the external auditor pursuant to article
  2:393

References to the Combined Code on Corporate Governance

B.2 Procedure
main principle
There should be a formal and transparent procedure for developing
supporting principles
The remuneration committee should consult the chairman and/or chief executive

B.2.1 The board should establish a remuneration committee of at least   51

B.2.2 The remuneration committee should have delegated responsibility for setting remuneration   51

B.2.3 The board itself or, where required by the Articles of
B.2.4 Shareholders should be invited specifically to approve all new long-term

C Accountability and audit

C.1 Financial Reporting
main principle
The board should present a balanced and understandable assessment of
supporting principle
The board's responsibility to present a balanced and understandable

C.1.1 The directors should explain in the annual report their responsibility
C.1.2 The directors should report that the business is a going

C.2 Internal Control
main principle
The board should maintain a sound system of internal control   82

C.2.1 The board should, at least annually, conduct a review of   82, 83

C.3 Audit Committee and Auditors
main principle
The board should establish formal and transparent arrangements for considering

C.3.1 The board should establish an audit committee of at least   51

C.3.2 The main role and responsibilities of the audit committee should   51, 52

C.3.3 The terms of reference of the audit committee, including its
C.3.4 The audit committee should review arrangements by which staff of

C.3.5 The audit committee should monitor and review the effectiveness of

C.3.6 The audit committee should have primary responsibility for making a

C.3.7 The annual report should explain to shareholders how, if the

D Relations with shareholders

D.1 Dialogue with Institutional Shareholders
main principle
There should be a dialogue with shareholders based on the mutual   139
supporting principles
Whilst recognising that most shareholder contact is with the chief

D.1.1 The chairman should ensure that the views of shareholders are

D.1.2 The board should state in the annual report the steps

D.2 Constructive Use of the AGM
main principle
The board should use the AGM to communicate with investors   139

D.2.1 At any general meeting, the company should propose a separate

D.2.2 The company should ensure that all valid proxy appointments received

D.2.3 The chairman should arrange for the chairmen of the audit,

D.2.4 The company should arrange for the Notice of the AGM

SECTION 2 INSTITUTIONAL SHAREHOLDERS

E Institutional shareholders

E.1 Dialogue with companies
main principle
Institutional shareholders should enter into a dialogue with companies based   139
supporting principle
Institutional shareholders should apply the principles set out in the

E.2 Evaluation of Governance Disclosures
main principle

Main Cases and Reports

Addendum: Executive Directors' Remuneration in the Amended Version of The Dutch Corporate Governance Code

In the amended version of The Dutch Corporate Governance Code the provisions on executive directors' remuneration are largely overhauled and read:

> principle II.2[-1] The level and structure of the remuneration which the management board members receive from the company for their work shall be such that qualified and expert managers can be recruited and retained. When the overall remuneration is fixed, its impact on pay differentials within the enterprise shall be taken into account. If the remuneration consists of a fixed component and a variable component, the variable component shall be linked to predetermined, assessable and influenceable targets, which are predominantly of a long-term nature. The variable component of the remuneration must be appropriate in relation to the fixed component.
>
> The remuneration structure, including severance pay, shall be simple and transparent. It shall promote the interests of the company in the medium and long term, may not encourage management board members to act in their own interests or take risks that are not in keeping with the adopted strategy, and may not 'reward' failing board members upon termination of their employment. The supervisory board is responsible for this. The level and structure of remuneration shall be determined by reference to, among other things, the results, the share price performance and non-financial indicators that are relevant to the company's long-term value creation.
>
> The shares held by a management board member in the company on whose board he sits are long-term investments. The amount of compensation which a

management board member may receive on termination of his employment may not exceed one year's salary, unless this would be manifestly unreasonable in the circumstances.

II.2.1 Before drawing up the remuneration policy and determining the remuneration of individual management board members, the supervisory board shall analyse the possible outcomes of the variable remuneration components and how they may affect the remuneration of the management board members.
II.2.2 The supervisory board shall determine the level and structure of the remuneration of the management board members by reference to the scenario analyses carried out and with due regard for the pay differentials within the enterprise.
II.2.3 In determining the level and structure of the remuneration of management board members, the supervisory board shall take into account, among other things, the results, the share price performance and non-financial indicators relevant to the long-term objectives of the company, with due regard for the risks to which variable remuneration may expose the enterprise.
II.2.4 If options are granted, they shall, in any event, not be exercised in the first three years after the date of granting. The number of options to be granted shall be dependent on the achievement of challenging targets specified beforehand.
II.2.5 Shares granted to management board members without financial consideration shall be retained for a period of at least five years or until at least the end of the employment, if this period is shorter. The number of shares to be granted shall be dependent on the achievement of challenging targets specified beforehand.
II.2.6 The option exercise price may not be fixed at a level lower than a verifiable price or a verifiable price average in accordance with the trading in a regulated market on one or more predetermined days during a period of not more than five trading days prior to and including the day on which the option is granted.
II.2.7 Neither the exercise price of options granted nor the other conditions may be modified during the term of the options, except in so far as prompted by structural changes relating to the shares or the company in accordance with established market practice.
II.2.8 The remuneration in the event of dismissal may not exceed one year's salary (the 'fixed' remuneration component). If the maximum of one year's salary would be manifestly unreasonable for a management board member who is dismissed during his first term of office, such board member shall be eligible for severance pay not exceeding twice the annual salary.
II.2.9 The company may not grant its management board members any personal loans, guarantees or the like unless in the normal course of business and on terms applicable to the personnel as a whole, and after approval of the supervisory board. No remission of loans may be granted.

principle II.2[-2] The supervisory board shall determine the remuneration of the individual members of the management board, on a proposal by the remuneration committee, within the scope of the remuneration policy adopted by the general meeting.

The report of the supervisory board shall include the principal points of the remuneration report concerning the remuneration policy of the company. This shall describe transparently and in clear and understandable terms the remuneration policy that has been pursued and give an overview of the remuneration policy to be pursued. The full remuneration of the individual management board members, broken down into its various components, shall be presented in the remuneration report in clear and understandable terms.

II.2.10 If a variable remuneration component conditionally awarded in a previous financial year would, in the opinion of the supervisory board, produce an unfair result due to extraordinary circumstances during the period in which the predetermined performance criteria have been or should have been achieved, the supervisory board has the power to adjust the value downwards or upwards.

II.2.11 The supervisory board may recover from the management board members any variable remuneration awarded on the basis of incorrect financial or other data (clawback clause).

II.2.12 The remuneration report of the supervisory board shall contain an account of the manner in which the remuneration policy has been implemented in the past financial year, as well as an overview of the remuneration policy planned by the supervisory board for the next financial year and subsequent years. The report shall explain how the chosen remuneration policy contributes to the achievement of the long-term objectives of the company and its affiliated enterprise in keeping with the risk profile. The report shall be posted on the company's website.

II.2.13 The overview referred to in best practice provision II.2.12 shall in any event contain the following information:

a) an overview of the costs incurred by the company in the financial year in relation to management board remuneration; this overview shall provide a breakdown showing fixed salary, annual cash bonus, shares, options and pension rights that have been awarded and other emoluments; shares, options and pension rights must be recognised in accordance with the accounting standards;

b) a statement that the scenario analyses referred to in best practice provision II.2.1 have been carried out;

c) for each management board member the maximum and minimum numbers of shares conditionally granted in the financial year or other share-based remuneration components that the management board may member acquire if the specified performance criteria are achieved;

d) a table showing the following information for incumbent management board members at year-end for each year in which shares, options and/ or other share-based remuneration components have been awarded over which the management board member did not yet have unrestricted control at the start of the financial year:

    i) the value and number of shares, options and/or other share-based remuneration components on the date of granting;

    ii) the present status of shares, options and/or other share-based remuneration components awarded: whether they are conditional or unconditional and the year in which vesting period and/or lock-up period ends;

    iii) the value and number of shares, options and/or other share-based remuneration components conditionally awarded under i) at the time when the management board member obtains ownership of them (end of vesting period), and

    iv) the value and number of shares, options and/or other share-based remuneration components awarded under i) at the time when the management board member obtains unrestricted control over them (end of lock-up period);

e) if applicable: the composition of the peer group of companies whose remuneration policy determines in part the level and composition of the remuneration of the management board members;

f) a description of the performance criteria on which the performance-related component of the variable remuneration is dependent in so far as disclosure would not be undesirable because the information is competition sensitive, and of the discretionary component of the variable remuneration that can be fixed by the supervisory board as it sees fit;

g) a summary and account of the methods that will be applied in order to determine whether the performance criteria have been fulfilled;

h) an ex-ante and ex-post account of the relationship between the chosen performance criteria and the strategic objectives applied, and of the relationship between remuneration and performance;

i) current pension schemes and the related financing costs; and

j) agreed arrangements for the early retirement of management board members.

II.2.14 The main elements of the contract of a management board member with the company shall be made public after it has been concluded, and in any event no later than the date of the notice calling the general meeting where the appointment of the management board member will be proposed. These elements shall in any event include the amount of the fixed salary, the structure and amount of the variable remuneration component, any agreed redundancy scheme and/or severance pay, any conditions of a change-of-control clause in the contract with a management board member and any other remuneration components promised to the management board member, pension arrangements and performance criteria to be applied.

II.2.15 If a management board member or former management board member is paid severance pay or other special remuneration during a given financial year, an account and an explanation of this remuneration shall be included in the remuneration report.

Index

EUROPEAN COMPANY LAW SERIES